S0-AEV-593

The Lion on the Freeway

Studies of World Literature in English

Norman R. Cary
General Editor

Vol. 5

PETER LANG
New York • Washington, D.C./Baltimore
Bern • Frankfurt am Main • Berlin • Vienna • Paris

Theodore F. Sheckels, Jr.

The Lion on the Freeway

A Thematic Introduction to Contemporary South African Literature in English

PETER LANG
New York • Washington, D.C./Baltimore
Bern • Frankfurt am Main • Berlin • Vienna • Paris

Library of Congress Cataloging-in-Publication Data

Sheckels, Theodore F., Jr.
The lion on the freeway: a thematic introduction to contemporary
South African literature in English/ Theodore F. Sheckels, Jr.
p. cm. — (Studies of world literature in English; vol. 5)
Includes bibliographical references and index.
1. South African literature (English)—History and criticism. 2. South African literature (English)—Themes, motives. 3. English literature—20th century—Themes, motives. 4. South Africa—In literature.
I. Sheckels, Theodore F. II. Series.
PR9359.6.L56 820.9'968—dc20 94-28219
ISBN 0-8204-2625-3
ISSN 1043-8580

Die Deutsche Bibliothek-CIP-Einheitsaufnahme

Sheckels, Theodore F.:
The lion on the freeway: a thematic introduction to contemporary
South African literature in English/ Theodore F. Sheckels.–New York;
Washington, D.C./Baltimore; San Francisco; Bern; Frankfurt am Main;
Berlin; Vienna; Paris: Lang.
(Studies of world literature in English; Vol. 5)
ISBN 0-8204-2625-3
NE: GT

Cover design by James F. Brisson.

The paper in this book meets the guidelines for permanence and durability
of the Committee on Production Guidelines for Book Longevity
of the Council of Library Resources.

Printed in the United States of America.

For Emily Annette & Kathryn Marie

Contents

Preface

My model for this book is, oddly, **not** an earlier study of South African literature. Rather, my model is Margaret Atwood's curious 1972 book entitled *Survival: A Thematic Guide to Canadian Literature*. Let me explain. *Survival* met a need. Northrop Frye had announced that need in his challenging conclusion to the second edition of the *Literary History of Canada*. In it, he called for Canadians to, first, take their literature seriously and, second, explore what makes their literature Canadian. Atwood's *Survival* was a response to this call. She, quite deliberately, did not address her study to specialists in "Can. Lit."; rather, she spoke to those in and out of academe who wanted a guide to what "Can. Lit." is. She chose to structure that guide by examining several sorts of survival, since she had found, in her own experience as a reader of Canadian literature, that survival was its dominant theme. She confessed that a thematic approach was not the only approach one could take to understanding the territory. Furthermore, she noted that she was not going to argue that the thematic approach was the "right" or "best" approach. Rather, she suggested that exploring the recurring themes of Canadian literature was **a** way of gaining some control over the subject. Her endeavor was, of course, premised on an assumption about her audience: that there were many nonspecialists, in and out of academe, who wanted this control.

She was not the only writer to answer Frye's call: D. G. Jones, for example, wrote a guide (also thematic) to "Can. Lit." a year earlier. But this study, *Butterfly on Rock*, had a different audience: it was pitched at those who reside in the higher echelons of academe. As a result, it did not have the effect on readers that Atwood's book had. Atwood's *Survival* and the thematic approach it exemplifies have not been met with universal acclaim: as early as 1983 Robert Kroetsch was attacking Atwood's "naming" of themes as an inadvertent continuation of

Canada's colonial and post-colonial subservience to the literary traditions of the United Kingdom and the United States. Nonetheless, Atwood's book provided many, many readers with a way "in." And that's really all that Atwood intended the book to do.

My intention is quite similar; so is my assumption about my audience. But I do lack the clarion call of a Northrop Frye. The call I have is the general recognition that has emerged over the past decade among students of English literature that the field extends beyond–way beyond–the U. K. and the U. S., that English is an international language and that English literature is, as a result, an international literature. Although most undergraduates still study, at least to a large extent, "the canon" and although graduate students are still trained as specialists in a traditional period of British or American literature (and although most job announcements are still framed in these traditional terms), an increasing number of students want to know about the "other" English literature. So do their professors, the ones who teach Chaucer or Milton or the American Romantics. These undergraduate and graduate students and these professors are the intended audience for *The Lion on the Freeway*. Furthermore, the book is *not* intended to be a "scholarly" introduction to one of those "other" English literatures, that of South Africa, but rather a thematic introductory guide, much like Atwood's *Survival*. As such, it refers to existing scholarship sparingly–at those points where the references truly enrich the discussion.

Atwood derived her book's title from her experiences as a reader; I have derived my title from my experiences as a reader and a teacher of English South African literature. My title is borrowed from a short story by Nobel laureate Nadine Gordimer. I have read (as one would expect) widely in South African literature, but I have yet to encounter a single work that offers a better brief initial glimpse at the South African situation and, thereby, English South African literature than Gordimer's story. I have read many works that I think are "better" literature, but quality as a literary work is not the issue here. Rather, the issue is what can give readers an "in."

The story features a white South African woman who is trying to go to sleep in a hotel room in a large South African city—we presume Johannesburg. She is restless, disturbed by many noises: by the love-making couple in the adjoining hotel room; by the roar she thinks she hears of a lion that has escaped from the zoo and is now roaming the city. This lion is, in her imagination, traveling down the freeway. This thought leaves her (and us at the sketch's end) feeling quite anxious.

Gordimer's story can be read allegorically. The city is white South Africa; the zoo is the legal imprisonment of apartheid; and the lion is the black South Africa. Appropriately, Gordimer chooses an image, the lion, associated in much black African literature with the continent's native people, as her image for her nation's oppressed majority.

Just as the motif of survival gave Atwood her structuring principle for her guidebook, this story's simple but nonetheless rich allegory gives me my structuring principle for my guidebook. Thus, I consider, in **Part II**, "The Roar of the Lion," the various ways the oppressed black majority has chosen to voice its feelings. Gordimer spends some time in her brief sketch talking about how the lion's voice seems to change from moment to moment in the restless sleeper's imagination. Similarly, the black voice in South African literature seems to have four different sounds. Chapters 3 through 6 consider these sounds, beginning with the least threatening and ending with the most.

Thus, Chapter Three, "Loving," focuses on three works, Bessie Head's novel *When Rain Clouds Gather* (1969), Ahmed Essop's collection of short fiction *Stories* (1978), and Gcina Mhlope et al.'s play *Have You Seen Zandile* (1987), that suggest that a loving expression of the human needs of all people, regardless of color, is at least one facet of the lion's complex cry. The inclusion of a discussion of Essop's stories set in Fordsburg, the former Indian section of Johannesburg in this chapter suggests that human needs transcend the Black community and may represent a basis for overcoming South Africa's racial divisions.

Chapter 4, "Restlessness," examines works that suggest that the lion's love is tempered by the oppression he feels. As a result, the lion–i.e., the oppressed people–feels ill at ease, on-edge, restless. Chapter 4 examines three very different literary works that voice this emotion: Alfred Hutchinson's play *The Rain-Killers* (1968), Modikwe Dikobe's novel *The Marabi Dance* (1973), and Ezekiel Mphahlele's autobiography *Down Second Avenue* (1953). In these works, we see the two different environments in which the oppressed blacks restlessly endure oppression–the improverished homeland and the urban slum.

The uneasiness that emerges from these works turns to pain in Chapter 5, "Suffering." This chapter surveys several literary works. Five, Dennis Brutus' *Letters to Martha* (1968), Workshop '71 Theatre Company's *Survival* (1976), James Matthews' *Pass Me a Meatball, Jones* (1977), D. M. Zwelonke's *Robben Island* (1977), and Lewis Nkosi's *Mating Birds* (1986) deal with political prisoners; three others, all collections of verse, Oswald Mtshali's *Sounds of a Cowhide Drum* (1971), Mongane Wally Serote's *No Baby Must Weep* (1975), and Mafika Gwala's *No More Lullabies* (1982) deal heavily with the men, the women, and, especially, the children who suffer not because of any political or criminal actions they have undertaken but simply because they are black. Another work, Matsemala Manaka's play *Egoli* examines the suffering in South Africa in a slightly earlier period–when Johannesburg's gold mines were still booming. One last work, Athol Fugard's play *A Lesson from Aloes* (1981) suggests that apartheid has caused other racial groups, whites and coloreds, to suffer as well. Although not focused on "the lion" *per se*, this play demonstrates that its suffering cry is echoed in some of the nation's other quarters.

Chapter 6 completes Part II of the book. In this chapter, the lion's cry turns violent. The six works treated in Chapter 6, "Attacking," have very different tones. Poems from Sipho Sepamla's *The Soweto I Love* (1977) reflect disillusionment in the wake of the 1976 Soweto riots whereas poems from Keorapetse Kgositsile's earlier *My Name is Afrika* (1971) satirically attack the white establishment and envision revolution. More militant is the voice heard in James Matthews' collection of poetry, *Cry Rage* (1972); more Marxist are the lessons received from Miriam Tlali's novel *Amandla* (1980). Quieter but still militant is the tone of Alex LaGuma's *In the Fog of the Seasons' End* (1972).

The lion's cry then has many facets, ranging from loving to restlessly enduring to suffering to attacking. Those listening to this cry, as represented by the sleepless woman in Gordimer's story, also react but **not** in a simple, single way. Part III of this study, entitled "Listening to the Lion," studies three very different reactions.

The first reaction is really not a reaction at all; rather, it's ignorance. Chapter 7 examines works that reflect the white community as ignorant of the nature or depth of the problems facing South Africa's oppressed people. All three works discussed are satirical. Sheila Roberts' novel *The Weekenders* (1981) satirizes the coarse ignorance of hedonistic white South Africans; Nadine Gordimer's novella *Something Out There* (1979) satirizes the silly ignorance of affluent white suburb-dwellers; and Richard Rive's radio play *Make Like Slaves* (1971) satirizes the white liberals who think they "get it" but really don't. They are ignorant not of the existence of oppression but of what it really means.

In Gordimer's short story, the white woman is initially unaware of the lion's presence "out there." Once she thinks she hears it, she reacts in a manner that exhibits both fear and guilt (although she is unable to articulate what it is she is guilty of). Many white South Africans reacted in just this manner when confronting "the lion" that they had imprisoned in a zoo of apartheid laws and now no longer find safely there. Two guilt-informed works are studied in Chapter 8, "Guilt", J. M. Coetzee's *Waiting for the Barbarians* (1980) and Athol Fugard's *"Master Harold" . . . and the Boys* (1982). In the former, the focal character acts–in vain–to assuage his guilt; in the latter, the focal character is only just discovering his guilt. His acting based on it takes us outside the text.

Guilt prompts Coetzee's magistrate to act, but the way he acts in his strange attempts "to make up for" oppression has a disturbing quality to it. Less disturbing are the actions of the central characters of the two novels discussed in Chapter Nine, "Action": Benjamin DuToit from Andre Brink's *A Dry White Season* (1979) and Rosa Burger from Nadine Gordimer's *Burger's Daughter* (1979). These two hear the lion and eventually, after wrestling with their personal needs, commit themselves to the lion's cause.

Chapter 9 then is far more optimistic than the other chapters in Part III, for it suggests that the political turmoil in South Africa might end well. Ending well will, of course, entail the freedom of South Africa's Black majority from oppression. As Gordimer sees it in her short story, the lion is already "on the freeway." The question then is whether the lion–whether Black South Africans–will complete their free-way journey through war or through peace. Part IV of this book, "The Freeway," explores both possibilities, for the writers of South Africa see both as equally likely.

Chapter 10 looks at two nightmarish predictions–that in J. M. Coetzee's *In the Heart of the Country* (1976) and that in Nadine Gordimer's *July's People* (1981). These novels are not presentations of violence *per se*; rather, they are psychologically complex portraits of people, black and white, trying to come to terms with new political realities . . . and failing.

Chapter 11 analyzes two very different predictions, two "dreams." The first is presented largely through images in the poems of Mazisi Kunene's *The Ancestors & the Sacred Mountain* (1982); the second is presented through the story of a puzzlingly apolitical heroine in Nadine Gordimer's *A Sport of Nature* (1987).

The bulk of this book looks at the lion, those who hear (and are disturbed by) its cry, and what waits at the end of the path the lion is taking. Prior to this thematic journey, the book offers Part I, entitled "A Map." This section deals with two separate matters that readers may need to acquire an initial understanding of contemporary South African literature in English.

Chapter 1, "The Sociopolitical Environment," presents a by-necessity abbreviated account of South Africa's political history. Then, it examines the nation's four racial groups (once defined by law) in order to pinpoint the differences among them in such areas as income and education and health. That there are marked differences is a reflection of the failure of the policy of apartheid to bring about the promised separate development.

Chapter 2, "The Landmarks," examines four earlier works of South African literature. These works, very different from each other, foreground any discussion of the post-1960 writing. In turn, the chapter examines Olive Schreiner's 1883 *The Story of an African Farm,* Sarah Gertrude Millin's 1924 *God's Step-Children,* Peter Abraham's 1946 *Mine Boy,* and Alan Paton's 1948 *Cry, the Beloved Country*.

Throughout this book, I have made every effort to present both the historical-political material and the literature objectively. Like Atwood, I have tried **not** to let either my politics or my chosen themes determine what I do with the numerous works of literature this book surveys.

The questions I have asked of the literature are the critical ones the works seem to require. Given my audience's diverse (and in some cases) limited background in criticism, I have borrowed from a variety of critical approaches (but not from any obscure corners) to come up with the questions that lead to answers that provide an introductory guide. Thus, sometimes I will sound like a New Critic, asking questions about imagery and other formalistic matters, while at other times I will sound like a post-colonial critic who has been influenced by feminist criticism*s* or a reader response critic who stopped reading Stanley Fish et al., while there was still a text in the class, one constructed by a highly conscious rhetorical artist. My critical perspective then is probably most influenced by R. S Crane and Wayne C. Booth in so far as I tend to ask questions of a rhetorical sort and I tend to incorporate the insights of theoreticians of several sorts into my "pluralistic" approach **if** those insights assist in reading and interpreting a text.

If one is looking for a theoretically "pure" work, this study is not it. Again, my model is Atwood's *Survival*. She could have adopted the *ethos* of an academician, of a critic of a particular sort, but she explicitly chose not to. She chose her persona and her methods because she intended *Survival* to be reader-oriented: to give readers an easy-to-grasp, easy-to-apply framework for studying "Can. Lit." That her readers might, later on, choose to depart from either her framework or her particular interpretations of literary works, I'm sure, did not bother Atwood. When they so departed, they no longer needed *her* guidebook; they were ready to make a guidebook of their own.

The same is true in this study. My persona and my intention match Atwood's. And I will not be disturbed if, after benefitting from what I present, readers choose to see texts and groups of texts differently or through different critical lenses. The guidebook I present is designed to provide those who are curious but not yet well acquainted with access to a fascinating and important body of literature. Once they gain access, they may, of course, pursue their own courses.

None of this, of course, means that I don't still see these many literary works the way I present them. As the many students I have introduced to South African literature can attest, I do teach these works pretty much the way I discuss them here. And it is my success in teaching them and thereby giving undergraduates a good "feel" for this one particular "other" English literature that caused me to write this book. So, I'd like to thank these many students for learning so well—and expressing a great deal of enthusiasm for what it was that they were learning. I'd also like to thank Nancy Newins and JoAnn Snapp, reference librarians at Randolph-Macon College for helping me locate and then acquire through inter-library loan many of the works of South African literature that I discuss in this book as well as many book-length and article-length studies of them. Finally, I'd like to acknowledge the financial assistance I received from Randolph-Macon College. In the Summer of 1989 and in the Summer of 1991, I received small grants from the College's honors program to develop and then further develop a seminar devoted exclusively to a study of contemporary South African literature in English. A more substantial 1990 grant from the Walter Williams Craigie Endowment funded much of my reading of the primary and secondary material relevant to this book and my drafting of a prospectus for and two sample chapters of this book. An even more substantial 1993 grant from The Rashkind Family Endowment, coupled with sabbatical leave from my teaching duties, funded not only the time necessary to complete the project but a trip to South Africa—to see the land and the people I talk about in class and now in print. On that trip, I took several guidebooks, and I used them. I hope that readers interested in contemporary

South African literature in English will use **this** guide, just as I used those.

TFS
Randolph-Macon College
Ashland, Virginia
Fall 1994

Acknowledgements

To succeed in meeting my goal of introducing and interesting readers to the English literature of contemporary South Africa, I felt I must quote the representative works surveyed in this study rather generously. Below I list the permissions secured for the more extensive quoting of these works.

Peter Abrahams, *Mine Boy*. London: Faber & Faber Ltd., 1946, 1963. Reprinted with the permission of the publisher. All rights reserved.

Alan Paton, *Cry, The Beloved Country*—Reprinted with the permission of Scribner's, an imprint of Simon & Schuster from CRY, THE BELOVED COUNTRY by Alan Paton. Copyright 1948 Alan Paton; copyright renewed © 1976 Alan Paton. Reprinted with the permission of Jonathan Cape Ltd., Random House UK Ltd.

Bessie Head, *When Rain Clouds Gather*—Reprinted by permission of John Johnson Ltd., London. Copyright © The Estate of Bessie Head, 1968.

Ahmed Essop, *Hajji Musa and the Hindu Fire-Walker: Stories*. London: Reader's International, 1988. Reprinted by permission of the publisher. All rights reserved.

Modikwe Dikobe, *The Marabi Dance*. Oxford: Heinemann Publishers Ltd., 1980. Reprinted by permission of the publisher. All rights reserved.

D. M. Zwelonke, *Robben Island*. Oxford: Heinemann Publishers Ltd., 1977. Reprinted by permission of the publisher. All rights reserved.

Dennis Brutus, *Letters to Martha*. Oxford: Heinemann Publishers Ltd., 1968. Reprinted by permission of the publisher. All rights reserved.

Oswald Mtshali, *Sounds of a Cowhide Drum*. Oxford: Oxford University Press, 1971. Reprinted by permission of the publisher. All rights reserved.

Mongane Wally Serote, *No Baby Must Weep*. Jeppestown, South Africa: Ad. Donker, 1975. Reprinted by permission of Mongane Wally Serote and Ad. Donker Ltd.

Mafika Pascal Gwala, *No More Lullabies*. Johannesburg: Ravan Press, 1982. Reprinted by permission of the publisher. All rights reserved.

Keorapetse Kgositsile, *My Name Is Africa*. New York: Doubleday, 1971. Reprinted by permission of the publisher. All rights reserved.

Sipho Sepamla. *The Soweto I Love*. Claremont, South Africa: David Philip, 1977. Reprinted by permission of Sipho Sepamla. All rights reserved.

Sheila Roberts, *The Weekenders*. Johannesburg: Bateleur, 1981. Reprinted by permission of Sheila Roberts. All rights reserved.

Nadine Gordimer, *Something Out There*. Copyright © 1979, 1981, 1982, 1983, 1984 by Nadine Gordimer. Used by permission of Viking Penguin, a division of Penguin Books USA Inc. Reprinted by permission of Russell & Volkening as agents for the author. Copright © 1979 by Nadine Gordimer.

J. M. Coetzee, *Waiting for the Barbarians*. Copyright © 1980 by J. M. Coetzee. Used by permission of Viking Penguin, a division of Penguin Books USA Inc. Reprinted by permission of Reed Consumer Books Ltd., London.

Athol Fugard, *"Master Harold" and the Boys*. Copright © 1982 by Athol Fugard. Reprinted by permission of Alfred A. Knopf Inc.

Nadine Gordimer, *Burger's Daughter*. Copyright © 1979 by Nadine Gordimer. Used by permission of Viking Penguin, a division of Penguin Books USA Inc. Reprinted by permission of Russell & Volkening as agents for the author. Copyright © 1979 by Nadine Gordimer.

Andre Brink, *A Dry White Season*. Copyright © 1979 by Andre Brink. Reprinted by permission of William Morrow & Company, Inc., New York, and Andre Brink.

J. M. Coetzee, *In the Heart of the Country*. Copyright © 1976, 1977 by J. M. Coetzee. Used by permission of Viking Penguin, a division of Penguin Books USA Inc. Reprinted by permission of J. M. Coetzee.

Mazisi Kunene. *The Ancestors & The Sacred Mountain Poems*. Oxford: Heinemann Publishing Ltd., 1982. Reprinted by permission of Mathabo Rachel Kunene.

Nadine Gordimer, *A Sport of Nature*. Copyright © 1987 by Nadine Gordimer. Reprinted by permission of Alfred A. Knopf Inc.

PART I

A Map

1

The Sociopolitical Environment

Once upon a time, students majoring in literature were routinely told to enroll in courses in history. Then, perhaps prompted by the New Criticism's stress on literature as ahistorical texts, literature and history split apart. If students, however, tried to read most South African literature without some sense of the land's history and politics, they would have a great deal of difficulty, for South African literature—at least the English language literature—more often than not deals, directly or indirectly, with the country's political problems. The political problems result in social problems, and all of these problems are rooted in history. And these problems are so overwhelming that it is difficult for writers to *not* reflect or confront them.

There are several full-length introductory histories of South Africa in print: two are listed at the end of this chapter. Some students *might* want to study these. However, most students need only a brief treatment—light on names and dates—to gain access to the literature. This chapter offers such a brief treatment, ending with a discussion of the social consequences of recent South African political history.

The history of southern Africa, as far as the white man is concerned, begins in 1652 with the Dutch settlement at Table Bay. The Dutch saw this settlement near the Cape of Good Hope as a way-station for its merchant ships sailing between Europe and "the East." However, the way-station grew into a small colony, and the residents farmed and raised livestock.

There were black Africans in the region when the Dutch arrived, and, in less than a decade, hostilities began between the Dutch or Boers and these black Africans (the Khoi and San), probably prompted by their poaching of the Boers' livestock, which the black Africans saw as wildlife not property.

These Black Africans were, pretty much, eliminated as a presence in what was becoming the Cape Colony in less than a century. Some were killed; some died of smallpox (especially in the epidemic year of 1713); and many inter-married or "inter-related" with the Boers. From these many sexual liaisons arose the mixed-blood "colored" people of South Africa who are especially numerous in the present-day Cape Province.

Throughout the eighteenth century, the Boer presence in southern Africa grew, and the territory they occupied expanded in a northeastwardly direction from Cape Town, the original Table Bay settlement. As the Boers moved northeastwardly, they encountered other groups of Black Africans, who for hundreds of years had been slowly migrating southwestwardly in search of better land. Conflict between the white settlers and these black African people began in 1779 and lasted for over fifty years. The (white) historians refer to the several outbreaks of conflict as the Kaffir Wars, and, during the fifty year-plus period, there were six Kaffir Wars.

By the time these wars ended, four other "events" had changed the colonial picture: first, more and more slaves were imported into southern Africa to help work the growing Boer farms; second, more and more British missionaries and British colonists joined the Boers in the Cape colony; third, in 1795, the British government took official control over the colony; and fourth, some years later, the British government abolished slavery. No civil war was fought in the Cape between the Boers and the British: the colony changed hands because of events back in Europe. The Boers, however, were angry enough to fight (but they did not). Then, when the British freed their slaves, the Boers became even angrier. But rather than fight, they fled.

In 1836, the Boers began their "Great Trek" out of the Cape Colony into the interior of southern Africa. They founded what would become the "Orange Free State." Some Boers went farther into the interior: some crossed the Drakensberg Mountains into the area that became Natal; others crossed the Vaal River and founded what would become the Transvaal.

Meanwhile, the British were preoccupied with extending their influence up the Indian Ocean coast. They eventually turned their attention to what is the present-day province of Natal. As the British settled this region during the nineteenth century, there was conflict between the colonists, British and Boer, and the Zulu people whose land was being slowly usurped. There was also large-scale importation of Indians as indentured servants into Natal. It is from these imported Indians (many of whom left Natal for the growing Transvaal cities) that South Africa's Asian or Indian population stems. And this population group is still to be found primarily in Natal, especially in and around the port city of Durban. As Natal became increasingly British in character, many Boers left and moved into the Transvaal.

In 1867 and in 1872, momentous events occurred in the Boer-dominated interior that caused the British to cease leaving those who had treked across the Orange and Vaal Rivers pretty much alone. In 1867, in the Orange Free State, diamonds were discovered; in 1872, in the Transvaal, gold was discovered. Both "finds," it was clear from the beginning, were *significant* ones. The British, desiring that the new-found mineral wealth of the Orange Free State and the Transvaal belong to the Empire, began trying to control and/or annex these two regions. The Boers did not want to have control of their new lands taken from them. Thus began the two Anglo-Boer Wars. The first was in 1880; the second extended from 1899 to 1902.

The Boers or Afrikaners (as they are known in this century) have not yet forgotten the Anglo-Boer Wars. They resent what ultimately proved to be a British victory. They remember that the British had to bring in troops from elsewhere in the Empire (for example, from Australia) to overcome the Boer forces; they also remember that the British shipped many Afrikaner women and children off to concentration camps. Although these British acts can certainly be questioned if not condemned, their behavior after the wars should probably be questioned and commended, for an "enlightened" new British government did not annex the Boer-Afrikaner colonies but, rather, granted them self-government. The grateful Afrikaner leaders proved able to put any anti-English anger aside and to work with British leaders elsewhere in southern Africa. The result was, in 1910, the creation of the Union of South Africa, which merged the four existing colonies or lands: the Cape, the Orange Free State, the Transvaal, and Natal. This new nation, with a combined Afrikaner and English leadership in the political and economic spheres, would become part of the British Commonwealth, and all would seem peaceful until after World War II.

At the turn of the century, in the Transvaal cities, the British began acting against the Indian population, denying political rights to the people they, the British, had brought to South Africa. Among other anti-Indian acts, the British compelled Indians to carry pass books certifying where they could live and work. In the first decade of the twentieth century, Indians in this province began practicing passive resistance to the pass book and other laws. A young lawyer named Gandhi learned his initial lessons about passive resistance in South Africa in 1906.

Gandhi was not the only one who learned from what the Indians were doing in Natal. Blacks elsewhere in South Africa were inspired by the Indians, and, by 1919, a black organization known as the African National Congress (ANC) was using passive resistance against pass book laws that had been passed in the new Union of South Africa. Beginning with this activity by the ANC in 1919, we can trace a pattern of black activism followed by white suppression followed by black activism followed by white suppression. And, each time, the black activism became more militant and the white suppression became more violent. Unfortunately, intermixed with the black activism were Marxism and communism. I say "unfortunately" because the Marxist-communist dimension of black activism in South Africa seems to have prevented Western Europe and the United States from attending to the black cause in South Africa until the 1970s.

Parallel to this pattern of black activism and white suppression was the slow increase in Afrikaner economic and political power. Historically, the Boers-Afrikaners were a rural, farming people. They not only were not involved in the business of South Africa, but believed that involvement would be spiritually debilitating. The land would nourish their souls; the city and the city's business would corrupt them. Believing that they were "saved" and the British were just this side of the devil, the

Boers-Afrikaners left the non-agricultural economy of South Africa to the English. Gradually, during the twentieth century, the Afrikaners became "comfortable" in the growing urban centers and in business. With an increased involvement in the nation's urban economy came an increased involvement in the nation's politics. More and more frequently, the Afrikaners in politics became members of the National Party. This very conservative political group had as its primary goal the preservation of the Afrikaner people and culture. This group believed that the British had tried to eliminate them during the Anglo-Boer Wars; this group believed that the other groups presently in South Africa, especially the blacks, represented a threat to the purity and the nobility of the Afrikaner people and their culture.

The year 1948 is a crucial year in the history of South Africa, for in 1948 the Afrikaner National Party gained control of the nation's government. Initially, the National Party was aided by a provision in South African law that gave Afrikaner-dominated rural areas proportionately higher representation in the Cape Town parliament than still heavily English urban areas. Once in power, the National Party increased its hold and has been dominant in South Africa from 1948 to the recent past, when a split between "enlightened" and "hard-line" factions characterizes the political group.

Shortly after ascending to power in 1948, the National Party acted to ensure the survival of the pure, noble Afrikaner culture. The party leaders believed that the only way to protect this culture from other groups that might threaten it or pollute it was to separate the racial groups in South Africa from each other. The leaders began erecting an official government policy of separateness, the Afrikaans word for which is "apartheid." A number of laws passed in and after 1950 implemented this policy. One, the Population Registration Act, declared all South Africans to be members of one of four racial groups, white, Asian, colored, and black. Where one could work and where one could live would hereafter be tied to which group one was in; where one could eat lunch and where one could see a movie or a play would hereafter be tied to which group one was in.

The apartheid laws can be conveniently ranked along a continuum. At one end would be the "petty apartheid" laws that forbade interracial dating (the so-called "sweetheart laws") and insisted on separate accommodations (hotels, restaurants, buses, theatres) for the different racial groups. At the other end of the continuum would be the denial of voting rights to all racial groups other than whites. In between are three sets of laws that I wish to deal with specifically because they figure so heavily in the English literature of South Africa. In 1950, the Afrikaner-dominated government passed the Group Areas Act. This Act attempted to physically separate the four racial groups. Certain regions of the urban areas would be white-only; other areas black-only; etc. Thus, Johannesburg *per se* became a white-only city. Townships that almost ring Johannesburg—with a "no man's land" buffer zone in between—became a black-only city. Black and colored and Asian workers were needed in the white cities, so the government did not want to separate these groups from the white group by too great a distance. If it were not for this economic necessity, the National Party might well have insisted on greater separation. This likelihood is seen in what the government did indeed do to many of the most threatening groups, the blacks, who comprise close to three-quarters of the nation's population. The government decided that as many blacks as economically feasible ought to be returned to their native regions. The government then determined that the blacks were really ten tribes; then, the government determined where these tribes were from. Coincidentally, the tribes all seemed to be "from" some of the worst land in South Africa. Then, blacks were forcibly removed from where they had been living and transported to their tribal *homelands*. The government appointed tribal chiefs and proposed that these men could eventually lead their tribes to independence from South Africa. Four of these ten homelands, the Ciskei, the Transkei, Bophuthatswana, and Venda, have been "granted" independence by the South African government. However, the rest of the world *does not* recognize these four homelands as independent entities but rather sees them as still economically and militarily *and politically* under the control of the South African government.

But not all black South Africans were transported to these remote, impoverished homelands. Many were granted passes that allowed them to live in the urban townships and work in the white-only urban centers. Since the urban centers required far more male labor than female labor, families were often split up by the government: the men were to stay in townships like Soweto and live in dormitory-like hostels; the women and children were to go off to the homelands. The white-only cities (and their posh suburbs) did require some female labor. So, in some cases, the situation was reversed: the women (and their children) stayed either in the townships or in backyard "servants' quarters" in the white areas while the men went to the homelands.

Black family life was largely destroyed as a result of these government actions. Township-residing men frequently would have a township wife and a homeland wife and have children by each; township residing women would have a township husband and a homeland husband and have children by each. But the "pattern" in the townships was "messier" than this polygamous/polyandrous picture suggests. Many resisted the government laws and lived (from the beginning or eventually) in the townships so as to keep their families intact. Many men, unable to thrive (even exist) in the homelands, came illegally to the townships and tried to either get a pass entitling them to live there and work in the city or get by through illicit activities. Even before this influx of males to the townships and especially afterwards, males outnumbered females there. And the hostel-living men were prone to heavy drinking and violence. The problems that had existed at the black male-only workcamps that had been set up near the diamond and gold mines in previous decades were exacerbated by the "separate development" policy pursued by the National Party-controlled government.

The Group Areas Act (and associated other pieces of legislation) helped create the homelands and townships that (still) dominate the South African scene and play a major role in the English language literature, especially the literature authored by black South Africans (who write in English or a native tongue, *not* in Afrikaans). The second set of laws I've already glanced at: the pass laws. If one was black or colored or Asian, one had to carry, at all times, a passbook. This book indicated where one could work and where one could live. Carrying a passbook (and presenting it upon demand for inspection) was a sign of second-class (or lower) citizenship. The passbooks were, as a result, resented and figure in many literary works as a symbol of oppression. The passbooks were also one's route to privileges: if one's passbook had the right stamps or if one could steal or otherwise acquire someone else's passbook that had the right stamps, one had access to the few opportunities and privileges available to people of the non-white racial groups. That the passbooks had a contradictory quality–symbol of oppression *and* route to opportunity and privilege–gives them a multifaceted richness as a symbol or plotting device in much of the literature.

In 1950, the government passed another law, the Suppression of Communism Act. This law and others that followed gave the South African government, especially the police, considerable power to act against anyone or any group suspected of being communist. And, as I already noted, black activism was always treated by the government as communist. Detention without trial, torture while in prison, and the suppression of rights during frequently declared states of emergency were justified as necessary anti-communist measures. It is important to note that South Africa has no written bill of rights. This absence made it especially easy for the government to act in whatever manner it deemed necessary. Many works of literature, authored by English White and Black South Africans, show the government using its various security laws to oppress black South Africans and members of other racial groups who choose to sympathize with the plight of their Black countrymen/women. These works of literature also suggest that a suppress-communism-at-any price mentality has led the police and the armed forces to act behind-the-scenes in many sinister ways. The laws of apartheid are numerous. The three clusters I have discussed at some length–the laws that determined where the different races could live; the laws that required some races to carry passbooks; and the laws that granted the government and the police unbridled power to suppress communism–are important in general and are important in the literature. But they represent only a part of the "structure" of apartheid that the National Party began erecting in 1950.

As one might expect, there was considerable resistance to these laws. The ANC protested; the even more militant Pan-African Congress (PAC) demonstrated. Fire bombs were thrown; passbooks were burned. Finally, in 1960, the anti-apartheid sentiment erupted in riots in the township of Sharpeville in the southern Transvaal. The government squashed the rioting, *violently*, and proceeded to ban the ANC and PAC and throw their leaders in prison. Among them was, of course, ANC leader Nelson Mandela, who would spend the next twenty-one years of his life on Robben Island off the Cape Province's southwest coast.

Opposition to apartheid went underground for several years. It emerged in 1970 with the South African Student Organization (SASO) led by Steve Biko. What differentiated SASO's action from that of previous anti-apatheid groups was its emphasis on building pride among the members of the black community. A great deal of the English language poetry written by blacks at this time reflects both Biko's emphasis on "black consciousness" and similar movements in French Africa and the United States. The South African government, however, did not treat SASO and Biko differently from their anti-apartheid predecessors. Refusing to understand the "black pride" message and upset by SASO and Biko's rallies celebrating the Marxist revolution in Mozambique, the government banned Biko. Then, when he violated the restrictions placed upon him as a banned person, he was thrown in prison, where he was tortured and died.

In the mid 1970s, the South African government began to see that suppression alone was not going to quiet the unrest in the Black townships. The government began repealing some of the "petty apartheid" laws, hoping that these repeals would have a symbolic quality and soothe angry tempers. Unfortunately, not to appear weak in the eyes of the extreme right-wingers of the National Party, the government insisted that some of the edicts of the (white) Minister for Bantu (black) Education be carried out in the schools of the black townships. One of these edicts was that blacks learn Afrikaans; another was that a specified portion of the post-elementary schooling be conducted in Afrikaans. The attempt to carry out this edict led school children in several townships to go on strike and demonstrate against being forced to learn and learn in what they called "the oppressor's language." In June 1976, South African police opened fire on one such demonstration in the large township of Soweto (southwest of Johannesburg), killing many unarmed children. Riots ensued for days in Soweto and elsewhere in the country; overall, close to 500 black South Africans lost their lives. These riots figure in much of the nation's English language literature; these riots also effect a definite change in the tone of the black poetry, as many poets abandon "black consciousness" for revolution.

The Soweto riots also destroyed the anti-Communist facade behind which the South African government had oppressed its non-white people for twenty-five years. No longer did the world community, especially Western Europe and the United States, uncomfortably accept what was going on in South Africa as necessary to combat global communism. South Africa became a pariah state, progressively weakened by international sanctions. Black South Africans were probably hurt more by the sanctions than white South Africans, but, white South Africans were hurt as one of the world's richest nations slid into a deep recession. At the same time, black militancy increased. And, in the eyes of most observers, civil war—bloody civil war—was imminent.

At this point, leadership in South Africa changed hands: Botha went out of office; De Klerk came in. Seeing no alternative, De Klerk began dismantling the structures of apartheid. He freed political prisoners, including ANC leader Nelson Mandela, and legalized banned black political organizations such as the ANC. He then embarked on the very rocky path toward a new Constitution for South Africa, one that embraced the non-white racial groups.

Those negotiations led to a provisional Constitution and the first all-races elections in April 1994, elections that brought the ANC and Nelson Mandela to power. The elections were accompanied by violence, especially in Natal; and the elections will certainly be followed by violence—in Natal and elsewhere. This violence reflects several tensions that continue to exist in contemporary South Africa, tensions that the new government will have to address.

The first is a tension within the Afrikaner community. Many feel that a transition to shared power within the context of a black majority government is necessary if not proper. However, some fear for their property, whereas still others believe that they are a superior people and therefore ought to rule. Their superiority is proven, in their eyes, by the modern South African nation that *they* built. Furthermore, they are entitled to the wealth they have accumulated because their expertise generated this wealth. Many Afrikaners who embrace this very pro-white view have or have had ties to the nation's military and security forces. These ties make pro-white counter-revolutionary terrorism or military action a very real possibility in South Africa's future.

The second tension is between the ANC and the Inkatha Freedom Party and their respective leaders Mandela and Zulu chief Buthelezi, who competed during the pre-election period for the role of spokesperson for the Black South African people. De Klerk recognized the ANC and Mandela, turning his back on the man the Afrikaner government had earlier installed as the chief of the KwaZulu homeland. Buthelezi claims considerable support among perhaps the one South African "tribe" that maintains a strong tribal identity, the Zulus. Considerable unrest exists as a result in Natal and in the Jo'burg townships, such as Soweto, to which many Zulu men have gone seeking work and where they must live in cramped hostels side-by-side with ANC-supporting others. Polls show that the ANC is indeed the party of choice of the vast majority of black South Africans; however, Buthelezi does indeed have a considerable following, especially in Natal. The supposed solution to the Mandela-Buthelezi rivalry was federalism, with the provinces (now numbering nine) having far more power under the new constitution than under the old. Under a more federal system, Buthelezi could play a major role, but in Natal, not in the central government. Buthelezi, however, after calling for just such a federal system, seems discontent with the extent to which federalism has been incorporated into the provisional constitution. His role in the future of South Africa is, at this point, unclear. Based on the results of the April 1994 elections and Mandela's desire to embrace all political groups in the new South Africa, Inkatha will dominate the new province of Natal-KwaZulu, and Inkatha will have some role in the federal government. Precisely where Buthelezi himself will fit in is uncertain—probably because he has not yet determined where he can gain the most political advantage.

The third tension is between the ANC and some considerably smaller, more militant black groups (as well as a more militant faction within the ANC). These more militant blacks reject compromise and sometimes advocate anti-white violence—their rallying cry being "One Settler, One Bullet." They also, rather unrealistically, expect their economic circumstances to change *dramatically* once South Africa becomes Azania (the black African name for the nation). They view the negotiations as a selling-out, and they think that ANC leaders such as Nelson Mandela have become complacent in their advocacy of the black cause once they began enjoying the limousines, five-star hotel suites, and silk sheets once reserved for the privileged, power-holding whites. Mandela's most difficult task may well be convincing these militant Black South Africans—and the many they might incite—to be patient and realistic. Some immediate tangible improvements in the lives of township-residing Black South Africans will, however, probably be absolutely necessary: patience and realism will probably have to be purchased.

Thus far, what I've presented is a narrative—fast at times; slow at others: always with the needs of readers of the English language literature in mind. Now, I'd like to offer a different perspective—a static one. Although the laws establishing racial groups in South Africa are no longer extant, there are still important differences to note among these groups. I'd like then to look at five groups (the four racial categories with the whites split into English and Afrikaner) socioeconomically.

The English white South Africans have, since World War II, shrunk in numbers as well as in importance. Once the backbone of the booming South African economy, the English are increasingly "off on the side." They are to be found in sizeable numbers in the Cape Province, Natal, and the Transvaal. Always an urban people, they have become even more urban over the past half century. Their language is, obviously, English. They are affluent. They belong to a wide variety of churches. They do seem to be a divided lot on the compelling political questions facing South Africa. Many are activists who have fought to dismantle the Afrikaner institution of apartheid; many are also comfortably non-involved, hoping the problems somehow go away. (Most of the significant white English language writers are from the activist group.)

The Afrikaners are also a shrinking presence in South Africa—particularly when one looks at what percentage of the total population they comprise. However, unlike the English, the Afrikaners have increased their political and economic power and, until very recently, they were becoming increasingly affluent. The countrywide recession experienced since 1976 and the prospect of black majority rule (and property redistribution) have caused the Afrikaners' prospects to look dull, not bright, in recent years. The Afrikaners are traditionally a rural people, and there are still many Afrikaners residing in the rural areas of the Orange Free State and the Transvaal. However, over the past half century, the Afrikaners have become increasingly urban dwellers—dominating many neighborhoods in Johannesburg and Pretoria, the two larger cities in the Transvaal. The Afrikaners speak Afrikaans, a language that descends from seventeenth-century Dutch but is probably closer to present-day German than present-day Dutch. Afrikaans newspapers, radio stations, and television shows exist to serve the Afrikaans-speaking population, and these media tend to be more conservative and more highly censored (on political and on obscenity grounds) than the comparable media serving the English-speaking population. This conservatism and censorship is a reflection of the Afrikaners' overwhelming membership in the rather puritanical Calvinist Nederduitse Gereformeerde Kerk (NGK). Uniformity in religion does not translate into uniformity in politics. Afrikaners run the continuum between enlightened reformers, such as De Klerk, and self-proclaimed Neo-Nazis.

The English and the Afrikaners share some characteristics. The government spends about the same amount *per capita* on the education of English and Afrikaner children. The doctor-patient ratio (1:400) and the hospital bed-person ratio (1:96) are the same in English-dominated and Afrikaner-dominated areas of the country. These numbers are typical of highly developed countries, as is the age distribution of the English and Afrikaner populations and the diseases that tend to kill them—cardiovascular problems and cancer.

The colored population is small and predominantly in the Cape Province. Once a rural people, working the farms of their Boer masters, the coloreds are increasingly urban. Their average income is 20 percent of what the whites make, resulting in their living just at the poverty line. They tend to speak Afrikaans, a reflection of their past close association with the rural Afrikaners. However, many have deliberately chosen to use English, not Afrikaans. This choice reflects a marked split among the coloreds between those who are still allied with and supportive of the Afrikaner society and those who have sought solidarity with black South Africans. Many in this latter group now refuse to call themselves "colored," prefering "black" or "African" or "People of Color." Given the close relationship that existed between the coloreds and the Afrikaners, one might expect coloreds to be members of the NGK. Instead, the coloreds tend to be either Anglican or Roman Catholic.

The small Asian population is, as one might expect, Hindu. They are to be found predominantly in Natal and have been, since their arrival in South Africa as indentured servants, an urban people. Thus, parts of the Indian Ocean port of Durban have a distinctive Indian flavor. They fare economically slightly better than the coloreds—23 percent of the white per capita income—but are like the coloreds, right on the poverty line. But this figure is an average, and in the Indian community, there is quite a range—from rather affluent merchants to impoverished street people. Once there was a great deal of class conflict among the South African Indians or Asians; however, it has been fading as they have increasingly found a measure of common cause in opposing the provisions of apartheid that have affected them.

Apartheid has had negative effects on South Africa's colored and Asian peoples; however, apartheid has had, as the preceding narrative suggested, its most devastating effects on the country's black population. This group comprises close to 75 percent of the nation's population. The ancestors of the present-day blacks settled the eastern half of the country in a rather even pattern. However, their interactions with the white colonialists and post-colonialists tended to draw them into pockets of dense population—mining towns, homelands, townships—and make them an urban people. Blacks use English, a variety of native languages, and often a mixture when speaking; they tend to use English when writing, reflecting their desire to communicate to an audience that extends beyond fellow black South Africans. They belong to a variety of religious groups, with Methodism and several Black Christian churches dominating the urban scene and native religions still finding some adherents in rural areas. They are, as a group, impoverished, their per capita income being only 10 percent of that of the white South Africans. Their prospects are not, under Afrikaner rule at least, bright, for the Afrikaner government spends ten times more on each white child's education as on each black child's. In addition, their health needs are not met well by the government, with the doctor-patient ratio among blacks being 1:40,000 (as opposed to 1:400 among whites) and the hospital bed-person ratio being 1:186 (as opposed to 1:96 among whites). Blacks, together with most coloreds and some Asians, have very different health problems from those of the whites. Like many Third World populations, the blacks suffer from tuberculosis, malaria, and nutritional deficiencies, not heart attacks, strokes, and cancer.

The black population may well be united in its opposition to Afrikaner policies; however, there are some marked tensions in black communities. I've already mentioned the tension between Inkatha and ANC members and the tension between more militant black groups and the ANC. One must superimpose this tension on several others. There has long been tension in the South African black population between those who have embraced Western ways and those who, by choice or because of where they have lived, have held to native African customs and beliefs. Somewhat paralleling this tension is another between those who are educated and those who are not. There may also be some tension among tribes. Although tribal differences may have diminished in the urban areas, they still exist there and especially in rural areas. These differences are to some extent entrenched because the tribes still use different African languages and these languages figure these peoples' relationships to other peoples, to the environment, and to the divine differently.

Finally, there has long been tension in the townships between those "entitled" to reside there and those who have migrated there and live there illegally. This tension has been a "have" vs. "have not" one, exacerbated by the tendency of many migrants to live a less "settled" life-style and to drift into violence and crime. The laws that labeled some black township residents as "Section 10" and others as illegal are, of course, no longer in force; however, the tension between the two groups remains.

Students of South African literature in English may well need to know more about the history, politics, and demography of the nation, and resources can be found in most university libraries to help them acquire that knowledge. The information in this chapter should give these students a solid start–enough to understand what is in the background–and often in the foreground–of most contemporary literary texts. Students of this literature probably do, however, need to do one thing beyond reading this chapter: read the newspaper to keep up with the *very* volatile situation in South Africa *today*. This chapter has offered–more accurately, implied–some forecasts; however, they are nothing more than educated guesses. They may prove wrong. The literature of contemporary South Africa that post-dates this book will reflect what really happens, not necessarily these guesses. Therefore, as students proceed onward from the literature discussed here to other, more recent literature, they need not just the story and the socioeconomic profile presented here but the rest of the story and an updated profile.

Works Cited

Davenport, T. R. H. *South Africa: A Modern History*. 4th ed. Toronto: University of Toronto Press, 1991.

Nelson, Harold, ed. *South Africa: A Country Study*. 2nd ed. Washington, DC: Government Printing Office, 1981.

Omer-Cooper, J. D. *History of Southern Africa*. London: James Currey, 1987.

2

Landmarks

South African literature in English, of course, did not begin in 1960 after the riots in Sharpeville and the subsequent suppression of black political groups such as the ANC. This book focuses on the contemporary, because it is out of the turmoil of the post-Sharpeville period that a particularly large, particularly rich literature emerges. This chapter, however, looks at four works of South African literature written earlier than 1960. These works serve as landmarks. They are similar; they are different. Two come from earlier times; two from the late 1940s. Put together, they raise many themes and many issues that continue to surface in the post-1960 literature. Thus, in ways that are sometimes subtle, these four works, Olive Schreiner's *The Story of An African Farm* (1883), Sarah Gertrude Millin's *God's Stepchildren* (1924), Peter Abrahams' *Mine Boy* (1946), and Alan Paton's *Cry, the Beloved Country* (1948), foreground the literature that this thematic introduction focuses on.

The Story of An African Farm

Olive Schreiner's novel has received considerable praise–in and out of South Africa. However, it will probably strike a reader today as a book that is good in parts. In writing the novel, Schreiner blends herself, people she had encountered in the South African colony, and several stereotypes and gives the reader several memorable characters. She discusses these characters' lives against two backdrops: a philosophical backdrop informed by much nineteenth-century European thought and a geographical backdrop that simultaneously offers local color and plays off of a land-based mythology. The novel lacks structure; some of its reflective passages are tediously long. Nonetheless, through its characters and through its two backdrops *The Story of an African Farm* does provide the reader with a good sense of the South Africa that is emerging, as a place and as a state of mind, in the later nineteenth century.

The novel features two sets of characters, each drawn from different generations The older generation characters in Schreiner's novel are stereotypes. The one truly older character, the German overseer, may well be drawn by Schreiner partially using her father as the model. But Schreiner gives the sketch a stereotypical nobility and a simplicity that suggests characters such as Wordsworth's Michael (in "Michael") and Hardy's Gabriel Oak (in *Far From the Madding Crowd*) and other romanticized pastoral figures. The duplicitous Irishman, Napoleon Blenkins, who manages to bring about the ruin of the overseer, is a diabolically comic not a noble stereotype. The conflict between these two characters dominates the initial third of the novel. The conflict reveals the obvious about the overseer and Blenkins: that the one is noble and the other not. What is more important is the effect that the conflict has on the third stereotype, the Boer woman Tant' Sannie. She has been widowed twice and is looking for a new spouse. Her role in life is to be housewife and baby producer, and as she pursues this role, without skill or success, she gets fatter and fatter. Nonetheless, she assumes that her possessions and her person qualify her as a prize catch. She knows her Bible; nonetheless, she finds cruelty toward others as amusing, not as inspiring Christian charity. Books other than the Bible she finds suspicious. Her second husband's books (English books, since he was English) have been crated and stored in the loft. These characteristics are those of the Boer "aunt" stereotype: domestic but unkempt, fecund but not maternal, coarsely fat, attuned to the Bible but not its Christian message, and stupid. Blenkins exploits her prejudices, her false vision of herself, and her stupidity and easily–very easily–dupes her into almost accepting him as her third husband. When she discovers him "making love" to her younger, much more attractive, and richer niece, she realizes what his game has been. However, prompted by Blenkins, she has already destroyed the noble German overseer and psychologically damaged the children living on the farm.

Schreiner's portrayal of Tant' Sannie suggests that *The Story of An African Farm* is, at least in part, a satire of nineteenth-century Boer life. This satire has resonance beyond 1883 because throughout the twentieth century, the Boers/Afrikaners have created and held to a myth based on their earlier rural life. Rather than living in wise and noble harmony with nature (what the myth suggests), the Boers, presented through Tant' Sannie, are far removed from wisdom and nobility. They are coarse, falsely proud, narrow-minded, cruel, stupid people. They live on the land, but they seem to have no relationship to this land. It's there; they're there. And that's the end of it.

The land itself is often portrayed by Schreiner as territory that one would probably not want to have a relationship with: hot, dry, sparsely green. This view further contradicts the myth of their past that present-day Afrikaners have created. Their rural homelands (to use the Afrikaners' term) are not at all the great farms of their myth. But far more important in Schreiner's novel is that their relationship to the land is not at all the beautiful one of their myth.

Others in the novel see the land quite differently. These others are the novel's younger generation characters. In fact, to varying degrees, these characters, whom we meet as children and see mature, see many matters quite differently. The Boer mentality oppresses them. Symbolic of this oppression would be the time Tant' Sannie locks the young girls Em and Lyndall into their room and the time Blenkins, with Tant' Sannie's approval, beats and then locks young Waldo in the fuel house. As in many nineteenth-century novels, physical structures and imprisonment within them function symbolically. But, despite this oppression, the children still manage to reflect on such matters as beauty, freedom, love, God, and the land. The bulk of the novel is the story of this reflecting.

The four younger characters are very different from each other. Em is Tant' Sannie's niece. The Boer blood seems to be in her veins, for despite being surrounded by the others, she seems to be settling into her aunt's life-style. We witness Em accepting the proposal of Gregory, although she really does not love him as much as she thinks she should (or as much as she loves her cousin Lyndall). When Gregory obviously falls in love with Lyndall, we witness Em sacrificing her immediate domestic comfort and ending the betrothal. Then, after Lyndall's death and Gregory's return to the farm, we witness Em settling for a sadly complacent life as Gregory's spouse. Their prospective union will be forever clouded by the death of Lyndall, whom they both loved more than each other, as well as by Gregory's latent homosexuality, something Schreiner hints at heavy-handedly. All along, we see Em getting fatter and fatter—becoming the Boer "aunt." Her tragedy then is that she cannot escape the shaping power that her culture exerts on her.

Lyndall's tragedy is quite different. Lyndall is English—the child of Tant' Sannie's second husband. She is drawn to questions philosophical and social. And she is drawn to those who ask such questions, such as Waldo. Everyone on the farm loves Lyndall—except 'Tant Sannie, but it is the English latecomer Gregory who expresses that love in a proposal of marriage. She does not love Gregory; however, she sees in his total devotion to her a way to maybe be married but still retain her freedom. So she agrees to marry him. Shortly before the wedding, she runs off with another man, a man she does indeed love. He wants to marry her, but she wants their relationship to be different. She wants to be lovers and companions until their passion (inevitably) fades; then she wants the freedom to abandon the relationship. They take off for the Transvaal together. Along the way, she becomes pregnant; also along the way, she loses her feelings for him and wants her freedom. So she abandons him. Then, alone in a hotel, she gives birth to a baby who lives but a few hours. Weakened by childbirth and further weakened by crying in the rain over the baby's grave, she falls ill and dies.

Lyndall is a rebel: not only does she not become trapped in the Boer culture, as Em does, but she rejects it—in a manner that would have, of course, been shocking in her time. She does not understand why her freedom must be diminshed, and it is clearly her freedom both as a person and as a woman that she is talking about:

> "It is not what is done to us, but what is made of us," she said at last, "that wrongs us. No man can be really injured but by what modifies

> himself. We all enter the world little plastic beings, with so much natural force, perhaps, but for the rest—blank; and the world tells us what we are to be, and shapes us by the ends it sets before us. To you it says, *Work!* and to us it says, *Seem!* To you it says, As you approximate to man's highest ideal of God, as your arm is strong and your knowledge great, and the power to labor is with you, so you shall gain all that human heart desires. To us it says, Strength shall not help you, nor knowledge, nor labor. You shall gain what men gain, but by other means. And so the world makes men and women." (222-23)

Her rebellion, however, does not lead to happiness; rather, it leads to death.

It is easy—too easy—to focus on her death and conclude that Schreiner's point is that someone with a philosophy like Lyndall's cannot be happy and cannot survive in Boer-defined South Africa. Schreiner is perhaps making this point; however, she is more strongly making the larger point that someone—a woman—like Lyndall cannot (yet) find a place in a world where she can be truly free. Lyndall thus stands beside two other heroines of her time, Australian (Stella) Miles Franklin's Sybylla Melvyn of *My Brilliant Career* (1899) and American Kate Chopin's Edna Pontelier of *The Awakening* (1900). Lyndall's story then is not simply an indictment of the Boer mentality. Furthermore, Lydall's story is not entirely tragic. The passages in which she communes with nature and sees a beauty in it that escapes the others' notice are powerful and beautiful. She found something in the land the supposedly land-loving Boers could not. Her death does not diminish that which she found during her brief lifetime. Furthermore, she lives on—beautifully—in the memories of those whose lives she touched. Her death has something of the quality of the death of a child, when the sadness is deep and the memories are especially beautiful. Throughout the novel, Schreiner describes Lyndall as a child, emphasizing her small hands and small feet. In a way then, growing up, in her Boer society and in her late nineteenth-century world, killed her, for that society and that world could not tolerate her desire to be free.

Lyndall's intelligence is obvious in the many passages in which she reflects; furthermore, that she has used that intelligence to shape a somewhat coherent philosophy for herself is also evident. Waldo, the son of the German overseer, reflects as much (if not more) than Lyndall does. His basic intelligence is obvious, but so is the fact that he is impeded from shaping a coherent philosophy by a number of factors: his questions are difficult ones; his anger and his despair intrude; and his intelligence is simply not great enough to think matters through as well or as fully as Lyndall.

He is drawn to nature more powerfully than Lyndall is, and, even though he cannot articulate what he feels, he *feels*—profoundly so. A passing stranger's allegorical tale gives Waldo clues, so does his study of Herbert Spencer's *First Principles*. In frustration and with the encouragement of Lyndall, he leaves the farm and goes to the burgeoning cities. Much like Fielding's heroes, he is driven back to the farm by the cities' wickedness. Once back in rural South Africa, he begins to attach himself to the life force that unites him and the other animals to the land:

> He was an uncouth creature, with small learning, and no prospect in the future but that of making endless tables and stone walls, yet it seemed to him as he sat there that life was a rare and very rich thing. He rubbed his hands in the sunshine. Ah, to live on so, year after year, how well! Always in the present, letting each day glide, bringing its own labor, and its own beauty,—the gradual lighting up of the hills, night and stars, firelight and the coals! To live on so, calmly, far from the paths of men; and to look at the lives of clouds and insects; to look deep into the heart of flowers, and see how lovingly the pistil and the stamens nestle there together; and to see in the thorn-pods how the little seeds suck their life through the delicate curled-up string, and how the little embryo sleeps inside! Well, how well, to sit so on the one side, taking no part in the world's life; but when great men blossom into books, looking into those flowers also, to see how the world of men too opens beautifully, leaf after leaf. Ah! life is delicious; well to live long, and see the darkness breaking, and the day coming,—the day when soul shall not thrust back soul that would come to it; when men shall not be driven to seek solitude, because of the crying out of their hearts for love and sympathy. (373-74)

Once he achieves that unity, in the novel's last sentence, he dies.

His death at a young age is, of course, tragic, but Schreiner presents Waldo's death in ambiguous terms. First, you have to pay very close attention to how Schreiner describes the behavior of chickens to even realize that Waldo has died. Second, since no creatures but the chickens know he is dead, you have no commentary in words or action by the other characters about his death. You are left with a picture: Waldo, in harmony with nature and the life force, dead; Waldo, at the successful conclusion of his philosophical struggle, dead.

Lyndall and Walso die; Em survives, but her survival is sad. Joining her in sadly surviving is Gregory. Gregory does not strike the reader as being as philosophical as Lyndall and Waldo are; rather, he is aesthetic, searching for beauty. He found beauty in Lyndall. His gushing proposal to her, although it may have sounded a great deal like his earlier gushing proposal to Em, proves to be based on an aesthetic love he could never have had for the rather plain-looking Em. And it was not just Lyndall's physical beauty that appealed to Gregory; it was her beautiful soul as well as her beautiful child-like hair, face, hands, and feet. And even Lyndall's physical appeal was rather "un-bodied," for, in assessing her beauty, Gregory jumps from her head to her extremities, not noting her sexual being. When Lyndall fled the farm, Gregory took off after her. He traced her path, town by town. Finally and accidentally, he found her dying in a hotel room. He then goes off to a dry riverbed, transforms himself from male to female (putting on Lyndall's mother's clothes), and returns to the hotel to nurse her until she dies. Then, he returns to the farm. There, he finds a four-word note Lyndall had written to him: "You must marry Em." He does. But, as I observed before, this union is one that we must have very reserved feelings about. It certainly is not the conventional happy-ending marriage of the nineteenth-century novel.

The younger generation in South Africa comes across in *The Story of An African Farm* as a more hopeful group than the one that preceded it. However, even this younger generation ends the novel sadly. The younger generation is beginning to question; the younger generation is rebelling; the younger generation desperately wants a **new** relationship to the land. However, the forces arrayed against this generation are still too strong to permit it.

God's Stepchildren

Those forces are numerous in Schreiner's novel. One fairly minor force is the city. It figures more in Waldo and Gregory's stories than in those of Em or Lyndall. The city will, however, play a stronger role in Sarah Gertrude Millin's *God's Stepchildren*, which presents the familiar city vs. the land dialectic of Western literature in terms that are distinctively South African insofar as it superimposes the nation's race relations on this city vs. the land motif.

In Schreiner's *The Story of An African Farm*, the land offered something, a "life force," to those who were sufficiently reflective. In Millin's *God's Stepchildren*, the land offers the very sad comfort of knowing who you are–in terms of race. It is away from the land in the city that those with some Black blood aspire to the life-styles of the white South Africans and try to pass as white; it is away from the land in the city that these colored people fail–sometimes immediately; sometimes eventually. The failures are traumatic, for both the colored characters and for the novel's readers, who feel the injustice of their situation. And for both these characters and the readers, the countryside offers at least a clearer sense of identity within the emerging racist schema of South Africa. Those who are black know they are black; those who are colored know they are colored; etc. Within the world that Millin constructs, there is a sad comfort to be found in living where one's place and one's identity are clear.

That the clear racial lines of the countryside offer this sad comfort suggests that *God's Stepchildren* takes an ambiguous moral stance. The novel is about miscegenation. We begin with the story of missionary Reverend Andrew Flood, who, to surmount the barriers that he believes exist between himself and his Hottentot people, marries a Hottentot woman. We then follow the successive generations of colored people who trace their origin to this union: Deborah, Kleinhans, Elmira, and, finally, Barry. As we follow the generations, the African blood decreases. Still, it is present. So, when Barry, now an Anglican minister, marries a young English girl named Nora and she becomes pregnant, he sees what he has done—passing on his tainted blood—as sinful, as criminal:

> As the train traversed the empty vastness of the land, the thoughts of Barry ran ceaselessly backwards and forwards from the past to the future. His ancestor, the Rev. Andrew Flood, had thrown away his white heritage, and for a hundred years at least one branch of his descendants had struggled to reach it again. They had diluted the blackness of their blood with whiteness until it was more white than black, until the whiteness was just barely tinted with black, until it was almost undistinguishably white, until there had resulted, in short, himself. And he, again, had followed the family tradition and had married upwards, and his child. . . . A spasm of terror passed over Barry Lindsell's face. His child. Nora's child. The vagaries of heredity. Who knew but that he, Barry, had made poor innocent Nora the vehicle for the vengeance of the Lord for the sins of the fathers? Who knew but that his child might be the sacrifice? His mind stood still for a moment, then began feverishly grinding out thoughts again. And yet it did not happen. And yet it might happen. And yet. . . . Ah, what was God going to do with them all? (294)

He sends her back to England, punishes himself by declaring that he will never see his child, and decides to go back to Canaan, the village the Reverend Andrew Flood had tried to bring to Christianity, to help the people there. His return to Canaan has two motives: to punish himself for his sin and to expiate his great-great-grandfather's sin. The sin is clearly mixing blood, or, as it is at times expressed, adding the dangerous, inferior taint of black blood to white blood. Either way, the novel's focus on this "sin" reinforces the racist mentality of the nation that Millin presents.

Millin does indeed criticize those who deny these colored South Africans fair treatment. Thus, the novel's moral stance seems somewhat enlightened; however, Millin does seem to criticize the Reverend Andrew Flood for mixing blood more severely. Furthermore, she seems to criticize those among his descendants who do not marry within their colored group. Kleinhans, for example, who marries the colored Lena, is treated throughout the novel as noble. Those who consort with whites, Deborah, Elmira, and Barry, are treated ambiguously: yes, they are victims of a racist state; however, they add considerably to their tragedy by not accepting their colored status. So, what is the moral stance of Millin's novel: opposed to racism or opposed to miscegenation? *God's Stepchildren* tries to oppose both and is thus internally morally contradictory.

One thing the reader of "early" South African literature will find is ambiguity. The land is ambiguous in *The Story of An African Farm*: it is not what the Boers make of it, but it is indeed a powerful, beautiful force. Racial barriers are ambiguous in *God's Stepchildren*: the discrimination that Kleinhans experiences in Kimberley and that Elmira experiences when she is asked to leave her Cape Town boarding school are unjust, but, given the existence of these barriers, mixing blood is reprehensible. And, when Millin's characters talk about the taint of black blood, it is very difficult for readers to distinguish between a racist attitude that her characters have internalized and a racist attitude that she may have internalized:

> He [Barry] was never comfortable with other children. He felt himself to be different. He had the contempt for black blood which is one of the nails in the cross that the black-blooded bear. . . . Never would Barry forget the horror of those brown people who had claimed him as their own—him, the Little Baas to all that was dark on Lindsell's Farm! Now there was not a day but he remembered the secret degradation under his skin. (249)

These ambiguities, however, do not, in and of themselves discredit either of these novels as literature. The novels do, however, have flaws. In fact, as far as flaws are concerned, the novels are opposite cases. Whereas Schreiner's novel was structurally loose and philosophically verbose, Millin's novel is structurally over-tight and philosophically empty. *God's Stepchildren* begins with the story of the Reverend Andrew Flood, "The Ancestor." Then, in Book II, which is titled "Mixed Blood," there are four parts, each one devoted to a different generation of Flood's colored descendants. And with the story of the Reverend Barry Lindsell, the novel comes full circle back to the Canaan where "The Ancestor" had gone mad trying to teach the gospel. This structure is not only "neat," but it reinforces two of the novel's morally ambiguous messages—first, that the taint of black blood will continue on, generation after generation after generation; second, that someone must return to the scene of the original sin and expiate it. One should not push the Biblical elements in Millin's novel too hard, but, in a sense, the promised land of Canaan was lost when Andrew Flood committed his original sin of having sexual intercourse with a black woman, and now Barry must renounce his white woman and his mostly white child and return to the promised land and redeem it. Throughout the novel, there are references to the Biblical story of Abraham: references to the patriarch and to his wife Sarah and her handmaid Hagar; references to the children the patriarch had with both. Throughout the novel, as we pass through the generations, there is a vague evocation of Abraham yielding to Isaac, Issac yielding to Jacob, etc. This line, of course, brings us to Moses and the Israelites' return to Canaan.

But *God's Stepchildren*, just as it was morally ambiguous on other matters, is morally ambiguous on the question of what is this Canaan place. Is it the place the Reverend Flood travelled to at the novel's beginning, where the Hottentots danced naked before the full moon and laughed at the missionary behind his back? Or is it the Christianized, but racially stratified promised-land nation that the Boers (and others) in the nineteenth century were trying to create? The novel fails to answer this question, and that failure is not at all surprising, for the same dilemma is at the heart of *apartheid*. We have come to understand *apartheid* as a pernicious system of stratification and oppression, but, the Afrikaans word means "separateness," and some of the documents associated with the early history of *apartheid* suggest that at least some of its creators saw it as a way of allowing the Afrikaners to have their culture and the black tribes to have their cultures. Respect for "multi-culturalism" was present in the doctrine of *apartheid*, but not, of course, in the way the doctrine was applied.

Given South Africa's confusion about what will characterize its "promised land," the novel's failure to answer the question of Canaan's identity within the book's *very* loose Biblical allegorical subtext would **not** then be especially problematic if it were not for the fact that the novel's tight structure suggests resolution where there isn't any. The novel then encourages its readers to be naively complacent at the end: all is well—no more miscegenation (at least in South Africa); no more injustice towards Andrew Flood's brown descendants (for Barry's baby will grow up in racism-free England); and the sins of the fathers and the mothers will be *somehow* expiated by Barry's return to Canaan. Curiously, this naive complacency that readers are lulled into by the structure of the novel has the same quality as the complacency that the colored characters and the novel's readers find in the rural areas the novel depicts. Things are understood there; the tension and the conflict of Kimberley, Cape Town, or even Kokstad are at bay.

This complacency, however, is *not* peace. If the characters reflected on their situation, they would not be at peace. If readers reflect on either the charaters' situations in the rural areas or the novel's "neat" ending back in Canaan, readers will not be at peace. Millin's text, however, does very little to encourage such reflection. It is "light" reading—too "light." We receive vivid portraits of the major characters; we get a good sense of what the various places in South Africa that the novel takes us to were like. However, we are not encouraged to think matters through. In fact, the novel's structure encourages us to settle complacently for a very easy to construct interpretation.

If we do think just a bit, we realize that the novel, like *The Story of An African Farm,* raises questions but provides very few answers. Both early novels offer us characters who know that answers are necessary (Lyndall, Waldo, Barry), but the two novels do not lead us to answers. Schreiner's novel shows us the characters searching their souls and struggling; Millin's shows us the characters stuck very much on the surface of profound matters. Schreiner's novel gives us a glimpse of what might be the seed of an answer: the recognition that we are all (*all*) part of the force or the soul of created life. Unfortunately, the two characters who are most able to catch this glimpse, Lyndall and Waldo, die. Millin's novel gives us what seems to be an answer—embodied in Barry's return to Canaan—but this supposed answer really is not clear enough to be one. Schreiner had a vision that enabled her to see beyond the troubles of South Africa; Millin seems to have been unwittingly trapped within her world.

Mine Boy

Schreiner and Millin are, of course, white writers. But it was not only white writers who were trapped in the ambiguities of the South African situation. Although Peter Abrahams' *Mine Boy* is able, in the end, to offer a fairly clear moral and political statement, it does explore the themes we have already explored–the land; rural vs. urban; race relations–with some ambiguity. What distinguishes Abrahams' book from those by Schreiner and Millin is that it is written later and told from the perspective of a young black South Afican.

Mine Boy has a focus that *The Story of An African Farm* and *God's Stepchildren* lack: Abrahams' novel is the story of Xuma, a black young man who comes from the farmlands of the northern Transvaal to Johannesburg in search of work. He finds work in the gold mines that are enrichening Jo'burg, but he also finds many friends and two lovers. Through these friends, he learns about the dynamics of modern, increasingly urban South Africa; through these friends, he learns the meaning of nobility.

Those first turning to South African literature or, more broadly, culture expect to find an attachment between the Afrikaners and the land, for that attachment has become something of a myth. What may then surprise some readers is the depth of attachment that exists between the country's black people and their land. Xuma had grown up in close harmony with the land. He finds the city large, confusing, and threatening. We see him early in the novel on a weekend excursion with the always laughing Maisy into the countryside surrounding Johannesburg. He enjoys the excursion: he enjoys the company of Maisy and her friends; he enjoys the country-brewed beer (which he distinguishes from the city brew which only gets you drunk); and, most important, he enjoys being close to the land:

> They were in open country. It reminded him of the open country of his home. The stillness and the peace of it. And the good soft earth. Not hard, macadamized roads, but soft clinging earth. . . .
>
> "It is beautiful," Xuma said and took a deep breath.
>
> "I was sure you would like it," Maisy said.

> "It is the land, the earth, it is good," Xuma said.
>
> "Come," Maisy said and ran down the footpath.
>
> She ran nimbly and easily, jumping over stones and dodging jutting rock points. Xuma followed more slowly, sucking in the fresh air and looking around with hunger in his eyes. He had longed for the land more than he had known. And there it was now, stretches of it. And again the sky was close to the earth. (93)

Later on, he and his lover Eliza plan their city life together. Now, they will live in his single room in the Malay Camp slum of Johannesburg, but she will do her best to make the room pleasant, pretty; later, they will have two rooms. Xuma invests in this dream because Eliza is city-born and wants the life-style of the whites she has seen all around her all her life. That life-style entails not just the dream of moving from one room to two, but the impossible dream of moving from two rooms to the posh neighborhood she takes Xuma to on a stroll the evening before she leaves him and Johannesburg. Xuma's investment in this life-style is, however, limited. He is much more enthusiastic at the prospect of taking Eliza home with him to the farmland of his youth.

The land then has intrinsic value for Xuma. Unfortunately, living close to the land seems less and less possible for him and his people. The jobs are in the urban centers; and those urban centers are booming. *Mine Boy* offers us several positive views of the booming urban center of Johannesburg. Xuma walks fairly freely through its golden streets lined with expensive shops, restaurants, and apartments; the evening before she leaves, Eliza takes Xuma to the top of a tall hill, shows him the glittering lights of downtown Jo'burg, and insists that he make love to her there. That glittering downtown is always depicted as teeming with life–fashionable life. The slums of Vrededorp and Malay Camp are also depicted as teeming with life; however, it is not a fashionable life. The life of the slums is not altogether negative in *Mine Boy*: people laugh, people dance, and some people genuinely care for other people. However, there are urban problems evident in these slums.

Three "images" are strongly associated in the novel with these urban slums. We more often than not see these slums in the dark. Sometimes this darkness is threatening, sometimes not; but it always has the potential to engulf and destroy. The novel's initial scene, which has the newly arrived Xuma roaming the streets of Malay Camp in the pitch black, establishes darkness as a dominant image in the novel. The numerous other night scenes as well as the night-like scenes deep in the mines reinforce this image. The characters escape this darkness primarily through alcohol. "Daddy" is always drunk; other characters seem to be almost always drinking; Skokiaan or shebeen queens like Leah support themselves (and others) by illegally providing beer and liquor to the slum residents. Alcohol and alcohol-induced states of gaiety and numbness seem to be the norm. Either consume alcohol or—and this is the third image—become the victim of a kind of sickness. Eliza resists alcohol, and she becomes so "sick" that she must leave Jo'burg; Xuma resists, and he also starts getting "sick." The nature of this sickness becomes apparent only gradually in the novel. When Eliza is said to be "sick" because she wants the "things" of the white man, the sickness sounds like a species of envy. Only late in the novel do the full characteristics of the sickness become clear: the envy must be mixed with a sense of injustice and a feeling of despair. One becomes sick when one realizes that the whites are enriching themselves and, simultaneously, constructing barriers that insure that they will be the only ones who become richer. One despairs when one realizes that, increasingly, there is very little one can do to change the emerging situation. Remember that *Mine Boy* predates the official beginning of *apartheid* by a few years; remember that the freedom to roam Jo'burg that Xuma and Eliza exhibit would be impossible a few years afterwards.

Passbooks appear in the novel, so does racist rhetoric at the mines. The white police vary in their treatment of the black urban dwellers—respectful and friendly toward Leah; respectful and fearful of Dr. Mini; brutal towards an anonymous man they are chasing along the rooftops and the "striking" black mine workers. Race relations then are not as bad as they will get. Discrimination exists; barriers are going up. However, there still seems to be the possibility of the races living together.

Early in the novel, Xuma runs into his white superior at the mine, an Irishman nicknamed Paddy or the Red One, while roaming the streets of downtown Jo'burg. Paddy invites Xuma to his apartment. There, Paddy and "his woman" Di try to entertain Xuma as if he were just another person. Xuma resists: in Xuma's eyes, color is far more than a superficial distinction. Throughout the novel, "Red" tries to bring Xuma to the point where he is first and foremost a man and only incidentally a black man:

> "It is good to love one's people and not to be ashamed of what one is. But it is not good to think only as a black man or only as a white man. The white people in this country think only as white people and that is why they do this harm to your people."
>
> "Then I must think as a black man."
>
> "No. You must think as a man first. You must be a man first and then a black man. And if it is so you will understand as a black man and also as a white man. That is the right way, Xuma. When you understand that you will be a man with freedom inside your breast. It is only those who are free inside who can help free those around them." (172-73)

Towards the novel's end, Xuma begins entertaining a vision of racial harmony:

> The vision carried him along. He could see himself and Eliza and Paddy and Paddy's woman all sitting at a little table in one of those little tea places in the heart of Johannesburg and drinking tea and laughing and talking. And around them would be other people all happy and without colour. And everywhere in the land it was so. On the farms it was so. People worked side by side and the earth was cheerful and rich and yielded a fat crop and there was food for everybody and work for everybody and there was singing while people worked and there was much laughter. And in the cities too it was so. People worked. People ate. People were happy. And oh the laughter! It was like a huge wave that swept over the land. And all eyes shone with it as they worked in the sun, and there was a new brightness in the sun. . . . (174)

This vision captures his imagination. He cannot share it with others—even with Maisy; however, it fills him as a possibility. Crucial to achieving this dream is doing what "Red" says—being first and foremost a man. At the end of *Mine Boy*, he chooses to follow this advice. He stands up for the black workers he is in charge of and refuses to lead them down into an unsafe mine. He is joined in defying the (white) mine officials by Paddy, who chooses to be first and foremost a man and only incidentally a white man. Then, Xuma chooses to go to prison with "Red." Together, they are men. If others would only join them, the novel's dream of racial harmony might be possible.

It is very difficult to read *Mine Boy* as someone in 1946 might have. We, unfortunately, know that this dream was not only not possible but turned into the nightmare of *apartheid* and the anti-*apartheid* violence of the '60s and '70s and the suppression of dissidents of the '60s, '70s, and '80s. Perhaps, in 1946, one could finish *Mine Boy* and have hope. The image of Red and Xuma together in jail and the image of Xuma and smiling, loving Maisy living their lives together after Xuma's release ***may*** counteract the darkness, drunkeness, and disease that the novel associates with being black in modern, urban South Africa.

Cry, the Beloved Country

A similar problem is posed by Alan Paton's 1948 novel *Cry, the Beloved Country*. It presents a hopeful possibility of racial harmony at its conclusion. One reading Paton's novel *today* responds sadly to this vision, for one today knows that events did not follow the course Paton had hoped for. In fact, Paton himself said, in an interview in 1971, that he would not have concluded the novel as he did in 1946 if he had written it in 1971. We are, however, more confident that the intended effect of the novel was optimistic, whereas we wonder if early readers of *Mine Boy* did not feel the ambiguities of that slightly earlier novel's images and events.

Cry, the Beloved Country is strikingly similar to *Mine Boy* in so far as raises the themes of the land, rural vs. urban, and race relations. (We will discuss each in turn.) Paton's novel goes beyond Abrahams' in so far as it uses language and style to create a work that is more a prayer than a realistic portrait. In large measure, it is the language and the style that still make *Cry, the Beloved Country* a moving reading experience. Time may have clouded the particular vision that Paton presents; however, time has not changed the emotions that the novel evokes.

The land is clearly sacred in *Cry, the Beloved Country*. We learn a great deal about its topography and about how that topography varies with the seasons. We learn that, for most of the year, the land is such that both raising crops and raising animals are problematic ventures. Nonetheless, all who live on the land—Afrikaner, English, colored, black—see in it something more than just rock and dirt and very little water. It is almost as if they see—in their imaginations or souls—what the land could be if a baptismal rain could redeem it:

> There is a lovely road that runs from Ixopo into the hills. These hills are grass-covered and rolling, and they are lovely beyond any singing of it. The road climbs seven miles into them, to Carisbrooke; and from there, if there is no mist, you look down on one of the fairest valleys of Africa. About you there is grass and bracken and you may hear the forlorn crying of the titihoya, one of the birds of the veld. Below you is the valley of the Umzimkulu, on its journey from the Drakensberg to the sea; and beyond and behind the river, great hill after great hill; and beyond and behind them, the mountains of Ingeli and East Griqualand.
>
> The grass is rich and matted, you cannot see the soil. It holds the rain and the mist, and they seep into the ground, feeding the streams in every kloof. It is well-tended, and not too many cattle feed upon it; not too many fires burn it, laying bare the soil. Stand unshod upon it, for the ground is holy, being even as it came from the Creator. Keep it, guard it, care for it, for it keeps men, guards men, cares for men. Destroy it and man is destroyed. (3)

In the early novels by Schreiner and Millin, the city is a weak but nonetheless negative force opposed to the something the characters see or feel in the land. In Abrahams' *Mine Boy*, the opposition between rural and urban is considerably stronger. Yet we still do see Jo'burg, especially the Jo'burg of the whites, as a golden, lively place. In Paton's novel, however, the opposition is not only strong but stated in stark terms. If the rural scene—the land—is beneficient, the urban scene is damning. Unfortunately, more and more of the young (of all races) are leaving the land and heading to the city because there are jobs there. The young zulu man Absalom Kumalo has taken this path. He is now in trouble, so his father, the Reverend Stephen Kumalo goes to Johannesburg to help him. *Cry, the Beloved*

Country is the story of the Reverend Kumalo's journey to the city and back.

The Reverend Kumalo finds the city a sinful place. He finds that his son was not only living in sin with a woman but sitting in jail charged with and then convicted of murder. The city has clearly been young Absalom's ruin.

Absalom's story is not, however, all that the Reverend Kumalo discovers as he explores Johannesburg. He sees, in person, the racial injustice that will soon become systematized in *apartheid*. Being a "man of the cloth," he is treated better than most blacks. Ironically, this better treatment allows him to get beyond the surface of racism that batters most blacks in Jo'burg and to confront the attitudes that characterize those who perpetrate, condone, or tolerate injustice.

In the end, the Reverend Kumalo loses his son. He loses more, however. As he suffers his way to and through urban South Africa, he loses his innocence, an innocence that the land, despite its dryness, nurtures. He could have easily despaired. However, feeling a need to do something within him, he turned apologetically to the father of the young man Absalom had murdered. Miraculously, these two men, one black and one white, find fellowship in their both having lost their sons. Their fellowship, in terms that are highly symbolic, leads to the building of a dam that will provide water for the land that they and many others of all colors share. The dam becomes a new covenant: their sons will not have died in vain; rather, their sons' deaths will help redeem the land and the people still on this land from the evil that has turned it dry.

This brief account of *Cry, the Beloved Country* resonates with religious connotations. One should not try to force the novel into the straitjacket of a Biblical allegory; rather, one should be alert to the suggestiveness of the Biblical allusions and the overall liturgical tone these allusions give the novel. This tone has been noted by most readers of the novel. These readers have further noted that it is not just names or words *per se* that give Paton's novel this tone. The prose rhythms of the novel are those of ornate seventeenth-century English, the ornate seventeenth-century English that King James I and his fellow scholars used when creating the "King James Bible":

> Yes, God save Africa, the beloved country. God save us from the deep depths of our sins. God save us from the fear that is afraid of justice. God save us from the fear that is afraid of men. God save us all.
>
> Call oh small boy, with the long tremulous cry that echoes over the hills. Dance oh small boy, with the first slow steps of the dance that is for yourself. Call and dance, Innocence, call and dance while you may. For this is a prelude, it is only a beginning. Strange things will be woven into it, by men you have never heard of, in places you have never seen. It is life you are going into, you are not afraid because you do not know. Call and dance, call and dance. Now, while you may. (225)

These rhythms are not always present or always heavy in the novel. As one might expect, they fade in Johannesburg; they rise to crescendos when the novel deals with the land.

The novel's language is not only religious but archaic. This quality might be explained as simply an accidental effect of using the seventeenth-century English syntax of the "King James Bible" if it were not for how the novel handles the Zulu language that its black characters are imagined to be speaking. Readers are not offered Zulu; rather, they are offered an English that is marked in such a way that we imagine that the words were really uttered in the native tongue. As novelist J. M. Coetzee has suggested in his 1988 study of a host of "older" white South African writers, Paton could have marked the English in any number of ways to signal "Zulu." What Paton chooses to do is consistently mark the English with archaic-sounding formulations in such a way that the Zulu we imagine being spoken sounds as archaic and noble as the seventeenth-century English that Paton uses to celebrate the land.

Through prose style and language then, Paton is giving the novel a traditional, noble tone along with the liturgical. The suggestion is strong that returning to one's cultural roots (pun intended) is *the* route to follow in solving the problems of South Africa. Modernization, urbanization, and perhaps the power and glory of diamonds and gold have so warped the people that neither white South Africans nor black South Africans have much humanity and morality left in them. Whereas it is true that the whites have lost theirs and the blacks have, in many cases, had theirs taken away, the path for both groups is back to their traditions, which are as noble as the novel's Biblical English and the novel's imagined Zulu.

We, of course, know the events that will ensue in South Africa *after* these novels are written. That Paton's *Cry, the Beloved Country* was published in the same year as the National Party gained political supremacy is a sad irony. We know that the hopeful vision of the novel will be almost totally destroyed by the realities of National Party action.

There is another irony that I wish to close this chapter with.

Schreiner's novel offers only incipient hope. The older characters fade into caricature; two of the younger characters, Em and Gregory, settle for a life that seems uninspired. The only two characters who have some vision die young. There was hope—through Lyndall and Waldo—but the environment was such that very little nourishment was available to sustain that hope. Similarly, Millin's novel offers very little hope. In fact, the novel's moral stance is so confused—so dangerously confused given how neat the novel makes some matters seem—that any hope that the novel offers insofar as it implicitly condemns racial injustice is entirely muted.

Our historical view of South Africa suggests that as the nation and its people move from the colonial and early post-colonial times of Schreiner and Millin to the latter half of the twentieth century, the nation's internal troubles increase. Given this circumstance, one would expect the not very hopeful view of Schreiner and Millin to become increasingly bleaker. The opposite, however, occurs, for in both Abrahams' *Mine Boy* and Paton's *Cry, the Beloved Country*, there is considerable hope. Although it may be muted a bit in the former novel, it is not at all muted in the latter.

One can conclude that this mismatch between history and literature is simply ironic. However, I think there is another explanation—one that is conjectural, beyond proof. I think both Abrahams and Paton sensed that their nation was at a crucial point in its history, that their nation would turn either toward or away from its racism. I think they both feared that their "beloved country" would take what they saw as the wrong turn. Given this context, the hopefulness of *Mine Boy* and *Cry, the Beloved Country* is their somewhat desperate attempt to exhort their fellow countrymen in the right direction. Whether it be Xuma and "Red" or Kumalo and Jarvis, the vision is a noble one, one that rejects race for humanity. The nation needed this vision in the wake of World War II; unfortunately, the nation did not embrace it. The results of this failure to respond to the hopefulness embodied by Abrahams' *Mine Boy* and Paton's *Cry, the Beloved Country* will be seen throughout the remainder of this book.

Works Cited

Abrahams, Peter. *Mine Boy*. 1946; rpt. Oxford: Heinemann, 1963.

Coetzee, J. M. *White Writing: On the Culture of Letters in South Africa*. New Haven: Yale UP, 1988.

Millin, Sarah Gertrude. *God's Step-Children*. New York: Boni and Liveright, 1924.

Paton, Alan. *Cry, The Beloved Country*. New York: Scribner's, 1948.

Schreiner, Olive. *The Story of an African Farm*. 1883; rpt. Harmondsworth: Penguin, 1979.

PART II

The Roar of the Lion

3

Loving

The lion evokes fear, especially in a non-African observer. But, lions, like most animals, have their domestic side. They mate; they bear young; they raise the young. They do indeed kill, but they kill for food, not out of innate viciousness. The lion will not, of course, necessarily behave in this domestic manner: the caged lion will behave differently, as will the provoked lion. This chapter, however, is not about the caged or the provoked. Rather, it is about the lion—the black South African—in more or less his or her domestic surroundings.

Given South Africa's history and politics, it is virtually impossible to look at the Black South African's life without also seeing how this lion has been victimized. However, some South African writers are able to push that victimization into the background and focus primarily on the lion's day-to-day existence. We will consider the work of three writers who, in very different ways, have managed to do so. This first is Bessie Head, who in 1968 celebrated the redemptive power of love in *When Rain Clouds Gather*. Head's novel, even though it presents the hardships of living in the bush in stark terms, is as joyous in tone as Paton's *Cry, the Beloved Country*. Different in tone is the short fiction of Indian Ahmed Essop. His *Stories* (1978) are gently satiric portraits of life in the Asian sections of Johannesburg. He reveals how the white man has victmized the non-white; furthermore, he reveals how men of color victimize each other. However, beneath the surface of his simple stories is the brotherhood that his characters are so close to embracing. His satirical portraits cause readers at least to see and maybe embrace this simple, loving feeling. Different in approach is Gcina Mhlophe, Maralin Vanrenen, and Thembi Mtshali's 1986 play *Have You Seen Zandile?* Using very autobiographical vignettes based on Gcina Mhlophe's life, the authors weave a garment of innocence and love that we wish the young Zandile could indeed always wear.

When Rain Clouds Gather

As a young adult, Bessie Head left her native South Africa for neighboring Botswana, where she was for fifteen years a refugee before gaining citizenship in 1979. Her novels are all set in Botswana. If one glances at a map of Africa and finds Botswana on it, one notices very quickly that the bulk of that nation's population lives in a narrow strip that borders South Africa. That the population lives there is the result of geography, for the Kalahari Desert which dominates western and central Botswana is uninhabitable. The population's location, however, causes Botswana to be both a haven for fleeing black South Africans and a close-by third world counterpoint to the developed South African nation.

Head's *When Rain Clouds Gather* is really two stories in one, and these two stories relate to these two different roles Botswana can play. Head's novel is, on the one hand, the story of young Makhaya, a dispirited black South African revolutionary, who flees to Botswana seeking safety, time to reflect, and a new life. On the other hand, Head's novel is the story of the village of Golema Mmidi, an experimental rural cooperative led—agriculturally, not politically—by a young Englishman named Gilbert Balfour. The stories intertwine when Makhaya accepts a salaried position in the village as teacher of new agricultural practices to its women.

Two of the most often repeated words in the novel, "love" and "hate," give the work a neat (perhaps too neat) binary structure. This structure is reinforced by the way in which those things natural allign themselves in the novel with "love" and those things political allign themselves in the novel with "hate."

"Hate" is the province of Matenge, the sub-chief nominally "in charge" of the region of Botswana that the village is part of:

> Matenge . . . it had always been his policy to transfer hate from one object to another, and if at last he found himself involved in the politi-

cal ideologies of Africa and the cauldron of hatred, it was because it was the last camp that reflected his traditional views.

> At first Matenge had hated his brother because he felt the chieftaincy should be his, and this hatred drove him to overreach himself until he was discovered in a plot to assassinate his brother. For this his brother smilingly and politely banished him to Golema Mmidi under the guise that he was being given an administrative post. The shock of it kept him quiet for some time, but soon he transferred his hate to the villagers, most notably Dinorego, who had refused to sit on his advisory council. For this he tried to get Dinorego banished from the area, but the banishment order was immediately rescinded by his brother. And so it had gone on. The villagers were aware of the tug of war, but they feared Matenge too much to take open advantage of it. They merely avoided him as much as possible. Then, along had come Gilbert Balfour, who, with his brother's backing, destroyed Matenge's lucrative cattle-speculating business overnight. The hatred, which had by now become a mountain, was once more transferred to Gilbert. (45-46)

Matenge then hates his brother, who is the jovial Paramount Chief, because his brother holds the position (and the privileges) he aspires to; furthermore, Matenge hates change because change might threaten the system that keeps him comfortable and the commoners impoverished. When Gilbert Balfour pushes through a change in the manner in which cattle are sold, a change intended to bring more revenue to the village, Matenge, who had personally profited from the old, corrupt system, starts to hate Gilbert Balfour and all who work closely with the Englishman on his various agricultural projects. Fortunately, Gilbert and his recruits have the support of both Paramount Chief Sekoto and "sheriff" George Appleby-Smith. As a result, Matenge's hatred, with no target upon which to vent itself, turns inward, leading to his suicide.

From the novel's beginning, we know that Matenge is a hateful person. Only gradually, however, do we discover how much hatred seethes inside the being of Makhaya. As we learn more and more about what his life was like in apartheid South Africa, we discover how embittered it left him. This bitterness causes him to often be on the brink of violence and to usually distance himself from the others in the village. Through interactions of various kinds, Makhaya is redeemed from this hateful state. Through his conversations with Gilbert Balfour, he discovers the white man's innocent generosity; by playing in the mud with Paulina Sebeso's little daughter, he reclaims a measure of innocence himself. Through his conversations with the wise old Mma-Millipede, he finds a faith that he can premise his life on; by making love to Paulina Sebeso herself, he joins the village and commits himself to its future prosperity.

"Love" is the province of several characters in Head's novel, most notably Gilbert Balfour and Paulina Sebeso. Their love, however, seems initially to be of different types. Gilbert's is intellectual: he will use his education in agriculture to help the impoverished people of Botswana. Paulina's, on the other hand, is physical: she will use her body to give herself and a man pleasure and fulfillment. Too proud to be promiscuous, Paulina sets her sights on Makhaya, and to win him, she commits herself to the tobacco-raising project he (and Gilbert) are promoting. Although she rallies the village's women to the project for selfish reasons (i.e. to "win her man"), one can detect in her utterances and her behavior a belief that the project will help the people.

Love, as embodied by Paulina and demonstrated by Gilbert, becomes associated with the natural—with sex and agriculture. The more pervasive association in *When Rain Clouds Gather* is, however, with the sun. The sun fascinates Makhaya because its rising and setting are dramatically different in the flat terrain of Botswana from what they were in his native South Africa. He spends hours studying the effects the emerging or disappearing sunlight have on the land and its sparse growth. He needs, however, to feel the sun within him:

> It was the face of a tortured man, slowly being devoured by the intensity of his inner life, and the tormented hell of that inner life has scarred deep ridges across his brow and down his cheeks, and the icy peaks of loneliness on which the man lived had only experienced the storms and winters of life, never the warm dissolving sun of love. (65)

Makhaya had too long lived in the "shut-away worlds where the sunlight never penetrated, haunted worlds, full of mistrust and hate" (81). He finally feels this sun when he unburdens his soul to Mma-Millipede and then embraces Paulina, "a passionate and impetuous woman with a warm heart" (77), who "was entirely unaware that her skirt was the same flaming colour as the sun" (117). "Ah," Makhaya thought to himself, "happiness . . . was dirt cheap in Botswana. It was standing still, almost in the middle of nowhere, and having your face coloured up gold by the setting sun" (141). And after thinking these thoughts, he turns to Paulina and her little daughter.

But the sun can be foe as well as friend: it can dry up the limited water supply and transform the people's livelihood (their cattle) into the vultures' feast when the rain clouds do not gather in September as they are supposed to. Similarly, love can be foe as well as friend: it can lead to heartache and heartbreak as well as to joy. The novel qualifies the symbolic significance of sun and its statement about love without appreciably weakening either symbol or statement. In the final analysis, the novel is as joyous—as love-filled—as Paton's *Cry, the Beloved Country*.

But, as in Paton's landmark novel, there is evil—political evil. As Head's novel makes abundantly clear, the political evil with which hatred is intertwined emanates from many quarters. Makhaya's story, once he tells it, points to the political evil in South Africa. He recalls "The terrors of rape, murder and bloodshed in a city slum, which was [his] background . . ." (97). Much of this violence is perpetrated by blacks upon blacks. He reflects often on the psychology behind this black-on-black violence:

> Things wouldn't have been so bad if black men as a whole had not accepted their oppression. . . . There were things like *Baas* and *Master* he would never call a white man, not even if they shot him dead. But all black men did it.
>
> He had seen it in the slums of all the cities of South Africa where black men had to live and how a man walked out of his home to buy a pack of cigarettes and never returned and how his seemingly senseless murder gave a brief feeling of manhood to a man who had none. Thousands of men died this way to boost up the manhood of a manless man. But there were many other reasons why a man became a murderer, and at one stage Makhaya had acquired enough hatred to become a mass murderer. (125)

Foremost among those "other reasons" are the indignities and the injustice blacks suffer in South Africa. But, before we get to the points in the novel at which Makhaya talks about life under National Party rule, we hear that political evil is rife as well in the black revolutionary movements that have developed throughout Africa:

> To many, Pan-Africanism is an almost sacred dream, but like all dreams it also has its nightmare side, and the little men like Jonas Tsepe and their strange doings are the nightmare. If they have any power at all it is the power to plunge the African continent into an era of chaos and bloody murder. (47)

Not only can these movements lead to "chaos and bloody murder," but they can defeat the progress that is necessary if people are to survive and thrive:

> On the one hand, you felt yourself the persecuted man, and on the other, you so easily fell prey to all the hate-making political ideologies, which seemed to him [Makhaya] to be the order of the day. Yet these hate-making ideologies in turn gave rise to a whole new set of retrogressive ideas and retrogressive pride. . . . (80)

The novel then is, in the final analysis, anti-political. Rather than supporting a black majority government over a white minority government (a common point in South African writing), Head's *When Rain Clouds Gather* calls for something other than government-as-usual. This "something other" returns the people to the land; it also shifts the focus from the battles among rival chiefs and other powerful individuals to cooperation among the people. This shift aligns Head's novel with much contemporary feminist theory. The novel, therefore, represents the first but not the last time we will see the philosophical position staked out by feminism coalesce with the situation of oppressed black Africans. Head seems to believe that this coalescence is necessary because, as Paulina Sebeso puts it, "a whole society had connived at producing a race of degenerate men" who were "wilting, effeminate shadows of men," a "spineless species" (93). As a result, "it [Botswana] was a country of fatherless children now" where "[e]very protection for women was breaking down and being replaced by nothing" (119). What *When Rain Clouds Gather* advocates, out of its mixture of the feminine and the African, is generosity and community. Head points to generosity fairly early in the text:

> If there was anything he [Makhaya] liked on earth, it was human generosity. It made life seem whole and sane to him. It kept the world from shattering into tiny fragments. (61)

She returns to this theme repeatedly, especially during Makhaya's soul-wrenching conversations with Mma-Millipede. "He [Makhaya] was never to know how to thank her [Mma-Millipede] for" these conversations that "confirm[ed] his view that everything in life depended on generosity" (132).

Head also sounds the communal note on many occasions. Gradually, as Makhaya moves from isolation to community, he realizes the importance of people. "Loving one woman had brought him to this realization: that it was only people who could bring the real rewards of living, that it was only people who give love and happiness" (163).

Stories

Ahmed Essop's *Stories,* which won the 1978 Olive Schreiner Award, also advocates community and generosity, but its approach is quite different. Whereas Head shows a character and a community moving toward those goals, Essop shows characters and a community sadly rejecting them. What makes Essop's satirical stories poignant is that these characters and the Johannesburg Asian community are ever so close to embracing a philosophy that would give their life the beauty (albeit perhaps utopian) of Head's Botswana village.

I cannot discuss all of the twenty stories in Essop's 1978 collection. I will focus on the handful that admittedly fit my thesis about Essop's fiction best. The others, however, do not contradict that thesis; rather, they show Essop playing variations on his basic theme.

Like many of Essop's stories, "The Hajji" deals with the crossing of the racial lines that the South African government established in the early 1950s. The story focuses on brothers Hajji Hassen and Hajji Karim. The latter had, earlier in life, made "the mistake" of abandoning his Indian people by crossing "the colour line" by marrying a white woman named Catherine. At that time, Hassen "had felt excoriating humiliation. By going over to the white Herrenvolk, his brother had trampled on something that was a vital part of him, his dignity and self-respect" (3). Now, Karim was dying, and Catherine telephoned Hassen to present him with his brother's dying wish: to be buried as a Muslim. All of Hassen's former feelings were brought to the surface again, so much so that he felt his recent pardon-seeking pilgrimage to Mecca might have been for nought. Hassen initially allows those hateful feelings to control his actions: he rudely denies his brother's request.

Catherine does not, however, give up. She comes to visit Hassen and, by blaming herself for all the "wrong" Karim had done, she convinces Hassen to visit his brother at the latter's apartment in the white Hillbrow section of Jo'burg. Hassen agrees to see to his brother's Muslim burial, but then refuses Catherine's offer of a ride home. "No, you stay here. I will take a taxi," (7) he tells Catherine. He proceeds to take the whites-only elevator, the elevator he and Catherine had taken earlier, to the ground floor, and, during the short trip, he is subjected to racist insults by three white youths. Shaken by the experience, he walks in a daze out of Hillbrow into downtown Johannesburg, where he takes a train back to the Indian section of Fordsburg. The experience in the elevator stirred up all of the hateful feelings of old and hardened him: he *would not* bury as a Muslim the brother who had betrayed his race and joined "them."

Many people from the Fordsburg community try to change Hassen's mind, but to no avail. So others take it upon themselves to provide Karim with the Muslim funeral and burial he desires. On the day of those ceremonies, Hassen flees Fordsburg and walks and walks eastward through Jo'burg and onward. Miles from the city's center, he experiences a dramatic change of heart.

> "Karim! Karim! he cried. . . . A fervent longing to embrace his brother came over him, to touch the dear form before the soil claimed him. He ran until he was tired, then walked at a rapid pace. His whole existence precipitated itself into one motive, one desire, to embrace his brother in a final act of love. (18)

Love finally triumphs—over barriers of color, over the past. However, as he is returning, the funeral procession passes and—the last words of the story—"No one saw him" (18). Love triumphs but too late.

Love and peace are often paired in Bessie Head's work; in Essop's, they are paired and given a particular South African Indian "twist" in so far as they evoke the non-violent philosophy of Gandhi. Essop's "The Betrayal" glances at the Orient Front, a non-violent political and cultural association for South African Indians that Gandhi played a role in founding. The story's central character, a Dr. Kamal, is the president of that organization.

The backdrop to the story is political: a new group for the Asian population is forming, and the Orient Front is upset. Although the Orient Front can point to disturbing differences in philosophy between themselves and the new group, what really disturbs Kamal and other Orient Front leaders is that they might lose power. Therefore, they hatch a plan designed to provoke a violent confrontation at the new group's initial meeting at Gandhi Hall. The irony of the plan does not escape Kamal: "He, the professed disciple of Gandhi, had unleashed a demon that would profane the hall commemorative of the master's name" (22).

As the plan unfolds and the meeting begins drifting toward violence, Kamal "experienced a sharp conflict within" (25). As he watches the violence that explodes, he realizes not only that he has violated Gandhi's non-violent creed but that he has destroyed something within himself by putting power ahead of principles: "The centre of his being that has been in turmoil during the past few weeks seemed to be undergoing a kind of physical rot" (26). He loses sight of Gandhi's message of love and peace and destroys himself in the process.

Dr. Kamal is one of the many hypocrites whom Essop satirizes in his *Stories*. In "Two Sisters," there are many hypocrites: by implication, the entire male population of the neighborhood, especially Mr. Joosub, a landlord.

"Two Sisters" focuses on two sisters, Rookeya and Habiba. These two have abandoned their Eastern ways. And with the

Westernization of their attire went what they thought was the Westernization of their sexual behavior. Young and naive, the two girls become the favorite sport of the narrator and his friend Omar. But the narrator and Omar become tired of the two sisters, and Rookeya and Habiba "hitched themselves to other men" (41). At some point, both girls become pregnant, and their promiscuity prevents them from pinpointing who the future fathers might be. Up until the girls begin trying to fix the blame on some of their lovers, the men found their presence in the yard acceptable. However, after they are pregnant, the men join the yard's women in a chorus denouncing the sisters' life-style and demanding their ouster: on moral grounds.

Landlord Joosub "expressed his willingness to oust the 'two bitches' from the yard. He was king of several backyards in Fordsburg and would not tolerate the presence of 'bitches' in his domains" (47). His attempt to oust them is described by Essop in a passage that mixes several tones:

> He stood at the foot of the stairs leading to the apartment of the two sisters and made several threatening pugilistic gestures. Excited people gathered around him. He struggled up the stairs, breathing hard and clutching the railing. When he reached the landing he paused to rest for a few minutes. . . . First he approached Rookeya and smacked her resoundingly on the cheek, shouting 'Pig! Bitch! Pig!" in Gujarati. Habiba, who tried to escape past him, received a blow on the head. She fell and nearly came tumbling down the stairs. Mr. Joosub then entered the apartment. The two sisters, shivering with fright, went towards the door to see what he would do next. Soon he appeared in the doorway, holding a primus stove in his hands; the brass contraption glinted in the sunlight as he flung it over the railing. It fell with a clanging sound and several parts were shattered by the impact. Next a chair came hurtling down, followed by a pot and a bath. Other household articles followed in quick succession as the mania for destruction gripped Mr. Joosub: crockery, linen, clothing. The two sisters, frightened, impotent, watched through the doorway as their landlord entered the apartment and gave way like marionettes as he emerged with some article.
>
> Then, suddenly, Rookeya and Habiba screamed as Mr. Joosub appeared in the doorway, holding one of the infants. (47-48)

Although the scene has comic qualities, the ominous prospect of infanticide makes one realize how dangerous Joosub's—and the community's—hypocrisy could be. The men were perfectly willing to make love to the two sisters but unwilling, along with the rest of the community, to extend love to them.

Many of Essop's *Stories* deal with male-female relationships; some with relationships that cross South Africa's "color line." "Black and White" is one such story. It centers on Shireen, another "Westernized" Indian girl, who has managed to acquire a poor white boyfriend. Her sexual appetite and/or what seems to be his purely sexual interest in Shireen probably dooms their relationship from the very beginning. However, "the psychology" of apartheid wrecks it sooner rather than later.

Shireen, seeing an opportunity to turn the power politics of race against the poor white boy, stages his public humiliation: "'I belong to everybody,' she declared, facing Harold. 'To everybody, you understand. That is, to blacks only, black boys only. Whites not allowed'" (93). Later, she changes her mind about Harold, but, Harold, humiliated by having the nation's racism turned against him, enacts his revenge by beating her. Love not only cannot triumph over the nation's racism, but is perverted by that systematic hatred.

"Gerty's Brother" is also about inter-racial love/sex, but it is a more optimistic story. A young man named Hussein takes up with an "easy" white girl named Gerty. Although he initially seeks both sex and the power that comes from sex with a member of the privileged racial group, Hussein seems to develop a fair amount of affection for Gerty. Unfortunately, the law of the land—the Immorality Act that prohibits sexual relations between members of different racial groups—comes between them. Hussein, believing that the police are watching him and gathering evidence against him, brings the relationship to what he says (to Gerty) will be a temporary end. Their love cannot triumph.

The real story, however, concerns, as the title suggests, not Gerty but "Gerty's Brother." The little boy develops a loving attachment to both Hussein and the narrator. When the affair between Gerty and Hussein ends, the little boy, Riekie, simply cannot understand: he is both too young and too desperately in need of love. As the story ends, we find Riekie at the gate to the yard where Hussein had resided:

> He was clutching two bars with his hands, and shouting for Hussein. I stood and watched as he shouted. His voice was bewildered.
>
> The ugly animal living in the yard lurched out of his room and croaked: "Go way, boy, go way, white boy. No Hussein here. Go way."
>
> Riekie shook the barred gate and called for Hussein over and over again, and his voice was smothered by the croaks of the old man. (128)

The narrator's reaction to this scene concludes the story. He recalls an earlier scene: while Hussein and Gerty had sought out the dark of a city park, the narrator had "baby sat" Riekie and taken him on a paddleboat ride elsewhere in that park:

> . . . I felt again the child's body as I lifted him and put him in the boat many nights ago, a child's body in my arms embraced by the beauty of the night on the lake, and I returned to my landlady's with the hackles of revolt rising within me. (128)

In those "hackles of revolt" there is some hope: perhaps someday love will come into Riekie's life and not be destroyed by South Africa's racial barriers.

One last story, "The Notice," also contains a note of optimism, although the plot, which is reminiscent of Boccaccio, takes the reader through many twists before it sounds that note. "The Notice" is set at that point in history when the government of South Africa was evicting members of the less privileged racial groups from the slums close to the center of Jo'burg so that both the white enclave could grow and white residents would feel less threatened. The story's central character, Mr. Effendi, tries to extend his stay in Fordsburg by always being out of town when the low-level government official, Mr. Hill, comes to his house to give him the required written notice of expropriation. Effendi is successful in avoiding Hill until, one day, Hill discovers him in bed. Mrs. Effendi, thinking quickly, confesses to Hill her marital infidelity, using Effendi's always being out of town as her excuse for her adulterous affair. After Hill leaves, lust overcomes him and he decides to connive his own way into Mrs. Effendi's bed. Hill tells his superiors that Effendi has gone to India for a visit and therefore cannot receive the notice of expropriation for months; then, Hill visits Mrs. Effendi, intending to use the favor he did the Indian couple to extract bedroom favors from Mrs. Effendi. Unfortunately for Hill, Mr. Effendi returns home to find Hill undressing in preparation for the encounter he assumes will soon commence. "In a paroxysm of rage, he [Effendi] rushed out of the house to call his assistant Charles—an ex-boxer still in fine fettle. . . . He shouted to Charles that there was a 'dog' in the house who must be killed" (145-46). After Effendi and Charles arrive, Mr. Hill escapes his fate (being beaten or killed): he cites the favor he had done the Effendis and transforms Mr. Effendi's anger into gratitude. As the story ends, Effendi and Hill find a peculiar solidarity in the deception. Effendi is delighted that he (with Hill's help) has fooled the government; Hill is delighted that he has been clever enough to foil an irate husband and avoid a beating. "'Come sit down, Mr. Hill. Let's have coffee,' Mr. Effendi said" (146). Stranger things have been known to bring people together in community!

Have You Seen Zandile?

Essop more often than not examines (satirically) the absence of community and love in South African life. When Essop portrays community and/or love, the portrayal is tinged with sadness ("Gerty's Brother") or peculiar humor ("The Notice"). As a result, the values of community and love come across in a much more qualified way than in Bessie Head's *When Rain Clouds Gather*. *Have You Seen Zandile?*, a 1986 play by Gcina Mhlophe, Maralin Vanrenen, and Thembi Mtshali, is a cross between the two. The play exudes loving; however, the portrayal is tinged with sadness.

Have You Seen Zandile? has a loose structure. It consists of fifteen vignettes. The first five celebrate Zandile's life with her grandmother Gogo in Durban. The next four, "The White Car Comes For Zandile," "Gogo Discovers Zandile is Gone," "Gogo Searches for Zandile," and "Zandile's Letter to Gogo" are transitional: they dramatize Zandile's kidnapping and her guardian's poignant reaction. The next five scenes find Zandile in a homeland with her mother, for it was Zandile's mother who arranged for her daughter's kidnapping. The final scene presents Zandile in Johannesburg after living six years in the Transkei.

This structure, albeit loose, provides an almost mythic pattern for the play's events. We begin in the paradise of the Grandmother's home and garden: the vignettes are idyllic; furthermore, they exude innocence. Especially touching is Scene 4a in which young Zandile plays teacher with the garden's flowers as her pupils.

Unfortunately, this paradise will be lost. However, at this point in the play, the creators twist the audience's expectations, expectations created by the Edenic first five scenes and by the portrayal of the white car as ominous, villainous. When we find Zandile in the homeland, we do not, however, find her in the antithesis of paradise; rather, we find her in a paradise of a different sort–less tame, more wild. And the scenes still exude innocence. Perhaps most striking is Scene 9, in which Zandile and her friend Lindi swim together in the river and discuss, naively, the topics of snakes, boys, and menstruation. *We* perhaps discern phallic imagery and echoes of the *Genesis* story, but the two girls simply talk innocently without any sexual or sinful hints. Even though our anti-paradise expectations for the homeland have been denied, we still "see" the mother, Lulama, as the villain of the piece. The homeland may not be hellish; however, living there does mean hard work in the fields and blisters, and Zandile certainly would have had the opportunities a "Western" or white audience would value if she had been able to stay with Gogo in Durban. Her mother has, in our judgment, deprived Zandile of these opportunities. But then, in scenes 8 and 10, Zandile and we really get to know Lulama. We hear her story: how she had to leave the Transkei and the man who had chosen her to be his wife originally because there were no jobs for her there; how she had found work as a member of a popular black singing group, the "Mtateni Queens"; how she fell in love with and became pregnant by a man she met in a shebeen in which she had been singing; how she was forced to leave the group and return to the Transkei in disgrace:

> I nearly made it. We were going to Johannesburg to cut a record and the people there were organizing a tour for us. We were going to sing

> in Cape Town, P.E., East London and all the other lovely places. But then we had to tell them that I was four-months pregnant. Intoni, they wouldn't hear of it. They wanted me replaced. My friends stood for me but the organisers said they wouldn't have a pregnant woman on stage—as if it was such a disgrace, or as if I had made myself pregnant. (55)

Her story, once we hear it, changes her role in our eyes from villain to victim. Still, we wonder why she *had* to kidnap her love-child. Zandile also wonders and asks her mother. Her mother explains that she had no choice but to leave Zandile in Durban after she was born, for her husband "would have killed me if I had come to his home with another man's child" (40). After twelve years, Lulama simply could stand no longer the thought that her daughter didn't even know that she existed. "Wait till you have a child, you'll know what I've been going through all the years" (40), she tells Zandile.

Love is very much apparent in the vignettes featuring mother and daughter, just as innocence was very much apparent in the river scene featuring Zandile and Lindiwe. *But* love and innocence were also very much apparent back in Durban with Gogo. The "problem" of the play is how to reconcile the love and innocence of the Transkei, which we surprisingly discover in the play's latter scenes, with the love and innocence of Gogo's house, which the initial scenes exude. The play's structure suggests that we will see a redemptive return to Gogo's at the end; however, because the Transkei scenes are not the loss of Paradise that we expected, the return must be not so much a redemption as a reconciliation. Zandile must tie together the separate loving and innocent strands of her life.

The last scene depicts Zandile seeking out Gogo—reversing the pattern of Scene 7. She discovers that her grandmother has died. However, Gogo knew Zandile would one day return. Gogo had left a suitcase for Zandile, and the play concludes with Zandile's opening this suitcase:

> Zandile is on her own in a pool of light, very quiet, very separated from her surroundings. She opens the suitcase and takes out all the little parcels her grandmother has been putting away for her through all the years. Zandile holds each of them for a moment, before laying them gently to one side. At the bottom of the suitcase she finds a dress, takes it out and holds it up against herself. It is a little girl's dress, which

> barely reaches beyond her waist. She puts it down, reaches for a second dress and repeats the action. She picks up a third dress and also holds it against her body. She then holds all three dresses closely to her, hugging them and sobbing. The lights slowly fade to black . . . (77)

These dresses (and the other gifts Gogo had set aside for Zandile) represent the innocence and the love of her early life. As she holds these dresses up to her eighteen-year-old body, the distance between her now and her at age twelve is apparent. When she hugs the dresses to her body, she bridges that distance emotionally and thereby merges the love and innocence of her days with Gogo with the love and innocence of her days in the Transkei. This love and innocence will protect her as she begins her own journey as a black South African woman. And perhaps, now that she is a woman, she can use these garments of love and innocence to garb–literally and symbolically–the daughter she might have. Her name, Ntombi Zandile, "means the number of girls has grown" (55). Her naming suggests that what we see in *Have You Seen Zandile?* is the passing on of the gifts of loving from generation of women to generation of women to generation of women. External forces may intervene, and they may make life rough and even drive a wedge between a particular mother and a particular daughter, but, nonetheless, the loving chain will continue. Love will triumph.

Women have played important roles in the works I have treated in this chapter. Three women created *Have You Seen Zandile?*, and the play deals with–celebrates–the power of loving that women can keep alive, even in South Africa. Bessie Head's novel also focuses on the love and the sense of community that the women of a Botswana village are trying to build a good life upon. And, if one stands back from Ahmed Essop's satirical *Stories* and looks for patterns that extend through several of the sketches, one sees that the men have fallen victim to the hatred that surrounds them whereas the women and children, although they are victims, seem more willing to love. Some of Essop's female characters seem to no longer know exactly what love is, confusing love and sex, but, nonetheless, they are much more attuned to the spirit of loving than Essop's males.

The lion's cries will turn less and less peaceful and loving as we proceed through the next three chapters. Curiously, seventeen of the eighteen works we will be discussing are authored by men.

The loving lion then seems to be a distinctly female creature.

Works Cited

Essop, Ahmed. *Stories*. 1978; rpt. London: Readers International, 1988.

Head, Bessie. *When Rain Clouds Gather*. 1968; rpt. Oxford: Heinemann, 1987.

Mhlophe, Gcina, Maralin Vanrenen, and Thembi Mtshali. *Have You Seen Zandile?* 1988; rpt. London: Methuen, 1990.

4

Restlessness

Loving and community will not always triumph. Sometimes, the lion will not lie down. Rather, the lion paces, restlessly, perhaps not fully knowing why. This restlessness is very much apparent in many works of contemporary English South African literature. As Chapter 1 revealed, the situation in South Africa is not as simple as perhaps the mass media make it out to be. It is the complexities of the situation that produce a large measure of the restlessness and the inability to know *exactly* why. The word *exactly* is crucial. It is easy for the three black authors I will discuss in this chapter to define their situation in terms of what the white man has done to the black man; however, all three authors—playwright Alfred Hutchinson, novelist Modikwe Dikobe, and autobiographer Ezekiel Mphahlele know that such a definition would be too simple, too easy. Thus, they try to go beyond the simple rhetoric of victimization in their works and to get at *all* that makes them feel restless.

The Rain Killers

Alfred Hutchinson's 1964 play takes us to the village of Mzindi in the eastern Transvaal. From the play's very beginning, we are introduced to the village's unfortunate situation: it is dry; the rain that is necessary for the village's meager crops to grow has not come. The drought functions in the play as a controlling metaphor: not only are the village's crops dying because of lack of rain, but the village as a community and the villagers as moral people are also dying because of various emotions that are out of control. Some during the play search for "the rain killers"—i.e., the witches who have cursed the village; what the audience discovers is that almost everyone in the community is a "rain killer" in the more symbolic sense.

Two events bring the villagers' ill feelings to the fore. The first occurs before the play begins: an important figure in the village's Christian church, Zwane, loses in his bid to be elected church treasurer. He believes the minister, Muruti, campaigned against him behind his back and is therefore looking for an opportunity to enact revenge. The second event occurs in the play's initial scene: a young girl named Mapule, whose deceased mother was a villager, returns there to visit her grandmother, Gran Shongwe. Mapule—we learn very quickly—is an attractive young woman. The men all seem to notice her beauty. She also has adopted many non-native ways, such as wearing makeup; and the village women are quick to notice this *and* the fact that their men are staring at the young girl. Despite her "Western" ways, the play's text gives us no reason to doubt Mapule's essential goodness. In fact, the play's text gives us, symbolically, testimony to her noble character, for she—we are told on several occasions—has just arrived from Lesotho where it was and has been raining.

The story that the play follows is that of Zwane's young son. He is very ill. The Mfundisi Muruti tries to convince Zwane and his wife to send the boy to the hospital. But they resist: they are suspicious of non-tribal ways; more important, Zwane wants to reject the Mfundisi's advice because he is angry with the Mfundisi. His anger also causes him to rally several of the village's women against Mapule, who is helping the minister. She is a bad influence on the children of the village, Zwane argues, and she must be banned from the Christian church. She is also, Zwane suggests to these women, having far too great an influence on Muruti, whose wife has gone to Durban to look after a sick parent. These women confront the Mfundisi. They tell him that the girl has "loose" morals and suggest to the minister that they will not be part of a church that has Mapule as a member. The Mfundisi tells the women that the Church is Christ's not his and that Christ welcomes sinners into the fold more warmly than those who have never strayed.

Zwane and his wife decide to turn to the tribe's elderly witch doctor Maziya for help with their ailing son. Maziya delights at this recognition of his power and tells Zwane and Ma-Zwane what he intuits they want to hear: that their son is bewitched and that the witch is Mapule. They then spread this lie, and, gradually, we see villagers, even the young children, turning against her.

Zwane himself had lusted after Mapule. Maybe this lust allowed him to see the lust in the Mfundisi's heart; maybe the thought planted in the minister's mind that she was perhaps "loose" brought incipient lust in his heart to the surface. In either event, the Mfundisi, in a melodramatic scene, attempts to seduce Mapule. She strikes him, symbolically knocking his minister's collar off and on the floor. Although she was personally disappointed in the Mfundisi, she promised to keep his indiscretion quiet for the sake of the village church. Unbeknownst to either of them, however, Zwane had witnessed the scene. He uses the information to get his revenge: he tells the Mfundisi that he had better leave the village.

Meanwhile, led by Zwane and Ma-Swane, villagers are quitting the Christian church and returning to the tribal beliefs represented by the old Maziya. This renewed power drives the old man into insanity. Tragically, he loses his sanity in a scene where he is ostensibly trying to save the Zwanes' son by driving the witchcraft out of him. He "bleeds" the child by slitting both of his wrists and his neck below the temple; then, he smothers the dying boy in smoke beneath a blanket. Zwane reveals through his actions that he never believed in Maziya, for Zwane runs for the police so that they can arrest the old witch doctor. Ma-Zwane, however, loses her wits in her grief and leads a mob toward the hut where Mapule is staying. This mob will destroy the witch that has killed the child and denied the village its needed rain.

Many elements from the tribal past are portrayed negatively in the play. However, at this point, two women, Gran Shongwe and Ma-Nkosi, summon up the spirit of their courageous (male) ancestors and prepare to defend Mapule against the mob. They do not need to, for, at this point, the Mfundisi comes forward. By confessing his failed attempt to seduce the girl and then by killing himself, he distracts the mob's attention from Mapule long enough for the mob to calm down and the police to arrive.

In a way, the Mfundisi substitutes himself as the scapegoat for her in the human sacrifice ritual that the village is about to reenact. His dying *for* her sins would be a very Christ-like action on his part *if* she had been guilty of the alleged sins and *if* he had been more Christ-like in other ways himself. The blurring of tribal and Christian in this, the play's final scene, is not, however, sloppy symbolism on Hutchinson's part; rather, it is a rather good reflection of the confusion that affects the village and makes it very difficult for the village to define its situation and thereby rest.

This confusion has two facets. First, the villagers are unable to grasp how they have indeed been victimized; second, the villagers are all too ready to victimize each other.

The village is in a tribal reserve. Gradually, we discover *why* there are so few men there. The land and the weather in the reserve being what they are, the men have been forced to go to the white-dominated cities in order to feed their wives and children. The women in Mzindi offer a few remarks about the situation that suggest their resentment of it; however, they hold the situation against their men, *not* against the political and economic forces, engineered by white South Africans, that have created this situation. The children in Mzindi have a view that is even more naive:

SAMUEL My father's gone to work in Jo'burg. He's going to bring me a present, Mfundisi.

MFUNDISI That's nice, Samuel.

JOHN My father's an *ilijoyini*. He works in the mines. Deep in the ground, digging out money. He's far away.

MARK My father works on the railway line. Chuff, chuff, chuff . . . P-e-e-p!

JOHN That's not the sound a train makes, stupid! Like this! (*He imitates a train whistle.*)

PAUL My father's a waiter in a hotel where white people stay. A big hotel with lots of white people. Eh, Elijah, your father's a stay-at-home . . . a woman's man! (23)

The children are not only proud of their father's servile jobs, but demeaning towards any men who do not go off to the white man's cities and be slaves.

Even the Mfundisi lacks a clear head on the matter of his people's plight. When he goes to Maziya to plead with the old man to tell the Zwanes to take their child to the hospital, the witch doctor, still sane, lectures the Mfundisi:

> Don't we starve now? And why? Because the white man took our country. All the big white farms you see around here were once tribal land. You know the ways of the white man. For all your schooling where has it gotten you? . . . Mfundisi, if you want to help the people, go and ask the white man for our ancestral lands. (54)

The minister protests that the problem is evil, not the white man. Maziya continues his lecture:

> They're using you, Mfundisi–using you to do their dirty work. Long ago they came here with their Bibles. Then others came asking for land. And Chief Sogasa gave it to them. Some took our daughters too. And while we were still asleep, came the police asking for taxes. Taxes! What for? We pay our tribute to the Chief. But the police don't listen. They throw us into prison. We cry and cry but they won't listen. (55)

Maziya's vision is clear. Unfortunately, greed–for money and power–get the better of him. He kills the Zwanes' child; he causes the mob to almost kill Marule. And it is left to the Mfundisi to lecture the people about how they are victimizing themselves:

> And you cry that the white man treats you badly because you're black; because you're not like him. You think it's a bad thing. But when you persecute this girl, then it's all right. You people are doing just what you say the whites are doing–but you're doing it to a black like yourselves! (*Uproar*) You don't like to hear it? Yes, it's the same thing. Don't think that because you're black you're better and can't do what the white man does. (75)

As the play ends, Mapule tells the police sergeant that "Maruti was killed by this beastly village; by people like Zwane" (78). The lesson of the play is that, until the village stops victimizing itself, it will not see its own victimization clearly. Without this clear view, confusion will still reign. And the fact that we leave the villagers arguing about whose prayers brought the rain

—the insane, murdering Maziya's or the dead, lustful Muruti's—suggests that they haven't quite grasped matters yet.

The Marabi Dance

The one character in *The Rain Killers* who has a clear head is Mapule. At the play's end, she says "It's God's rain" (80). She represents a younger, more worldly generation of black South Africans. As such, she is different from both those older and those who have experienced only the village. These two crucial differences—age and exposure to the world—also differentiate the characters in Modikwe Dikobe's *The Marabi Dance* (1973). The scene of Dikobe's novel is, however, quite different: rather than an African village in the rural eastern Transvaal, we find ourselves in rapidly-growing Johannesburg.

The Marabi Dance examines three different generations of Black Jo'burg residents. The novel does indeed indict the economic exploitation of black South Africans. This political point, however, seems secondary to the realistic depiction of the lives of these three different groups *and* the changes in attitude we see as we progress from the first generation to the second to the third. Whereas the first two are disoriented and restless, the last seems to have achieved a clear vision of the South African situation.

The Marabi Dance, along with other black novels of the '60s and '70s, provides the reader with a fascinating, realistic (almost naturalistic) glimpse of life in urban South Africa's slums. It is, therefore, of considerable sociological interest. The day-to-day operation of South Africa's notorious pass laws and the night-time routines of the shebeens would interest sociologists; more so would the inter-generational differences among the slum dwellers.

The older generation is torn between the tribal ways and the "western" mores, between rural customs and urban realities. Most members of this generation try to keep the tribal and the rural alive; however, they realize that keeping the ways and customs alive will require considerable adaptation to their new living situation. Sometimes they adapt with a quiet dignity; some times with an awkwardness that makes it all but certain that the old ways will die with them. This generation provides an important backdrop to the novel's more central story. One of Dikobe's implicit points is that this generation had values, even though they may not "work" especially well in the new setting. The mere presence of values, however, serves as a counterpoint to the comparative absence among those in the next generation.

This next generation is central to the novel. In many ways, *The Marabi Dance* is the story of a girl named Martha, who, early on in her life, shows a great deal of promise. Her parents, however, try to raise her in line with the ways of old—even to the point of arranging her marriage and marching her through the various tribal rituals associated with courtship and marriage. They talk in traditional terms that seem very out of place in a Jo'burg slum:

> "He is interested in his son marrying Martha and I also want them to marry. He has a lot of cattle and goats." (30)

But even the parents aren't sure how the rituals are to work. They turn to their elders for instruction:

> "There is only one law for the black man," intervened the old man. "If one marries a woman, one marries her for one's parents, and she must go and stay with them until the younger brother marries. The first child belongs to the grandparents and will not live with his parents, and when such a child marries, it is the grandparents who will have the final say. It is wrong for you, July, to say what your daughter will not like. If you like the boy's parents, it is not for your daughter to decide. The boy or girl has no right to refuse the proposals of the parents. The magadi might be paid without the couple even having met each other, and the bride can be taken to the man's parents even if she hasn't seen her man. What you should say now is that your cousin must send other people to have a look at your daughter and these people will return to say how much magadi is wanted. Then women from the man's house will come before the bogadi is paid to satisfy themselves of the looks of the bride. They may refuse the girl if she cannot cook or wash well or keeps the house in dirt." (38-39)

Knowing that Martha's heart is otherwise engaged, her mother turns to a practitioner of primitive medicine to help repell her present lover and attract her proposed husband:

> The doctor took from one of his bags raw reed-cotton and bade the woman coil a string. When it was completed he took out fat with his finger nails from ten horns of different animals and mixed it together and ran it along the string. Then he rubbed it into a skin that looked like that of a mouse:
>
> "Wash your hands after you touch it," he warned. "Take this and tie it around the hips of your daughter. Whoever touches her will die immediately, with his hand shrunk. It will make her smell like all the animals whose fat is on it and no man will want to touch her." (61-62)

Next, her father tries to instruct her in the subservient manners required of a wife in his tribe. During the instructions, it becomes clear that her own mother has slipped away from these practices:

> Martha had seen her mother sometimes kneeling before her father when giving him food, but never doing such things as her father had mentioned. The day her father's cousin had paid a visit, she had seen her father blush when her mother pushed a plate in front of the visitor without going down on her knees, and after meals she did not bring water until Ndala began licking the remains of food from his fingers. (64)

What emerges in the attempts of Martha's parents to enact the necessary rituals is the difference that is emerging between urban and rural in black South Africa. In the rural areas (where the proposed husband comes from), the traditional ways still hold sway, but in the urban areas, the traditional ways are fading fast. This urban vs. rural difference nags at Martha's mind:

> "Ma, I was born in town. I don't know the laws of the people at home and Sephai is not a boy like the town ones. He is what we call 'skapie-sheep.' He won't allow me to go to the Social Centre or bioscope." (67)

Ultimately, Martha rebels. She wants to be free–free from her family's dictates and her tribe's customs; free to "live." "Living" had its bright side in the Jo'burg slums, for despite the squalor, there was music, dance, drink, and sex. And many black South Africans of Martha's generation gave way to these pleasures. They led a carefree life; they very much seized the day. Martha did not pursue these pleasures alone: she pursued many of them with her marabi musician friend George. We, early in the novel, form a rather negative impression of George. He is a womanizer, and Martha, we fear, will be seduced and abandoned. And that is, pretty much, the plot. Martha, rather than fulfilling her promise and/or living the traditional life her parents charted for her, finds herself pregnant and about to be married to a man whom she knows is not the father of her child. She nobly—and as an expression of her desire for freedom—refuses to dupe the boy and confesses that she is pregnant by another man to Sephai's relatives.

George is not yet the "marrying kind," or so it seems. Whereas we discover a great deal about Martha's restless and confused behavior, we see George's comparable restlessness and confusion from a distance. We hear he has many women; we hear that, to some extent, he lives off of money these women give him; we hear that he has fathered many illegitimate children. We know that he is a talented and popular marabi musician—sought after by the shebeen queens and other black entrepreneurs for he attracts a crowd and sells beer. One especially puzzling scene involving Martha and George takes place the evening he impregnates her. The scene is puzzling because of the curious way it mixes the following of traditions and the flaunting of them and the very ambiguous picture it offers of George:

> "Martha! You and I have been in love since our school-days. I have been trying to make children by you and I couldn't. I want to make children with you so I have proof that you are a woman. We Zulus don't just take a woman before we know that she can get children. How can my father's cattle go for nothing? A woman must bear children to return the cattle the man has paid for her." George held her by her fingers. "Please honey let's sleep," he said in English. (78)

Is George truly devoted to the Zulu customs he cites, or is George being "smooth," handing the upset young girl "a line" to get her into bed one more time? The question becomes complicated when we follow the scene just a bit farther:

> George felt a piece of string around Martha's waist. She pushed his hands lightly from it: "Don't touch me on the waist. It is against our custom that a man touches a woman on the hips."

> George smelt the animal fat and sneezed. He pushed his hand forcefully back and ripped the string off: "I don't care for native custom. You are my woman. Tonight you are going to get me a child." (78)

So what *is* George's attitude toward "native custom"? First, he cites it; then, he rejects it. We never find out if George is confused or conniving. We do realize—as did Martha all along—that George was not ready to settle down *yet*. So Martha soon finds herself a single mother, moving from the Jo'burg slum to the new housing project the government is building for blacks farther outside the city toward the southwest. A faint note of hope is found in how "wonderful" this new township appears, compared to the inner-city slum where she had grown up:

> Martha felt for the first time the pleasure of living in a house with rooms. She had grown up in what was called a house, but here was a real house. Three rooms: a kitchen and two bedrooms, one which she shared with Tiny and her child and the other where the old Mapenas slept. The kitchen served as a sitting room for strangers and when she had important visitors she let them sit in her room. Sonnyboy and Tiny found a lot of space to play in the house. There was a big yard where vegetables and flowers could be grown. (112)

We find this depiction doubly ironic: we realize that Martha's new home is only nice *by comparison* with what she had previously known; we also know what this new township, Orlando, will be like ten and twenty years later when it is part of Soweto. Nonetheless, the home does provide her with the spirit she needs to push on and raise her child, Sonnyboy—"a child who, among millions of others, was to spend his life in and out of jail" (79).

Seven years pass; the novel is in its last few pages. One day, Martha receives a letter from George in Durban. In it, George asks if he could return; in the novel's two-page epilogue, we see Martha and George marry.

There is a sense of renewal in this epilogue. Not only do Martha and George (and Sonnyboy) renew their life together, but other characters—some from very early in the novel—are depicted starting over, with clean slates. The "happily-ever-after" quality of this ending makes one wonder how much editing the several non-blacks who helped Dikobe revise his novel did. The end of Chapter 8, the last in the novel, seems, in many ways, more authentic.

Chapter 8 ends with the future of Martha and George somewhat up in the air: we have the letter from Durban but not George from Durban yet. Chapter 8 also ends with two very important shifts.

The first shift is from *carpe diem* to political awareness. George had always epitomized the carefree approach to life that Martha and many others of her generation had found attractive. Yes, everybody knew that the nation's politics were unjust, but, unable to do anything about the political situation, they "lived." While they so lived, the political situation for their people worsened. Activism increased; the need for the white-controlled government to control blacks increased. The government used many techniques, among them the use of paid informers in the black community. The government had wanted George, in Durban, to play such a role. He was to spy on other bus company workers and inform the government who the trouble-makers were. He tells Martha that he "would rather walk the streets without work than sell his own people" (114). George wants to quit this job and return to Johannesburg. Assuming his family responsibilities, giving up the "marabi" life, *and* refusing any longer to be apolitical are interconnected in George's proposed return. Although Piniel Viriri Shava in *A People's Voice* finds George's reformation too abrupt and therefore unconvincing, there is no evidence in the text that we are to take his words less than seriously.

The second shift is brief: it is from the generation of Martha and George to the future generation of Sonnyboy. Chapter 8 ends with Martha's words to Sonnyboy:

> "My child, you are going to grow to be a man. George, your father, wants to leave work because he does not want to sell his people. I like him for that. Our people must talk without being heard by the white people. Some tell the white people what we have said and are given money. Last night the people talked about schools and high rent, and this morning some people were arrested. You, you my child, must be a man." (115)

In these words, Martha associated "being a man" for Sonnyboy's generation with action against the oppressing system, the oppressing white people. For George, "being a man" meant music, dance, drink, and sex; for Sonnyboy, hedonism must yield to activism. The prospect is not entirely pleasant: it indicates that the novel's third generation will finally figure out what's what in South Africa, but it also means that many in this generation will suffer. We end Chapter 8 as "She [Martha] rested her head on the table and wept" (115); we recall what we were told about the boy and prison right after he was conceived.

Down Second Avenue

Ezekiel Mphahlele's *Down Second Avenue* is not fiction; rather, it is writer Mphahlele's autobiography. He also passes through a long restless period during which he is not sure what course his life should take. We hear about his childhood and adolescence in the northern Transvaal and in Pretoria (living on Second Avenue) and at private church schools: during these years, he absorbed much that will return to his consciousness later in life. As he embarks upon his adult life, "passive resistance" is in vogue. He rejects this approach to the injustices he sees and experiences:

> Fellowship? Love? Obedience of the law? Suddenly I did not know what these meant in terms of my place in society, and I revolted against such preachments. How could I adopt an attitude of passive resistance towards the ruling clique and their electorate who a year later were to dedicate themselves to the cause of white supremacy by voting to Parliament a bunch of lawless Voortrekker descendants whose safety lies in the hands of sten-gun-happy police youngsters? How could I even pretend to myself that the United Party was better, when in 1945 the Smuts government had sent armed troops to quell a riot in a municipal compound near Marabastad, where Africans wanted better living conditions? How could I, when Sturrock of the United Party government had started to rebuild Johannesburg station so that whites and non-whites should enter segregated platforms through segregated entrances? How could anyone unashamedly ask me to do things constitutionally—in obedience to the dictates of an immoral constitution my people did not help formulate? (162)

The young man realized that "Something dramatic was taking place inside me" (162). His "personality revolted" (162); hate took over his mind and caused him to reconstruct his world. But he was not led immediately to activism: his hatred, according to Rowland Smith in *World Literature Written in English,* was a restrained one. Rather than act, he was thrown into a limbo in which he "suspended belief and disbelief indefinitely" (162).

Mphahlele becomes a teacher and confronts a government-dictated curriculum. In writing, he attacks this curriculum "as being for a race of slaves; for pupils who were not expected to change as well as be changed by the environment, but to fit themselves into it; for unsettled communities doomed for ever to shift from one place to another, without the necessity to become either a stable peasantry or urban communities" (166).

He cringes as he teaches from history books that distort the country's past in order "to glorify white colonization" (166) and Afrikaans grammar books that contain examples that are blatantly racist. He cringes more as he teaches Afrikaans literature that "was either lyrical vapourings about natural phenomena or fighting talk inspired by the Great Trek, the Transvaal War of Independence and the Anglo-Boer War" (166). To cooperate with the oppressor was bad enough but to glorify him! He continues crusading against the education being offered black South Africans, and, before long, this incipient activism costs him his job.

He, in an interlude with mythic and religious echoes, goes to the mountains of Basutoland. There, he

> went to the top of a high mountain. There I felt the touch of the Ultimate, but only for a fleeting dizzy moment. Below were the fields laid waste by rushing water: fingers and fingers of furrows with photographic unreality. Grey earth cried out in vain to the skies; as grey and fruitless as the cough of old men who cry for the migrant sons in mine pits of far-away lands, where their lungs began to rot. (184)

Still searching, Mphahlele's eyes rise in this scene to heaven but quickly fall back to the earth and how South Africa's black people are oppressed by the white nation's political and economic system. "My longing search continued" (185), he says; he realizes that his "dreams had long since taken flight and now hung dry in shining cobwebs to which my fermenting furies clung crucified . . ." (185). He talked through the night with a wise old man; then, "Dawn came and announced victory. The quest had come to an end . . ." (185).

During his soul's dark night, Mphahlele discovers bitterness and he embraces this bitterness passionately. This bitterness is because he now *knows* what the (his) situation is but also knows that there is very little he can do about it.

He continues living in South Africa, however. He feels physically oppressed—"Things close in upon you; you find yourself in a tightly closed-up room" (202). He offers us stark, disturbing portraits of the urban existence that is emerging for its black residents. He describes Orlando, the nice, new location that Martha was raising Sonnyboy in:

> Orlando. A glorified Marabastad. Saturday night is the same as it was twenty-five years ago in Marabastad minus the ten-to-ten bell because now the curfew law is only for the city and suburbs to protect a frightened and neurotic white population which keeps revolvers and narcotic drugs under pillows. Yes, it is still the same, the only tarred roads being those leading to white superintendents' offices. The township has been spreading west and south since 1934 in three-roomed units; not east because that's the direction in which Johannesburg lies, twelve miles away; not north because that's where the line of gold mines is. We have been paying a subeconomic rental of fifty shillings a month for four rooms without electric lights or water-borne sewerage, and now the rents have gone up a scale stopping at five pounds. Near us is one of the biggest electric power-stations in the world. As Orlando spreads into Meadowlands, Mofolo, Dube, Jabavu, Moroka, Molapo, Moletsane, with more than 200,000 souls altogether, it also develops ulcers in the form of shanty towns; like the one just below us. And still the Black metropolis grows, meeting other townships of refugees who have been removed from western towns which like Africans only as labourers. Faction fights must be a source of amusement to some white supreme chief of the Bantu who decided to force people into ethnic compartments and threw thousands of single men into huge dormitories in hostels with high fences around them. (203-04)

What Mphahlele is describing—vividly—is the emergence of the area we know today as Soweto. When Martha moved to Orlando, it did indeed hold some promise. Mphahlele looks beneath the township surface:

> There was a time when it was much better to be a tenant in a freehold township like Sophiatown than a municipal tenant, but the difference today is academic. Police continue to beat up and down the road in front of our house, not to protect human life and property but to look

> after the law and demand passes. . . . Comparative cleanliness and bigness blunt the edge of political discontent here but you know you're in a ghetto and God, those lights are so far away, too far for you to reach. Between you and them is a pit of darkness, darkness charged with screams, groans, yells, cries, laughter and singing. They swell and reach a frantic pitch, only to be suppressed by the spirit of the night. (204)

The distant lights become symbolic of all the black South African is denied. Years later, "The lights quiver as brightly as ever" (206) *in the distance*. And Mphahlele's children begin to become affected by the nation's institutionalized racism. His four year-old "sees the police take people down to the charge office and municipal police beat up a man or boy in the street"; he "clings to [Mphahlele] tightly when he sees a constable walk up or down the road and says *Ntate*, is the policeman going to arrest me is he going to take you is he going to take mamma?" (206). Then, the same boy ominously begins imitating the policeman's behavior:

> Another time Motswiri comes to you with imitation handcuffs crudely made of wire and shouts Bring your hands here, where's your pass I'll teach you not to be naughty again. Now he wants a torch and a baton and a big broad belt and a badge . . . (206)

It is time to leave South Africa . . . for Nigeria. After arriving in Nigeria in late 1957, Mphahlele reflects. These reflections are disconnected, suggesting that even though the writer has moved from restlessness to action, he has not yet assembled a coherent picture of his situation. He thinks back to the rural northern Transvaal of his birth; he thinks about Christianity and how empty it seemed when wielded by the white man; he thinks of "the white man's achievements" and how he "used to want to justify myself and my own kind to the white man" (218). Separated from that homeland, he now rejects Christianity and the white man and turns inward. He will move on—to what place or position or politics he is not yet sure, but he ends *Down Second Avenue* by declaring that at least now—out of South Africa—he has the right to move on.

The three works discussed in this chapter are different in kind (play, novel, autobiography) *and* different in the kind of restlessness they exhibit. Hutchinson's *The Rain Killers* presents a village that is confused, that cannot come to terms with its own victmization because it is still entrapped by superstitions and, more importantly, by human emotions such as jealousy, lust, and the desire for vengeance that cause it to victimize itself. The restlessness in the play is born of this confusion: something is wrong, but day-to-day life is so muddled that it is difficult to pinpoint that which is wrong. The first generation in Dikobe's *The Marabi Dance* are similarly confused, as traditional ways come into conflict with the new urban mores. The second generation, however, instead of finding clarity in that confusion, find pleasure in the life-style of the marabi clubs. It is left to the third generation, Sonnyboy's, to abandon the *carpe diem* restlessness that his parents fell prey to and pinpoint that which is wrong. Mphahlele is, in age, in between Martha and George and Sonnyboy. His upbringing, education, and work bring him to both bitterness and understanding. He is able to pinpoint much of what is wrong; however, he is not able to do much about the situation. He feels somewhat powerless against the white establishment. Just as importantly, he feels that he has not yet come to terms with who he is. And those terms, he feels, must be *black* terms.

Mphahlele, like many of his generation, left South Africa. From without, they suffered as they saw their homeland's situation and their people's situation worsen. Many *within* South Africa would suffer during the twenty-year period from 1965 to 1985. The next chapter examines some of the literature that emerged out of this suffering.

Works Cited

Dikobe, Modikwe. *The Marabi Dance*. Oxford: Heinemann, 1980.

Hutchinson, Alfred. *The Rain Killers*. London: Headley Brothers, 1964.

Mphahlele, Ezekiel. *Down Second Avenue*. Berlin: Seven Seas Publishers, 1959.

Shava, Piniel Viriri. *A People's Voice: Black South African Writing in the Twentieth Century*. 1989; rpt. Athens: Ohio University Press, 1989.

Smith, Rowland. "Allan Quartermain to Rosa Burger: Violence in South African Fiction." *World Literature Written in English* 22 (1983): 171-82.

5

Suffering

The cry of the lion has long been an anguished cry. Poets, playwrights, and novelists have presented this cry in a range of works that depict and/or express the suffering the people—primarily the Black people—have endured in modern South Africa. This chapter examines many of these works.

The first three works are by poets. Read together, the three, Oswald Mtshali's *Sounds of a Cowhide Drum* (1971), Mongane Wally Serote's *No Baby Must Weep* (1975), and Mafika Gwala's *No More Lullabies* (1982), form a progression. Although these works contain recurring motifs, their tone changes from sad and ironic in the case of Mtshali to angry in the case of Gwala. Gwala's work then provides, in tone, a good transition to the works discussed in the next chapter, in which anger yields to calls for action.

All three poets survey the conditions under which black South Africans lived in the 1960s and 1970s. The poets examine a range of conditions, ones they saw then and there. Lewis Nkosi's 1986 novel *Mating Birds* and Matsemela Manaka's 1980 play *Egoli* also deal with the circumstances of daily life; however, they differ from the poems in more than just genre. *Mating Birds* focuses more narrowly on interracial sex and explores how power politics corrupts sexuality. *Egoli* looks back in time and presents the life stories of two very different men who were chained together in prison and are chained together "now" as mine workers and, more broadly, as black South Africans.

Egoli's glance at prison life is a good prelude to an examination of four very different works that deal with the day-to-day suffering of the many Blacks who were imprisoned unjustly at the height of apartheid. Dennis Brutus' *Letters to Martha* (1968) is a poignant, frightening, but surprisingly quiet work of poetry.

Quite different in tone are the poems that comprise James Matthews' 1977 *Pass Me a Meatball, Jones*. D. M. Zwelonke's 1977 novel *Robben Island* is a rather matter-of-fact account of day-to-day living on this infamous prison island off the coast of Cape Town. Despite its usually restrained tone, it nonetheless succeeds in shocking, especially in certain scenes. More shocking is Workshop '71's 1976 production *Survival*, which was successfully performed before white and black audiences at venues as varied as the Space Theatre in Cape Town and the Dube YMCA in Soweto, where it was violently stopped by an attack by South African police.

All of these works clearly–sometimes graphically–depict the suffering the black majority have experienced in South Africa. And it should be noted–loudly–that the black majority are the primary victims of the "system" that dominated South African life and politics for decades. However, colored South Africans who made common cause with the blacks as well as whites who sympathized with the cause of the majority also suffered. Athol Fugard presents that suffering in all its complexity in his *A Lesson from Aloes* (1981). Before we turn in the next chapter to several works that attack white South Africans, it is useful to note that, sometimes, whites are fellow victims.

Sounds of a Cowhide Drum

Oswald Mtshali's *Sounds of a Cowhide Drum* was a landmark volume in the history of black South African poetry, for it represented an abandonment of colonial forms and a reembracing of traditional African rhythms. This dimension of Mtshali's poetry should be noted; however, it is more the content (for lack of a better word) that we are interested in here, for that content *is* the suffering of black South Africans. Not all of Mtshali's poems depict suffering. In fact, some of the more interesting poems in the collection–for example, "The Chauffeur Shuffle," "At the Seashore," and "The Detribalized" –are satires. And Mtshali is willing to satirize the people he sees regardless of their race; thus, whereas "The Chauffeur Shuffle" attacks the white businessman whose blood pressure is such that he is described as "Vesuvius" and "At the Seashore" attacks the affluent, hedonistic white man who escapes dusty, dangerous Jo'burg for Durban or the like resort, "The Detribalized" attacks the "Western" affectations of urban Black men and women. Even though these satires are effective and memorable and funny, they have less ultimate impact on the reader (or listener) than the poems that deal with suffering.

Mtshali presents the suffering of his black people in three general ways—directly, by setting up a contrast between white and black, and—perhaps most poignantly—by penning a song of innocence and then undermining it with concluding lines drawn from black experience. Some poems form a fourth category, that of laments.

In "This Kid is No Goat," Mtshali presents the emerging young generation of black South Africans who are emerging. Although some have gone to prison ("Gone to the Island of Lament for Sharpeville" [3]) and some have "Gone overseas on scholarship" (3), some remain. They were educated as Christians but have abandoned the lessons of traditional religion for the messages of jazz because their "higher" education "at Life University / whose lecture rooms were shebeens, / hospital wards and prison cells" (18-20) convinced them that they "can't be black and straight / in this crooked white world" (23-24). They make Duke Ellington, Count Basie, and Louis Armstrong their "High Priests" (35) because the music fits their "violent gusts of doubt and skepticism" (41). But these young blacks are not wallowing in these "gusts"; rather, the gusts have brought them to the point where they declare

> I want my heaven now,
> here on earth in Houghton and Parktown;
> a mansion
> two cars or more
> and smiling servants. (45-49)

Another portrait is presented by Mtshali in "Always a Suspect." Using the persona of a well-dressed young black man, he presents the day-to-day urban experience: being asked to produce his passbook ("the document of [his] existence" [8]); being viewed as a potential mugger by white women he walks alongside on the sidewalk.

Several poems depict life in Soweto. "Intake Night–Baragwanath Hospital" presents the township as a "battlefield" (1) and recites the wounds—"knife wounds / axe wounds / bullet wounds" (6-8)—the residents receive. Someone—it's not clear who—ends the sketch by declaring, ironically but sadly truthfully, that "'So! it's Friday night! / Everybody's enjoying / in Soweto" (22-24). "Nightfall in Soweto" makes it clear that blacks are wounding blacks—that something has happened to the residents of Soweto to transform man into beast. In another poem, "White City Jabavu," Mtshali finds nothing white in this ironically named section of Soweto, except, maybe, the chattering white teeth of hungry street waifs "Or the / white eye-ball / of a plundered corpse, / lying in the gutter" (11-14). Why do the black residents of Soweto pound and plunder each other so? Hints are found in "On Drowning Sorrow," when Mtshali explains why so many turn to alcohol, drugs, and sex. They do so in a futile attempt to banish sorrows, but "woe when they return / to capture my soul" (17-18).

Given how violent Soweto is, why do more and more blacks come to the townships of Soweto and other similarly nightmarish urban locations? In "Amagoduka at Glencoe Station," Mtshali tries to explain why by depicting the rural land of these Africans as "stripped naked" (51) and "gouged dry" (54). There, the "riverbeds [are] littered with carcasses and bones" (57) and "big-bellied babies / [are] sucking festering fingers / instead of their mothers' shrivelled breasts" (61-63). The men know what awaits them in Jo'burg:

> We come from across the Tugela river,
> we are going to eGoli! eGoli! eGoli!
> where they'll turn us into moles
> that eat the gold dust
> and spit out blood. (72-76)

However, the fate that awaits them in the Jo'burg mines is better than starving—and seeing their families starve—in their rural tribal lands. And they may not end up in the mines. Perhaps they'll end up like the men depicted in "A Roadgang's Cry." They will then become like their machines that "swallow the red soil / and spit it out like a tuberculotic's sputum" (4-5) and suffer the indignity of being called "Jim" by the whites, regardless of their true names.

This last poem, besides depicting the plight of black South Africans in naturalistic terms, also sets up a contrast between the black world and the white world. In this particular poem, the blacks are engaged in hard labor in the streets while the white businessmen and women shoppers (the sexism is in the poem) walk past—quickly—on the sidewalk.

A similar contrast is struck in "The Watchman's Blues." We are in Jo'burg; we see the skyscrapers and penthouses of the white man's "city of gold." Here sits a noble Zulu, reduced to chasing off "the wandering waif" and "hobo" (24-25)—"the rats that come / to nibble the treasure-strewn street windows" (8-9); reduced to being told, "'Here's ten pounds. / Jim was a good boy'" (20-21). Meanwhile, he is lonely for "the three wives and a dozen children / sleeping alone in the kraal / far away in the majestic mountains" (29-31).

Perhaps the greatest harm the various laws of apartheid perpetrated was to normal family life. Here and in "Amagoduka at Glencoe Station," men who come to the city to work are separated from their families who must remain in the tribal areas. There is this separation that blacks must bear. There is also the separation between man and woman that results when a black woman goes to work and live at a white family's home. "The Master of the House" is about just such a separation. Using the persona of the man, Mtshali describes—to the white master—how he the black man must come like an animal at night to see his beloved Lizzie.

The damage to normal family life is seen starkly in "An Abandoned Bundle." The poem begins with a vivid description of one of the Soweto townships as "a gigantic sore" with "thick yellow" "oozing" "pus" (4-6). Then, the poem shifts to a horrible scene: "Scavenging dogs" (9) mutilating the corpse of "an infant dumped on a rubbish heap" (18). Then, in a characteristic Mtshali gesture, the corpse is linked to the Christ child—suggesting how remote from salvation Soweto life is; then, in another characteristic Mtshali gesture, the poem shifts from baby to mother *and* describes the mother's face as "glittering with innocence" (24) and her heart as "as pure as untrampled dew" (25). Commenting on the poem, Piniel Viriri Shava describes the mother as indifferent (80). She may well be, but the poem's words stress her innocence as well. *How*—we are left to ask—can this woman who has abandoned her baby to the dogs be described in these terms? Such a description is possible *if and only if* the blame belongs not to her but totally to the system that has victimized her as well as her baby.

In "An Abandoned Bundle," Mtshali moves from experience to innocence—with a quickness that shocks. His more usual movement is in the other direction: from innocence to experience. In "The Shepherd and His Flock," we are offered an idyllic picture—punctured by a few words that we might not at first glance even notice—of a shepherd boy. Then, at the poem's brief transition point, we see him "salute / the farmer's children / going to school" (25-27) and then "dreamily" ask, "O! Wise Sun above, / will you ever guide / me into school?" (28-31) We then realize that the idyll was an illusion, that he is a member of an oppressed people.

"Boy on a Swing" works much the same way. The initial stanzas seem idyllic: a young boy plays; the poem's rhythm reinforces the to and fro motion. Only if we reread them do we pick up on the ominous note of his shirt being described as a "tattered kite" (7). Then, as if he is maturing before our very eyes, he asks questions. The first two are innocent; the third shocks us out of innocence:

> Mother!
> Where did I come from?
> When will I wear long trousers?
> Why was my father jailed? (13-16)

Mtshali's poems which shock us by taking us quickly from innocence to experience are perhaps his most memorable ones. Also memorable are poems in which his characters lament their situation. "The Washerwoman's Prayer" depicts how a poor black woman has suffered as a washerwoman serving a rich man for many, many years. More than halfway through the poem, she, in a manner that suggests George Herbert and in language that suggests Christ's from the cross, screams at God:

"Good Lord! Dear Lord!" she shouted
"Why am I so tormented?
How long have I lamented?
Tell me Lord, tell me O Lord." (15-18)

Then, again in a manner that suggests Herbert, God replies, "My child! Dear child" (19) and tells her to "Suffer for those who live in gilded sin, / Toil for those who swim in a bowl of pink gin" (20-21). She is essentially told to suffer, as Christ did, for the sins of the wicked–in this case, the wicked whites. She accepts this message. We, on the other hand, must question the justice of the divine words she hears. We are similarly taken aback by the references earlier in the poem to her employer as "her master" (5) and "lord" (6). We begin to see how the poem depicts the way Christianity is appropriated and abused by those in power to suppress those out of power. Early in the poem, she is kept in line because she views her employer as lord; when that twist gets old, she is kept in line because she views herself as Christlike and the whites as requiring her redemptive suffering. When that "twist" gets old, we suspect there will be another–until she realizes what we realize: that, as Shava notes, Christianity offers Black South Africa empty messages (82).

A more straightforward lament is the volume's title song, "Song of a Cowhide Drum." The drum's beat is "the Voice of Mother Africa" (32). The sound is heard despite how the conquering colonial forces and missionaries "trampled" and "destroyed" the African's "glorious past" (19-20). The sound is heard despite how horrible life is now for the African man–living and being raped in mine compounds; visiting the shebeens and catching syphilis from the prostitutes who ply their trade there; knowing that, back in the tribal lands, men who were too lazy to come to the city ("loafers" [47]) are fornicating with and impregnating their wives. The drum's beat is heard, but these men do indeed begin to doubt:

If the gods are with us–
Oh! beloved black gods of our forefathers
What have we done to you
Why have you forsaken us[.] (40-43)

There is, in this poem, no answer—neither one that further suppresses nor one that might ease their spirits. All we readers have are the probably empty allusion to Christ in the line, "Why have you forsaken us," and the fact that the drum's beat is not heard in the poem's last three stanzas. Has life become so oppressive that "the drum of [their] dormant soul" (12) has stopped beating? Mtshali's shift in tone in the later volumes of poetry he authored in exile, as Ursula Bennett notes, suggests that Mtshali's answer may well be a bitter "Yes."

No Baby Must Weep

Most would agree that black South African poetry—as well as that by other races—has succeeded more in short forms than in long forms. Mongane Wally Serote works in both short and long forms, and it is highly likely that short works such as "What's In This Black Shit" will be remembered long after his long works. The long works, however, are worth examining because they give the poet an opportunity to go beyond quick poignant descriptions of black life, especially that of children, and quick jabs at the white establishment and to explore how black life *feels*. Serote's *No Baby Must Weep* attempts just such an exploration.

Like Serote's earlier works, *No Baby Must Weep* is ultimately an optimistic poem. It begins, however, with a very pessimistic definition of "men." The love that ought to be within men is dead, Serote's autobiographical persona tells us. As a result, men are

> huge
> tall
> fat
> things
> outsmarted by cats in gentleness
> shamed by tigers in agility[.] (25)

Men "know nothing about songs," "are more petty than birds," and cannot "be moved / by the sight of machine-gunned children." They are often drunk, and they are always burning something be it cigarettes, dagga, or petrol. They either can't make love, or scare off the "cats when they make love in the dark" (26). They are greedy and likely to die of heart attacks inspired by their crazed chasing after wealth.

Serote's definition of "men" is interesting for at least two reasons. First, Serote keeps his definition a-racial: at times, he seems to be glancing at white men; at times, black men; at times, both. Serote's point then seems to be that all men have lost the love that ought to be within them. Second, Serote keeps returning to men's inability to hear songs. For a writer—for a poet, this inability is particularly troubling and frustrating. Serote's persona says

> shit
> i am fucking tired
> shitlessly tired of talking, writing hoping people can hear
> a song
> from a child whose heart was broken
> but nobody listens
> they want to jive
> seduce
> and i often caught me right in that shit[.] (26)

The discouraged, sometimes distracted poet finally abandons his condemnation of "men" and declares, numerous times, that "i am the man you will never defeat" (37). No matter how he suffers, he will not be defeated:

> if you walk this earth, where i too walk
> and you tear my clothes and reach for my flesh
> and tear my flesh to reach my blood
> and you spill my blood to reach my bones
> and you smash my bones and hope for my soul[.] (37)

He will sing, and those who join him in song will also not be defeated by loveless men. His song takes him to the source of love—the highly symbolic mother. "[W]eary from running," "bruised" by the wind, "burnt" by the sun, he tries to renew himself through the mother's smile, passion, and rhythm. The mother comes to symbolize Africa. The return to the mother is a return to the womb; the poem then transforms the sea-like womb into the sea, and the sea becomes a second symbol for Africa. As the second symbol is born from the within the first, there is a sense of renewal–available to the persona and to the reader.

But the sea is still distant. The persona must follow the river to reach the sea. A reader who has seen the townships that comprise Soweto can visualize the persona's problem: the river, which Barnett has suggested represents African (as opposed to Western) life, is only a near-dry creek or a ditch there. What dominates the scene, as the poem presents it, are the streets, which the poem describes repeatedly as dirty, dusty, "bloody muddy," and leading nowhere (45).

Serote's persona becomes trapped in this urban scene, these "squeaking blood-stained hungry-rat battlegrounds" (46). The scene is populated by whores, murderers, and "cops [who] shoot first and think after" (46). And victims! Serote chooses to emphasize how the children are victimized, how they suffer. The symbolic streets have "woven the children of this town into their dust" and have "made the children of this town gasp in their dongas" (46).

The "grannies," who comprise the oldest generation to be found there, remember the African past, and they embody that African past in their songs. Based on these songs and rooted in the slum-and-township suffering, Serote's persona will find the river and follow it to the sea. There, he will immerse himself in the water and sing and celebrate. But even at the point in *No Baby Must Weep* where he "say[s] hallelujah / and claps [his] hands / and do[es his] dance / and ring[s his] laughter" (58), he recalls the suffering of slum-and-township life. He especially recalls "shit like that / getting my children killed" (58). *Only if* people pursue the course that the persona has charted back to Africa will violence in general, violence against children, and the weeping of babies stop.

No More Lullabies

Mafika Gwala's 1982 collection of poems reads as a vivid catalogue of the ways the black people of South Africa have suffered. Gwala does propose a revolutionary course for his fellow blacks to take; in so doing, he goes *far* beyond the lamenting of Mtshali and the inward-looking exploring of Serote. He may even cease writing poetry and offer, as Shava has claimed, politics in verse (111). This departure from the "poetic" may be because *No More Lullabies* is a later work, one that post-dates the shocking events of June 16, 1976, in Soweto and the violent days that followed. One point that Gwala makes repeatedly (and many observers of South African history and politics concur) is that when the police opened fire on hundreds of unarmed schoolchildren, the police succeeded in changing the politics of South Africa dramatically—and permanently. Perhaps the police also succeeded in changing the poetics.

The sufferings of the black people can be lumped into two large categories: those that have been imposed from without (i.e., from white South Africa) and those that have been imposed from within (i.e., from black South Africa). Of course, those sufferings that blacks impose upon fellow blacks grow out of the situation that the white South Africans created.

Whites, in Gwala's view, have created a sad spectacle. In several poems, he depicts the urbanization of South Africa in negative terms. In "There is . . . ," nature is described as "Now threatened by pollution / and sprawling cities" (5-6). In "Words to a Mother," Gwala notes the way in which urban skyscrapers blot out the sun, and in "Exit Alexandra," he points to the economic cause of Jo'burg's growth, gold, as "The enrichening monster" that "pierces electric eyes into you, / Threatens everything black" (18-20). He indicts technology; he describes the white world as plastic. *His* Africa—his land—is lost, and, as he tells us in "Tap-Tapping," he is "still surviving / the traumas of [his] raped soil" (11-12).

The white city grew, of course, thanks to black labor. Alongside the white city developed the slums. Gwala glances at them, at the townships that replaced them when (as he notes in "Exit Alexandra") "greedy landgrabbers" needed more space for the growing white city. The forced removals seem especially to gall Gwala—both the removals to the townships and the removals to the distant homelands. In "Mother Courage on the Train Carriage," he refers to "the forced trek to KwaMashu / Then a diaspora to all kinds of new slums" (14-15), linking the black removals, with irony, to the Boers' great trek and, with bitterness, to the plight of another oppressed people, the Jews. And the new slums are no better than the old slums, and the homelands are described by Gwala in "The ABC Jig" as "the malaria-infested bushes / of the Boerewors Curtain" (8-9) and in "A Poem" as

> barren eroded valleys
> or sandtracked flats of impoverished reserves
> euphemistically called homelands,
> grandiloquently referred to as "Maziphathe"
> or "uZibuse[.]" (7-11)

The white South Africans, of course, did still more *to* Gwala's people. He refers to the many laws directed against non-whites (in particular, the pass and job reservation laws); he refers to the way the whites used Christianity to control the anger of non-whites; he refers to the way the whites tried to use family planning campaigns to control the number of non-whites; he refers to the way the whites tried to use the educational system to control the minds of non-whites; and he refers to the many black South Africans who were put in prison by the white government and the suspicious deaths that occurred there. In "In Defence of Poetry," Gwala refers to "long-term sentences and/ death in detention / for those who 'threaten state security'" (4-6); in "The ABC Jig," he recalls the story of Steve Biko; and in "No More Lullabies," he talks about the many who were detained after the Soweto riots in 1976.

In several poems, Gwala speaks more generally about the actions of the South African police. "Bluesing In" records events in South African history from 1894 to an Orwellian 1984 and a post-revolutionary 1994. The police are depicted as playing major roles in enforcing oppressive and discriminatory laws in the '40s and '50s and in silencing anyone who might "shout Viva Frelimo" in the '70s. "Afrika at a Piece" presents specifics about "deaths sometimes / called "accidental" (47-48) at Johannesburg's John Vorster prison and elsewhere. "My House is Bugged" details, in a somewhat comic way, the surveillance activities of the police against someone who dared to tell economics students to read Karl Marx and to preach against mass removals. Similarly comic (but not always) is "Looking at Saul," where the security police officer is described at length:

he haunts
        people's lives
    disrupts
        family peace
he'll say he has studied
    criminology
claims to know
the communist mind

he's mastered
the art of housebreaking
and revels in bugging devices
and transmitters
he's shot innocent children
brought me the bible
in detention cell[.] (1-15)

Gwala can be witty. However, the line about shooting innocent children stops the laughter, as does the comparison Gwala makes in "The ABC Jig" between "The S. B.'s" and "the Gestapo squads / on Jew hunts" (22-23).

All of the suffering discussed thus far embitters Gwala; however, it is the Soweto massacre of June 16, 1976, that seems to have galvanized the bitterness into an anger that eliminates all laughter. Gwala refers to the Soweto massacre often, and briefly. The brevity of the references should not be misinterpreted: they are brief because the very word "Soweto" had become so packed with meaning that merely mentioning it was enough to convey one's feelings. Thus, in "There is . . . ," Gwala refers to "the tears of Soweto" (21) before calling for "thunder" (22) and "guns" (25); in "Tap-Tapping," Gwala mentions only the place name (6) before declaring that an already wounded "Hope" has now been stripped of its banadages and left exposed to infection; and in "No More Lullabies," Gwala simply says "The spectre of Soweto '76 haunts" (9).

Not all of Gwala's poems indict white South Africans directly, however. Gwala is aware that his people suffer because of what they do to themselves. Although it is true that they might not do these things if the white man had not created the situation they find themselves in, nonetheless, they do act in a manner that causes suffering, and much of Gwala's poetry is a lecture to his fellow blacks, telling them to cease and desist.

South African blacks embrace "Western ways," thereby denying their African culture: "flushing Rand notes / down shopping centres/ in Africa-Adieu fashion" ("Circles with Eyes," 2-5). They also act *against* each other. In "A Poem," Gwala notes how many play-up to "the boss who drops Rand notes / so's you can play Judas on your fellow workers" (20-21). More ominously, in several poems, Gwala notes how his fellows attack and sometimes kill each other. In "Let's Take Heed," Gwala tells a young black boy

> Take heed, son
> the bag you just snatched
> from the black mama
> down in Cross Street
> is all she had in this money-world
> all she had to feed your own
> black brothers & sisters[.] (5-11)

More seriously, in "Bonk'abajahile," Gwala recalls, vividly, black-on-black killings. For example, "Bongi Ndlovu / She tried to run, to flee, to plead; / Whick! Whack! / Into flesh came the bushknife / On the sand dunes she collapsed" (65-69).

The black-on-black violence that concerns Gwala (and others) is rooted in some of the other ways the Black South African suffers. Many lose control of themselves because of drugs or alcohol. In "Words to a Mother," we hear how many young men "sink themselves / into the comforts of lounge furniture / in posh shebeens /—and drown" (V, 2-5) and how they are "smiting themselves with dagga / behind toilets in Warwick Avenue" (V, 6-7). In "Courage," we hear Gwala preach "Against the deceiving comfort / of Castle beer / Wimpy bars / and Kentucky Chicken" (25-28). Drugs and alcohol are problems indeed. Perhaps more pernicious is the self-hatred blacks inflict on themselves. In "Bonk'abajahile," Gwala notes that "we fear our blackness" (87) and "we hate our virtues" (89); more optimistically, in "Time of the Hero," the poet looks forward to the time "when blacks start / pissing on Mankunku's lament / refusing to bemoan their blackness" (2-4).

Ultimately, there is a great deal of hope to be found in Gwala's *No More Lullabies*. I have emphasized the sufferings

Gwala depicts; however, he builds, gradually, poem-by-poem, a revolutionary message. Like the hopeful message of Serote, it is one fit for music, as Gwala notes beautifully in his "To My Daughter on her 16th Birthday." The music, however, is specified in Gwala's poetry as jazz. The poet announces at the beginning of "For Bhoyi," "You raised your jazz banner." By the end of the poem, it is clear that jazz will inspire revolution; revolution will lead to "a liberated Azania," "the people's Azanaia" ("Words to a Mother," VI, 3-4). The revolution will involve violence: in "Lobotomies of a Party–May 1978," the poet "jazzes" to his "true self" in stanza six and the language turns suddenly military, ending with "flak guns." Furthermore, the revolutionaries will pass through some dark times, which Gwala describes in "Words to a Mother" as "moods / a shade darker than blue" (I, 6-7). However, in the end Azania will be triumphant. As Gwala declares at the end of "Bluesing In,"

> Blues, blues
> Azania blues 1994
> We buried Humpty Dumpty
> On a hill at Magaliesburg
> A monument marking his grave reads:
> "He didn't want change." (61-66)

The Soweto massacre and riots of 1976 were crucial in changing the tone in much Black poetry from the pained restraint of Mtshali's *Songs of a Cowhide Drum* and the inner struggle and triumph of Mongane Wally Serote's *No Baby Must Weep*. In "Road to Challenge," Gwala talks directly about this shift:

> We heard the hawking noises
> from the police ministry as a small plane
> zoomed above our heads and our minds,
> We listened to the vacillating voices
> On the Black Messiah,
> We also heard angry solitary pledges
> from Messrs Pink Opinion–
> as middleclass demeanours reneged on us:
> No "Eli, Eli lamma sabachthani?" blues
> Instead we bluesed "Take Cover"
>   we bluesed "Michochorodo."
> Signing off our trust in faded hopes. (28-39)

With this shift to a more revolutionary outlook, the "caged lioness" (III, 27) of "Words to a Mother" will be caged no more and will be well on her way down the freeway.

Mating Birds

Gwala's account of the sufferings of the black race in South Africa is thorough, touching many, many bases. Lewis Nkosi's 1986 novel *Mating Birds* is more focused. It deals with the controversial topic of interracial sex. Interracial sexuality finds its way into a large number of works of contemporary South African literature in English–so much so that Lewis Nkosi, in an essay published in 1963, criticizes this obsession with interracial sex, declaring it to be a reflection of the white man's psychological need to recreate the intimate bond he had once had with his black nanny. Curiously, years later, Nkosi gives way to the obsession. In his defense, he does seem to be suggesting that there is an important difference between the white man's desire for the black woman and the black man's desire for the white woman. The former may well be tied to the white man's desire for the loving embrace of the black nanny; the latter, which is the subject of *Mating Birds,* is tied to the question of power.

The tense drama of *Mating Birds* begins on a Durban beach, at that (white) man-imposed point separating the white from the non-white stretches of beach. On the white side is a young girl who seems to be teasing a young black man on the other side of the line. Day after day, she continues. The young man has some difficulty decoding her physical message: is she taunting him? does she want him? Finally, he decides to follow her to the cottage where she is staying. He watches from outside while she, seemingly aware of his presence, strips nude. He walks in; they begin to make love. All evidence in the text would indicate that their lovemaking was something they mutually desired. Unfortunately, some of her white friends show up, she screams "rape," and the young black man is arrested, tried and convicted, and imprisoned. It is from prison that he narrates the story, telling it, we are to imagine, to his amateur psychologist lawyer, who finds deviant behavior fascinating.

Told from the black man's point of view, *Mating Birds* provides us with a clearer sense of his feelings not only during the seduction but before and after. Afterwards, he feels he has been victimized–by her and, more broadly, by a racist South African society that found her story of rape far more believable than his story of enticement. The depths of his anger seem to make his time in prison even more agonizing. This "afterwards" portrait is moving; however, the "before" portrait is ultimately more revealing. In his monologue with his lawyer, the young man returns to the years during which he was growing up outside the city. During these years, he was drawn to white women.

The nature of this attraction was only partially sexual. The white women represented privilege, material possessions, status, and–most importantly–power. To be near a white woman was to be near all of that which he was denied as a black man. To be near a white woman provided him with a touch of these things. Thus, Veronica's exhibitionism, on the beach and in her cottage, offered the young man more than just a mere touch of privilege, material possessions, status, and power; rather, it offered him the potential of embracing intimately, if only for a few minutes, these desired entities.

If the young man's sexual desire for Veronica is seen in these terms, her turning on him becomes a devastating reassertion of white privilege, status, and power. Given how *Mating Birds* is narrated, we know less about Veronica's thoughts and feelings than the young man's. We do know enough to suspect that she meant him no harm. Her seductive actions on the beach were a game to her–something to entertain her. The same was true of her exhibitionist behavior later on. Having an audience, especially a black audience, seemed to excite her. When he entered her cottage and engaged her in intercourse, he was taking the game she had initiated to its logical end. And she seemed to accept this last play in the same "free" spirit that she had earlier shown when she enticingly undressed before his eyes. When her white friends arrived, her "free" spirit flagged in the face of potential embarrassment–in the face of potential loss, on her part, of privilege and status and power. Rather than be lowered by being recognized as a "loose" girl whose desire for adventure took her across the color line into the forbidden, she lashed out at her would-be lover. She lashed out in order to preserve her privileged position, her power. In other words, she did not maliciously victimize the novel's central character; rather, she became—in a moment—the instrument of her white society's desire to maintain its privileges, its status, and its power. In prison, awaiting execution, the young man comes to this very conclusion:

> This girl, for example, white, pretty, consumed by her own vanity and the need to escape from a life of numbing boredom, will be responsible, some will argue, for the dispatch of one more young African life to perdition. Such a view is quite mistaken. Veronica is responsible, of course, in a way, but only marginally, symbolically, responsible. The bearer of white skin. . . . , this English girl has simply been an instrument in whom is revealed in its most flagrant form the rot and corruption of a society that has cut itself off entirely from the rest of humanity, from any possibility for human growth. . . . All the same, the girl was there only by chance. But having been there, she became a convenient pretext for the state to indulge its well-documented appetite for murder and destruction; she became useful as the most seductive bait ever placed in the path of a full-blooded African. (180-81)

The young man concludes, as we do, that he is suffering in prison and will suffer execution *not* because of a particular young woman's actions but rather because of the way privilege, status, and power are distributed in South Africa—all to the whites; none to the non-whites. This division creates envy and desire. These emotions are just fine, in the eyes of the privileged whites, because these are the upward-looking feelings of those placed below, and, as such, these feelings reinforce the worth of the privilege, status, and power whites enjoy. But once envy and desire yield to action, the whites turn on the non-whites. You can envy, you can desire—whites are telling non-whites; however, if you try to seize even the slightest measure of what we whites enjoy, we will use our privileges, our status, and our power to oppress you. Read in this manner, Nkosi's *Mating Birds* becomes an essay on power, on the dynamics of the relationship between the empowered and the disempowered. The novel ends up being less about inter-racial sex and more about inter-racial power. And the ultimate sadness inspired by the book is the result not so much of Mr. Sibiya's prospective execution as the transformation—the degradation—of a beautiful, natural experience into something sullied by the intrusion of ugly, unnatural power.

Egoli: City of Gold

Like Nkosi's *Mating Birds*, Matsemela Manaka's 1980 play, *Egoli*, also deals with less territory than Gwala's all-encompassing poetry. The exploration of that smaller territory allows the author to turn the two experiences of prison and mine camp into twinned, interconnected examples of imprisonment and suffering at the hands of the white political and economic "system."

Like many of the plays Athol Fugard and his black compatriots have collaborated on, Manaka's *Egoli* features only two characters, John and Hamilton. Initially, all of our sympathy is with John. As the two relax in their room at the mine camp, they talk about their lives. We discover that they had been in prison together and that John was there because he was "arrested . . . under the Terrorism Act when [he] was only sixteen" (4) while Hamilton was there because he had "raped and killed a poor woman. One of our black mothers" (4). This difference does create some tension between the two men; it even leads to what (the stage directions tell us) is a "very serious" (4) fight between them. However, the tension does yield to solidarity because the two realize that they are entrapped *together*: "We escaped together," says John, "and we've got to live together in this compound" (5).

As the play progresses, we learn more and more disturbing aspects of life as a laborer in the Jo'burg gold mines. We learn that many of the men have come to the mines because there was no work for them in their native rural areas. Promised lucrative salaries, they slave for a pittance, and their wives and children still starve back in the countryside because the men are able to send so little money back home. Their ability to send money home is further limited by their consumption in the camp of the alcohol and the prostitutes that are readily available for a price. John, who begins the play as the noble character in *our* eyes, gradually becomes less and less noble as we realize the extent to which he has yielded to these temptations of the flesh.

As the two continue talking, we learn still more about the nature of work in white South Africa. John talks about a previous job he held in Jo'burg as a rubbish collector. He talks about how physically abusive the supervisor was and how he, having learned in jail *not* to take abuse, struck back and was then brutally beaten and sent home, a failure, to his starving family. Hamilton talks about their present supervisor: although black, he is just like John's Meneer Turnbull; Hamilton further talks about the work itself:

> A mineworker from the living grave. Look at his face, glittering with sweat, full of dust. This whirlwind within his muscles is turning Joburg into skyscrapers, pyramid-like buildings piercing the sky, castles and temples. . . . He is not enjoying the fruits of his sweat. (15-16)

Act Two of *Egoli* needs to be visualized. John and Hamilton recreate their escape from prison, chained to each other. There is no literal chain linking their legs together, but they act on stage as if there were. Similarly, there is no literal chain linking black South Africans together, but there are nonetheless the very real chains of the oppressive political and economic "system" whites created in South Africa, "chains that curse your manhood" and "chains that rust your brain" (18).

They mime the breaking of the chain; they treat the broken chain "like a dead snake"—beating it repeatedly, fearfully picking it up and "hurling it off-stage" (21). As they perform these actions, they sing a song of liberation.

The play, however, does not end at this emotionally "high" point that Ian Steadman describes for us in *Momentum*. The play continues, and we discover that any envisioned liberation will be too late for Hamilton and John and John's family. Hamilton and John are dying of tuberculosis or some other lung disease common to the black laborers in the mines; John's "children are eating soil and tree leaves. They are dying of hunger. They sleep with empty stomachs" (26).

As the play nears its end, John is in despair. Whereas at the beginning of the play we held John (the political activist) above

Hamilton (the rapist), we now hold Hamilton above John, for John has totally lost himself in alcohol. He vomits on stage and then collapses into his vomit. Hamilton not only has not lost his spirit, but he will not allow John to lose his. Hamilton pulls John up off the stage, shakes him, and tells him, "I would not escape from prison to imprison myself in another poison like liquor" (25); he pulls John up off the stage, shakes him, and tells him that his children need him. Hamilton then, ceremoniously, cleans John's face, and, when John accuses God of forsaking the African people, Hamilton asks "Why look to heaven?" and tells John to "Face the man!" (27)

John and Hamilton may well be dying. But we recall that the time of the play is the past. And, as the two end the play in a revolutionary declaration, we realize that the declaration's vision may be enacted by the generation of black South Africans of the present, the audience for whom the play was staged:

> For justice, freedom and peace to prevail in the country of our forefathers, we shall all have to stand up and face the enemy without fear. We shall all have to worship the spear and drink blood from the calabash until we all sing the same song–*Uhuru–Azania Uhuru Azania* [.] (28)

Before we get to these last words, however, we are reminded of the suffering that has preceded with the recurring images of "sweat," "blood," and black infants sacrificed to starvation so that gold and diamonds could be extracted from the mines at as low a cost as possible.

Letters to Martha

The mines provide black South Africans with one common experience; the prisons with another. And a great deal of contemporary literature deals with the suffering experienced in the latter. Dennis Brutus' *Letters to Martha* consists of eighteen brief poems and six equally brief postscripts that we are to read as the progressively darker reflections of an imprisoned man addressed to his wife or lover outside. As Shava notes, the style of these poems was decidedly simpler than that Brutus had exhibited in earlier work. And, as Barnett observes, the simpler style was due to Brutus' conscious decision to try to reach a larger audience with *Letters to Martha* than with previous volumes of poetry.

The first poem presents mixed emotions—"sick relief" (3); "apprehension" (4); "exultation" (8); "vague heroism" (11); "self-pity" (9); others. The prisoner does not yet know what to feel or what to expect. The second and third poems bring him face to face with one prison reality: violence. In the second poem, he wonders at how knives find their way in; in the third, he reflects on the confused motives that cause prisoners to use these knives against each other.

In the fourth poem, Brutus' persona reflects on the various ways religion plays a role in prison life: one can pretend to be religious to curry favor; one can "invoke divine revenge / against a rampaging injustice" (12-13); one can talk to God "in the grey silence of the empty afternoons" (24).

In the next four poems, Brutus' persona turns from piety to perversion. Prisoners turn to behavior other than praying in their empty hours. They turn to "Corpophilism; necrophilism; fellatio; / penis-amputation" (5-6), as well as to "suicide, self-damnation" (9). They turn to demands for sodomy, and in the sixth poem, the prisoner talks about the three ways to deal with these demands: imagine "romantic fantasies / of beautiful marriageable daughters" (9-10), have "fainting fits" (12), or flee "into insanity" (13). Some prisoners even "beg for sexual assault" (2), and in the seventh poem, the prisoner tries to understand the state of mind that would lead one to desire what he terms "absolute and ludicrous submission" (9). In the eighth poem, the persona's tone curiously shifts. Now jaded, he can joke a bit about homosexuality in prison and talk about "Blue champagne," "the most popular 'girl' in the place" (1-2).

The ninth poem shifts from inside to outside, as the prisoner reflects on how agonizing it must be for those outside not to know exactly what sufferings the men inside are enduring. The tenth poem presents another shift—from the sufferings of prison existence to the "benefits." One acquires a deep understanding of "one's fellow-men, / fellows, compeers" (5-6); one acquires discipline; one acquires the rest that comes after "honest toil" (10).

The eleventh poem talks about politics. The persona makes it clear that imprisonment radicalizes inmates not tames them.

The next three poems all deal with sounds. In the twelfth poem, the persona laments the absence of music. "Nothing," he says, "was sadder" "than the deadly lack / of music" (1, 3-4). In the thirteenth, the persona mentions how the inmates use words—empty "aphorisms and quotations" (9)—to hide from themselves the reality of their situation. But, lest one think that empty words abound, he makes it clear, in the next poem, that grandiloquent rhetoric had no place in prison.

The fifteenth poem seems to bring the prisoner back to the topic of the abuse the prisoners suffer at the hands of each other. Just as I avoided the word "penises" in the previous sentence, the persona avoids words that connote specific abuses. His refusal to name is psychologically interesting, suggesting that resorting to generalizations about how humans can "ennoble / or pervert" that which "is otherwise simply animal / amoral and instinctual" (5-9) is a way of defending himself against the harsh reality of forced sodomy.

The sixteenth poem begins what seems to be the prisoner's withdrawal. He seems resigned to his situation; he seems to give up on defiance. And, in the last two poems, he turns to the birds, the clouds, and the stars. Unable to face (as well as name) the prison realities, he turns his eyes upward. Unfortunately, the prison authorities can deny him even these sights, as the conclusion to the eighteenth poem makes clear when "anxious boots / and a warning barked / from the machine-gun post / on the catwalk" (18-21) interrupt his star-gazing.

The postscripts continue this withdrawal. In the second postscript, the prisoner talks, desperately, about how difficult it is to keep a sense of one's self worth alive. In the fourth, he talks about yielding to "some arbitrary will" (6). In the fifth, he realizes "how easily [he] might be damned" (6). He seems to be losing control over his fate. In the last postcript, the narrative perspective changes—from first person to third person. The prisoner has lost self-awareness; he now sees himself as an object. This self-objectification is described as offering him "safety" (8) "from the battering importunities / of fists and genitals of sodomites" (10-11). This self-objectification, we are told in the very last line, will lead to "a maniac world" in which "he was safe" (12).

Survival

Brutus' tone is surprisingly reflective in *Letters to Martha* for all of the indignities and abuse that the sequence of short poems reveals. One expects anger, but gets calm instead. Of course, the calm at the end may well be the calm of withdrawl into insanity. Also not angry is the tone of Workshop '71s 1976 theatrical creation, *Survival*. Although this play does at times assault the audience, less through its words and more through the confrontational manner in which it is performed, the actors maintain a sense of humor throughout. It may be a dark sense of humor—ironic and bitter, but it is humor nonetheless.

Survival is, very much, a play that needs to be seen: the staging, the lighting, the music, the choreography, etc., are all important elements of a theatrical experience. When I talk about the text that eventually emerged after months of workshop collaboration, I do not do the play justice. However, I feel I must discuss the play, because the play is a good example of the theme of suffering and because the kind of drama that the play represents has been one of the black people's most potent tools of protest.

The play begins with a frenzy—designed to disarm the audience. When matters settle down, we find ourselves in prison. We're promised a tour, but what we get is not an excursion through the prison place but rather an introduction to the kinds of people who end up "jailbirds."

We meet a young man fron Pietersburg in the northern Transvaal. His story is a common one:

> I came south on contract work. I've got a wife and four children. Well down south I found the wages I got weren't paying for my family and me. I spoke to the boss. Hy het gesqueal. [He refused.] So we organized a strike, me and some other contract workers from Pietersburg. It didn't work. People are weak. A few of the workers decided to give up and go back to work. We got angry and beat them up. That made it easy for them. The police arrested me for breach of contract, incitement to strike and assault. (143-44)

We meet a young man who has just been released from prison. It's 1976, and we're in Johannesburg. This Jo'burg is very different from the one the young man recalls from five years earlier. He meets a friend, Theo, who is staying at the Landros Hotel. In 1972, the Landros was "whites only," but not now. The young man decides to explore this new Jo'burg; he decides to get a bite to eat at the Zanzibar. He sees two black men eating there, so he sits down. Then, he discovers that the Zanzibar serves blacks from elsewhere in Africa, but not blacks from South Africa itself. Kicked out of the restaurant, he then goes to a public lavatory. When he tries to use the two toilets that look decent, the toilets (played by squatting actors) tell him they are reserved for whites; *his* toilet is the "contorted" one "over there" (148).

He now knows that the situation has not changed as much as it first seemed. He falls into a nightmare during which he is harrassed, first, by the discriminatory bureaucratic jungle of white South Africa and, second, by the absence of brotherhood and the presence of police in Soweto. When the police run him out of the Orlando police station, he, wanting "some peace and quiet," decides "to kill [him]self" (15). Unfortunately, the cemetery he chooses for his burial is "whites only." He feels so harrassed at this point that he demands to be arrested. He is, and he's sent back to prison—initially "for nothing" (155) and then, by the time the South African establishment reconstructs the events of his story, for terrorism.

We then meet a Leroi Williams and an Edward Nkosi. Leroi "was born in Sophiatown," but he's "never even seen it. It's some white suburb now" (158). Well-educated, he is nonetheless stuck with a poor-paying job. He quits and eventually joins a theatre group. In a cafe in a small Orange Free State town, he gets into an argument with the owner over a broken drink bottle. To get the goat of the cafe owner, Leroi "thrusts his fist in front of his face" and says "Remember Frelimo, dad!" (161). That reference to the Marxist revolutionaries in Mozambique was enough to get Leroi carried off to prison, a suspected outside "agitator."

Edward came to Johannesburg with his mother from Pietermaritzburg in Natal. When she lost her job as a domestic because she gave her young son meat and butter from the white family's refrigerator, he had to go to work. To just seek work, he had to get a pass. His mother ends up selling her body to "a sensual black pass official" in order to secure the necessary document for her son. "Don't blame her, Eddie. What else could she do?," a friend says, "You needed that pass. Mama had nothing but her body. She gave it and you got your pass. That's life in this stinking world . . ." (163). For Eddie's mother, unfortunately, this "prostitution" seems to have marked a turning point, for it drove her to drinking and sleeping around. As Edward remarks, "Mama was drinking the whole time, sleeping out almost every night with different men" (164). Some of the men were rather abusive. One night, angered by a man's behavior towards his mother, Edward beats him to death. Edward was sent to prison for life; his mother shortly thereafter drank herself to death.

After meeting these prisoners, the play dissolves into a second violent frenzy; then, the frenzy fades into a calm but sad discussion of family life and children. The prisoners want this "heaven," but "Oom Piet and Oom Jam," i.e. the Afrikaner establishment, won't let them have it. So, they call for an end to "the prison." But the prison is more than just the building they are in:

> Prison destroys. If no one can say which is the more destructive prison—jail or the system—then the whole nation should perish, the people should buckle, there should be chaos. (170)

They know, however, that this revolution will not occur immediately. In the meantime, they seek to triumph in survival:

> A people survive by grimly holding on. But at the same time they achieve what their oppressors cannot help envying them for. The strength lies with the people, who carry with them in their lives the justification for the struggle—the victory that is . . . SURVIVAL! (170)

The prisoners then march, fists raised, throughout the theatre, singing.

Robben Island

Less celebratory, more starkly realistic is the portrayal of prison and the sufferings there in D. M. Zwelonke's 1977 novel *Robben Island*. Early in the novel, we hear a litany of the abuses the black man suffers on the outside: an inferior education; curtailed freedom of movement; no freedom of expression; taxation without representation; no right to vote. But as the novel develops, we focus less on abstract political matters and more on the day-to-day sufferings of prison life.

We learn how cold Robben Island is; we learn how painful prison life can be for a man with a wife and children on the outside:

> The winter rain throbbed painfully on the roof. Bekimpi's body twitched in answer to my question. The cold had beaten him pale black. Cold did not agree with him. His eyes opened and shut, and opened and shut. He glared at the roof, a corrugated asbestos roof. The throbbing on the roof seemed to strike on the lens of his eyes.
>
> "My wife has been refused permission to see me," he said, changing the subject.
>
> I forgot to mention that Bekimpi was a married man and had two children. But this new subject was also bitter. I could see pain in his eyes. His mouth twisted. (49)

We hear repeatedly from the narrator and the other prisoners about the food—both its poor quality and its inadequate quantity. The quantity is so inadequate that, as one's days in prison progress, one's stomach starts becoming more dominant than one's mind:

> I had never thought until I went to jail that I would be reduced to a state when I would wrangle about food. A state when the arbitrator of disputes was the stomach; when the loudest and most influential part of myself, in all circumstances, was the stomach. We had the same full power of thought as before, but now it was channelled towards satisfying the riotous stomach. (133)

We hear about the "flogging and kicking," the "starving," and the "sapping of [the inmates'] energy by compelling them to do beastly tasks" (115). This physical abuse leads the narrator (whose voice is very close to that of the once-imprisoned Dan Zwelonke) to declare that "Jail teems with evil," that "it is infested with the germs breathed out by the devil himself" (115). The evil assaulted all the senses:

> Such was jail. It reeked of evil. If you opened your eyes, you could see it—a cryptogenic mass, worse than parasites. Prick your ears more sharply, you could hear it whining more painfully than a mosquito in the region of your ear. Clear your nostrils, you could smell it, more pungent than ether, a vomit-agent like the lav bucket full to the brim. (115)

But there was also the psychological abuse, and it was most intense when an inmate was placed in solitary confinement:

> That is the gruesome purpose of solitary confinement: to break a man completely, both morally and mentally. It is a kind of brain-washing. If a man wants to brood undisturbed, that is the place for it. If he wants to give himself up to meditation, that is the place for it. But it is also the place, whether you want it to be or not, for negative thinking: for fretting, self-pity, regret, and a crushing weight of remorse. You feel that the world has rejected you; relatives and friends, all have rejected you. Whatever attention your family and friends can give you, you feel it is not enough. You feel forsaken and forlorn, and finally you give in to melancholia. (85)

Plot *per se* is less important in *Robben Island* than the realistic portrayal of day-to-day life in prison. But towards the end of the novel, Bekimpi's story takes center stage. We witness his being tortured. We find him hanging upside-down, naked; his torturers make it clear to him that he will hang that way until he either tells them the particulars about terrorist operations in South Africa or dies. The torture is bad enough, but worse is the "fun" the torturers have with Bekimpi during their "off" hours:

> That evening, DuPlessis and two others came to have fun with the hanging man. They let him swing like a hunk of meat in a butchery.
>
> "No, here's better fun: cut the rope with this knife, and see him come down headlong to crash on the floor," DuPlessis said, and tested the rope with a pocket knife.

> One of them played with Bekimpi's testicles. "By God, this bastard has a big penis," he shouted merrily, "Just like a donkey's."
>
> Another one slapped Bekimpi's buttocks. Then he took a ballpoint pen and pushed it slowly down the helpless man's anus. The muscles there shrank inward like a snail into its shell. Bekimpi moaned. (145)

This sadistic scene yields to a poetic oration declaring the grievances and the rights of the black people of South Africa:

> Cry, O rational men:
> Thought is pigmented,
> Harmony of interests is sacrificed;
> Your inalienable right
> To free thought,
> To free expression,
> To free existence
> Within that scope that does not infringe
> On similar rights of others
> Is usurped.
> The right to till the land:
> The fertile pastures
> Of the coastal lowlands,
> Of the inland escarpment,
> Of the Limpopo valley,
> Of the Vaal valley,
> Of the Orange valley–
> The right to live in it
> Is usurped.
>
> The right to share the wealth of the land:
> The yellow metal in the belly of the Reef,
> The shining-as-glass metal in the bosom of the Vaal,
> The money these materials can buy
> By the sweat of man–
> Is usurped. (149-50)

Then, the oration having provided a broad political picture to frame Bekimpi's story within, we return to the torture room:

> Bekimpi hung still, cold. The mucus had oozed with foam. The foam came out scarlet with blood. His tongue stuck far out. His eyes were wide and bloodshot. (151)

His horrible death–a glaring example of how much the black man suffers in South Africa–ends the novel.

Pass Me a Meatball, Jones

James Matthews' 1977 sequence of poems written in prison has an irreverent title. The title belies the poems' content. Like Zwelonke's *Robben Island,* Matthews' poems expose us to the realities of prison; like Brutus' *Letters to Martha,* Matthews' poems present an inmate trying to deal with the suffering.

The early poems emphasize what the inmate has lost: he has lost the company of others; he has lost the belief that his hopes may one day be fulfilled. He still has the sky above: much like Brutus' persona, Matthews' finds solace in the freedom and beauty he feels and sees there. Initially, he "walk[s] around / flashing cellophane smiles" (3, 1-2), but these smiles mask "the nakedness of / my hidden fear" (3, 11-12). The fear is largely tied to the wailing that escapes from "subterranean / torture chambers" (10, 3-4):

> wails of
> souls suffering punishment
> writhing, squirming, screaming
> pleading release from
> mist entering chambers
> wresting from them
> tears as tribute
> pain unendingly inflicted
> by harsh overlords
> controllers of their
> confinement in hellholes (10, 10-20)

Matthews' persona settles into a coldness, that is both physical and metaphorical. Then, he becomes trapped in boredom.

Homosexual rape plays very little role in Matthews' poems, unlike in Brutus' *Letters to Martha.* Sexual desire, however, figures significantly. Matthews' persona loses himself in erotic fantasies that end in masturbation:

> my fantasy transports me
> from where i am
> to lose myself in
> sweet bird-note warbled
> the note tantalizingly aquiver
> in the still air

pursues an amorous bee
joined in orgasm with
willing flower petals unfurled
find contentment in caresses
offered by promiscuous breezes
and be partner to
the coupling of clouds
releasing showers of sperm
into earth's grateful loins (17, 1-25)

Interspersed among the poems that express unfulfilled sexual desire are three other recurring thoughts. The persona feels he is dying; the persona feels he is losing his mind; the persona longs for beauty.

Dreams then begin to figure heavily in Matthews' sequence. Sometimes the dreams are erotic; sometimes they are "dreams / of children at play / their voices treble-toned / as birds on summer's day" (22, 7-10). Increasingly, the dreams return the persona to his childhood, and in that childhood coalesce the beauty he longs for *and* the freedom he now so desires. Images recur in these dreams: the stars of the early poems in the sequence are joined by the moon.

But waking is "the return to loneliness" (24, 6). The colors blue and grey–increasingly more the latter–dominate the waking hours. Occasionally, "fear, a snake / wrapped around [his] throat" (37, 1-2), returns and seizes his body. This fear is exacerbated by his awareness of the sufferings of his compatriots in prison.

Finally and sadly, the dreams no longer provide a haven. "[D]reams / of childhood themes" are transformed "into / shattered freak scenes / phantasmagorical figures riotous" (41, 6-10). Matthews' persona then yearns for death, because the dead are free "to continue [their] / nightly sojourn among the stars" (42, 9-10). He sees death on all of the faces around him in the penultimate poem in the sequence. This poem strongly suggests that he is yielding to the same death-in-life that his fellows suffer from.

The last poem is different in many ways from the forty-three that precede it. The persona is less reflective; rather, he explicitly addresses an audience outside prison. He tells this audience to "think of me, sometime" in each of the six stanzas, and in each stanza, he strikes a contrast between life on the outside and life within prison. Those outside have hopes, the freedom to move, friendship and merriment, love, family, and the ability to enjoy the beauty of life; those in prison do not. And they suffer as a result.

The tone of Matthews's poems varies from poem to poem—sometimes quiet, sometimes rhapsodic, sometimes angry, sometimes scared. In all of the works we have looked at in this chapter, there is a range—sometimes as wide, sometimes not. Suffering is the common thread, even though the emotional response to the suffering runs the gamut. In the works examined in the next chapter, the emotion of anger will become dominant.

A Lesson from Aloes

The plays, poems, and novels examined thus far in this chapter depict, in various ways, the sufferings of the black people of South Africa. That the bulk of this chapter focuses on these people is indeed appropriate, for they are the most noteworthy —in numbers and in severity—sufferers. However, they are not alone. Playwright Athol Fugard's *A Lesson from Aloes* deals with the suffering of three people of other racial groups, a middle-aged Afrikaner named Piet Bezuidenhout, his wife Gladys, and his colored friend Steve Daniels.

The play depicts a reunion dinner. Piet and Steve were allied in earlier anti-apartheid campaigns, a white liberal and an enlightened colored. These campaigns, however, ended abruptly, shortly after the 1960 riots in Sharpeville: the government's security forces had, somehow, acquired information about the movement, and, using this information, they arrested many of those involved in it, including Steve. Steve's colored and black compatriots thought that Piet might well be the informer, the traitor. Steve himself wondered. In fact, Steve almost did not come to Piet's Port Elizabeth home for dinner. He came, he eventually tells Piet, because he still thought Piet might be innocent.

Fugard's plays usually involve two or three characters; they are typically quite conversational. *A Lesson from Aloes* is exemplary. Once Steve arrives at Piet's home, they begin a long, increasingly tense conversation. During this conversation, the question of Piet's loyalty to his friend Steve and to the larger cause of majority rights surfaces. More important than a resolution to this question, however, is the revelation of the suffering that Steve, Piet, and Gladys have suffered. The extent of this suffering also gradually surfaces during the conversation.

Steve is disillusioned. He no longer believes change will come in South Africa–except, perhaps, through violence. South Africa is his home: he loves it. Nonetheless, he realizes that continuing to reside there will deny him and his children both material success and personal fulfillment. Sadly, he has decided to leave South Africa:

> Tell me one thing we've achieved that makes it worthwhile staying here and messing up my children's lives the way I have mine. Because that's what will happen. We've only seen it get worse. And it's going to go on getting worse. But I know why now. We were like a bunch of boy scouts playing at politics. Those boer-boys play the game rough. It's going to need men who don't care about the rules to sort them out. That was never us. (68)

Piet tries to get Steve to stay. Steve gets angry. Piet makes his arguments–Steve believes–because he, Piet, has not experienced prison, is white, and still has hope. But Steve is only seeing the surface: he does not realize how wounded Piet is by not only the failure of their youthful political activity but the way Steve and the others suspected him after their arrest. Piet was so wounded that he withdrew into himself and into his house. He names that house "Xanadu," suggesting the fantasy retreat of Coleridge's poem; he spends his leisure time raising aloe plants. (More on those aloe plants in a bit.)

The third person in the play, Gladys, seems peripheral throughout much of the play. But toward the play's end, Gladys becomes increasingly important. After the raid that resulted in Steve's arrest and imprisonment, Piet and she were also subjected to harsh treatment at the hands of the Special Branch. Their status, because they are white, prevented their being arrested *per se*. However, they were questioned in a manner that was designed to be threatening, and their home was searched in a manner that was designed to be intimidating. In that search, the Special Branch officers seized and read the couple's private papers, including Gladys' diary. The seizing and reading of that diary is described by Gladys, earlier in the play, in terms of rape. "There were very initimate and personal things in those diaries, things a woman only talks about to herself" (27), she tells Piet. Having those "things" read has traumatized Gladys:

> It only needs to happen to a woman once, for her to lose all trust she ever had in anything or anybody. They violated me, Peter. I might just as well have stayed in that bed, lifted up my nightdress and given them each a turn. (28)

The experience led to her being institutionalized for a period at "Fort England," a sanitarium in Grahamstown. Piet was seeing to her care, without *fully* understanding her feelings, at the same time Steve was being tried and convicted. Piet's absence from the trial was, unfortunately, taken by Steve (and others) as further proof that Piet was indeed the informer.

Only at the play's end does Piet begin to grasp Gladys' feelings, because, then, she reveals how fully she blames Piet. She believes that Piet was the informer. Thus, she believes that the police harassment of Piet and herself was "for show," that she was "raped" "for show." Furthermore, she believes Piet could have protected her better—from the "rape" and from the indignities that she experienced when taken away to "Fort England":

> I don't need you! I don't need you to protect me anymore! You never did, anyway. When they took away my diaries you did nothing. When the others took away my false teeth and held me down and blew my mind to pieces, you weren't even there! I called for you, Peter, but you weren't there. (75)

As the play ends, Gladys reveals how empty all of her days since her return from "Fort England" have been by revealing that the diary she has kept since then is nothing but empty pages. She tells Peter that she has "got to go back" (78) to "Fort England" and that she'll "go quietly this time" (79). As the curtain falls, we envision her departure the next morning for the mental hospital (perhaps never to return) *and* Steve's departure the next morning for England (perhaps never to return). Piet is left staring at an aloe plant.

Throughout Fugard's play, there are references to the absence of rain. Rain becomes linked here, as in other works of South African literature, with both revolution and redemption. But, to borrow the title of Andre Brink's novel, there are only "rumors of rain" in Fugard's drama. The rain is not here yet. Not much can survive drought, but the aloe plant can. Thus, Piet's obsessive hobby of raising aloe plants can be interpreted symbolically as his holding onto the possibility of surviving (barely) until the rain—the necessary changes—come.

The "lesson" that we are to learn "from aloes" is to survive. Steve cannot; Gladys cannot; maybe Piet can. Oddly enough, this lesson is the same one that we end the play *Survival* with. The tone, however, is markedly different. The call for survival at the end of Workshop '71's theatrical experience is uplifting. The play is disturbing, but, in the end, we feel that, as the play tells us, surviving is triumphing. The picture of survival at the end of Fugard's *A Lesson from Aloes*—Piet, alone on a fairly dark stage, staring at an aloe plant—is depressing. We are left wondering if the rain will ever come, if Piet's suffering will not lead him nowhere. For Steve, there was England; for Gladys, there was "Fort England." Both were escapes, although sad escapes. Fugard stresses how Afrikaner Piet views South Africa as "home." Perhaps then, no "England" exists for him. No "Xanadu" either, for his "stately pleasure dome" has proven to be anything but. Perhaps, he has nowhere to go, nothing to hope for. And, as Sheila Roberts notes in an article in *English in Africa*, the fact that Piet's aloes are in tin cans, not wild on the Karoo, suggests that his survival will be in an imprisoned state.

Works Cited

Barnett, Ursula A. *A Vision of Order: A Study of Black South African Literature in English (1914-1980)*. Amherst: University of Massachusetts Press, 1983.

Brutus, Dennis. *Letters to Martha*. London: Heinemann, 1968.

Fugard, Athol. *A Lesson from Aloes*. New York: Random House, 1981.

Gwala, Mafika. *No More Lullabies*. 1982.

Manaka, Matsemala. *Egoli: City of Gold*. Johannesburg: Soyikwa-Ravan, 1980.

Matthews, James. *Pass Me a Meatball, Jones: A Gathering of Feelings*. Athlone: Blac Publishing House, 1977.

Mtshali, Oswald. *Songs of a Cowhide Drum*. London: Oxford UP, 1971.

Nkosi, Lewis. *Mating Birds*. New York: St. Martin's, 1986.

——. "Sex and the Law in South Africa." In *Home and Exile*. London: Longman, 1963. 37-43.

Roberts, Sheila. "'No Lessons Learnt': Reading the Texts of Fugard's *A Lesson from Aloes* and *Master Harold . . . and the Boys*." *English in Africa* 9.2 (1982): 27-33.

Serote, Mongane Wally. *No Baby Must Weep*. Johannesburg: Ad. Donker, 1975.

Shava, Piniel Viriri. *A People's Voice: Black South African Writing in the Twentieth Century*. 1989; rpt. Athens: Ohio UP, 1989.

Steadman, Ian. "Alternative Politics, Alternative Performance: 1976 and Black South African Theatre." In M. J. Daymond, et al., eds. *Momentum: On Recent South African Writing*. Pietermaritzburg: University of Natal Press, 1984. 215-32.

Workshop '71. *Survival*. In R. M. Kavanagh, ed. *South African People's Plays*. London: Heinemann, 1981. 125-71.

Zwelonke, D. M. *Robben Island*. London: Heinemann, 1977.

6

Attacking

The lion is a dangerous creature, especially when provoked. And, as the various works of literature discussed in the previous chapter reveal, the African symbolized by the lion in Gordimer's story has indeed been more than provoked. That provocation has led to calls for revolution, for violent revolution. In this chapter, we will examine five works that embody, in different ways, that revolutionary call.

Three of these works predate the Soweto massacre and riots of 1976. Keorapetse Kgositsile's 1971 collection of poetry *My Name is Afrika* is rich in imagery: a feast for the New Critic. In such rich language, the poems indict what the white man has done, criticize those blacks who have sold out to or become trapped within the white values, present a poetic vision of revolution, and then call for violence. The poems are also curiously post-modern in their discussion of language itself. James Matthews and Gladys Thomas' 1972 collection of poetry *Cry Rage!* presents a similar revolutionary message but in more direct terms. Alex LaGuma's 1972 novel, *In the Fog of the Seasons' End,* has a more restrained tone. In matter-of-fact language, LaGuma traces and justifies the day-to-day actions of those who worked, underground, against apartheid.

The last two works postdate June 1976. The first, Sipho Sepamla's 1977 collection of poems entitled *The Soweto I Love* was inspired by the events there. The poems, however, exhibit a range of topics and tones and styles. They seem, as a whole, to circle about the June 1976 events, offering different perspectives on them. All of these perspectives, however, lead to a hostile conclusion. Miriam Tlali's 1980 novel *Amandla* takes us inside Soweto. We learn about life there; we also receive, at some length, a Marxist-tinged economics lesson and a call for a people's revolution.

My Name is Afrika

Kgositsile's poems (which are virtually unknown in South Africa because of bannings and the poet's departure from the country) review much of the ground covered by the writers surveyed in the previous chapter, but, whereas the works discussed in the previous chapter lament the suffering of the South African people (almost always the black South African people), Kgositsile's poems go beyond laments and call for violent revolution.

In "Vector or Legacy," Kgositsile talks about what the white regime has done to the black children. Their "smiles [are] butchered to death long / before they meander out of their mother's womb" (5-6). Once born, they "hopeless[ly] search for crumbs" (8) and

> scramble for orange peel
> from garbage pail or sometimes
> a whole rotten banana from some
> fat-bellied bastard's trash can[.] (10-13)

The "fat-bellied bastard" is renamed "a shithead devil" in "Inherent and Inherited Mistrusts." He abuses blacks by "design," a major element of which is an education that tries to teach black children to be something they should not be–that is, white.

"Symptoms" describes white South Africa as an evil "empire," which is as unfeeling "as a frigid whore" (11-12). The poem mentions the "bloodstained sidewalks" (5); worse, the poem glances at the empire's torturous ways–the "heads" the police "bashed open / Or mashed to a pulp" (14-15) and the "genitals disembodied / For the amusement of some devil" (17-18).

"For Eusi, Ayi Kwei, & Gwen Brooks" takes an historical view of the white man's acts, referring to the "Centuries of systematic rape and ruin" (11). Kgositsile repeat this indictment in "Points of Departure: Fire Dance Fire Song," referring to the white man's acts as "The rape by savages who want to control / us, memory, nature" (III, 9-10) and present-day South Africa as "the ruins of the rape by white greed" (III, 8). Whites are called "murderers" who "butchered your flesh / As they butchered the flesh of our land" (II, 7-8) and "evil maniacs" with "greedy hands" shaping "vile creations" (III, 23-25).

Some blacks "sold out," in Kgositsile's view, to the white government. In coarse terms, he indicts these brothers and sisters in "Towards a Walk in the Sun":

You who swallowed your balls for a piece
Of gold beautiful from afar but far from
Beautiful because it is colored with
The pus from your brother's callouses
You who creep lower than a snake's belly
Because you swallowed your conscience
And sold your sister to soulless vipers
You who bleached the womb of your daughter's
Mind to bear pale-brained freaks
You who bleached your son's genitals to
Slobber in the slime of missionary-eyed faggotry
You who hide behind the shadow of your master's
Institutionalized hypocrisy the knees of your
Soul numbed by endless kneeling to catch
The crumbs from your master's table before
You run to poison your own mother. (11-26)

Many in the poet's generation, in his opinion, sold out, "claw[ing] / their way into the whitenesses of their desire / and purpose" ("Notes from No Sanctuary," 2, 6-8). Others were, unbeknownst to themselves, trapped within a white-defined world. In "To Mother," they are described as "old and impotent" (9) and "dazed" (24); in "To Gloria," "blindfold[ed]" (2). Fuller and more vivid are Kgositsile's descriptions of his black fellows in "Conditioned" and "For Sons of Sonless Fathers."

In the former poem, the poet's fellow blacks are compared, graphically, to "disembodied / penises on perverted college / toilets" (1-3). They are then, less graphically, called "Processed / echoes of papered hypocrisy / crumble[d] in programmed fate" (4-6). In the latter poem, they are "ghouls" doing "a death dance" (19-20); they have a "ball of transparent pus where / the manhood used to be" (11-12). They are

ghost[s]
more pale than faded junk

lighter than snowflake
not even swayed
by song or dance. . . . (1-5)

Not being "swayed / by song or dance" associates these black men and women with the antithesis of the vision Kgositsile offers of African revolution. This vision is presented through recurring images. The crucial image is that of rebirth. In order to be reborn, one must remember both the glory of the distant African past and the adversities of the not so distant colonial past. One must be able to laugh. Then, one can overcome the icy cold, associated with the white society, and, in the fiery warmth of the sun, one can sing, dance, and move to the rhythm of drumbeats. While so moving, one will be gently soothed by the wind.

Let's consider the elements in this vision one-by-one. Rebirth is *the* dominant image–present in too many poems in *My Name is Afrika* to name. Kgositsile speaks of "Vibrations in the womb" (1) in "Could Be"; of childbirth and nursing in "Tropics." In "New Dawn," the poet declares that his vision is not just for South Africa, but all of Africa and Asia, Latin America, and Afroamerica as well. The rebirth is, he tells us in "Points of Departure," "the rebirth of real men" (IV, 15), and it will involve–he makes clear in the collection's title poem, the spilling of blood.

To be so reborn, one must remember for "memory / defiant like the sound of pain / rides the wave at dawn" ("The Air I Hear," 10-12). One must, the poet tells us in "Tropics," nurse the "memories / Into upright method" (12-13); and, as he tells us in "To Gloria," attend to "the melody of memory / Lingered strained by bloodstained / Diamond, whiplash" (5-7). The melody will recollect these white-imposed horrors; it will also return the listener to the "roots [that] are heart [sic] in the depths / Of Afrika" ("The Long Reach," 16-17). Present-day black South Africans may well so remember, but, as the poet tells us in "Recreation," they are "remembering yesterdays without laughter" (8). The new generation can join memory *and laughter,* as this poem notes repeatedly in its latter lines.

The present generation's laughter, as "The Air I Hear" notes, is tinged with thoughts of death; the new generation's laughter, as "Mayibuye Iafrika" notes, is associated with the waking sun. Once reborn, Africans will be "Forever Laughing" ("Tropics," 2, 20); as the poet forecasts in "Epitaph," "Black children" will laugh and dance "To the rhythms of a new promise" (22-23).

Once reborn, they will move "From ice to sunlit bush" ("Tropics," 19). They will have real power, not that of the false black leaders Kgositsile satirizes in "The Lip Trick." These "magicians" (6) lack power: they "cannot see the ice / melt before [their] very eyes" (11-12); however, the reborn, revolutionary younger generation, wafted by the wind, spears the "splintered ice" ("The Spearhead Wind Strides," 14).

The younger generation has this power because they were born from "the fiery womb of sunrise" ("My People No Longer Sing," 8); they are "newly born" and able to "do the dance of fire" ("The New Breed," 15-16). The numbers of young blacks who are so reborn will grow: as Kgositsile tells us in "For Eusi, Ayi Kwei & Gwen Brooks,"

> In us and into us and ours
> This movement rises every day
> As the day whose fire informs
> The rhythm of the sons. . . . (1-4)

These young blacks will be "Panthers with claws of fire" ("My Name is Afrika," 15) who will use the fire of the sun to defeat "the cold enemy machine" ("Points of Departure," I, 33), to burn "these evil white maniacs" (III, 23).

Once so fired up, the younger generation will retrieve "songs almost aborted" ("My People No Longer Sing," 9), "moving songs" for which they must "recreate the music" ("The Nitty-Gritty," 21-22). To this music, they will "dance near the sun" ("For Afroamerica," 30); it will be "a new kind of dance / Awakening gods limp with slumber" ("Of Yesterday's Tomorrows," 8-9). This dancing will affect the gods of old and more, as the poet declares in "Bandung Dance":

> This dancer defies fatigue
> This dancer carries her fire,
> Dancing with Shaka's battered spear[.] (1-3)

Once singing and once dancing, the reborn blacks will move. Once reborn, they will be "speaking [the poet's] language, will / Say, today, we move, we move . . ." ("Random Notes to My Son," 38). As Kgositsile declares in "The New Breed," they will "Move in the air with air" (7). This moving is essential "Because," as the poet says in "Bleached Callouses, Africa, 1966," "a thing don't mean / A thing if it don't move" (50-51). This moving will be rhythmic, following a beat the poet associates with "armed peace" (37) in "Recreation," "laughter" (21) in "When Brown is Black," and "guts" (IV, 8) and "unchained Spirit" (IV, 11) in "Points of Departure: Fire Dance Fire Song." This beat, in a way reminiscent of Oswald Mtshali's *Song of a Cowhide Drum,* will be orchestrated by "a pregnant drum" ("Mayibuye Iafrika," 13); "the young talking drum" ("Sift and Shift," 10); "Drums [that] roll and peal a monumental song" ("My Name is Afrika," 10).

As Kgositsile says in "Epitaph," the younger, reborn generation will join him in "listening to the wind" (18). This wind will voice a condemnation of the whites who "ransacked the world" (20); this wind will also, as the poet makes clear in "Towards a Walk in the Sun," caress the reborn memories—noble and ignoble—of the reborn black people and, as he notes in "Points of Departure," orchestrate the fire of rebirth and revolution within them. "[T]he wind," in fact, "weaves this tapestry" ("The Long Reach," 11) of images that comprise Kgositsile's vision of rebirth and revolution.

This tapestry is quite poetic, in so far as it is woven out of images that recur in poem after poem. However, one should not think that because it is poetic it is in anyway soft. To the contrary, the tapestry depicts violence; the poems call for violence.

If one reads the poems in *My Name is Afrika* linearly as a kind of story, the violent note is not struck until more than halfway through the narrative—as if Kgositsile wants his readers to understand why violence is necessary before he calls for it. Furthermore, when he first sounds the violent revolutionary note in "Time," he sounds it as a global note, not just a South African one. But in "Symptoms," he focuses on South Africa, without naming the place, and declares that "there has been too / Damn talking much" (1-2). In "Brother Malcolm's Echo," he repeats that there's been "much too damn talking" (14) and wants to replace talking mouths with "grinning molotov cocktails" (10). In "Axiomatic," he says not to talk but to "SCREAM NOW!" (7) and advocates "burning / pants off false guardian gods / scorching their iced phallus" (8-10). Here, as elsewhere in *My Name is Afrika*, Kgositsile associates the white South African establishment with ice and with the raping penis.

For those who may think that revolution is ungodly, Kgositsile writes—with some wit—"In the Nude," in which he depicts the naked god—not the god clothed by the white man's interpretations—as "an assassin" with "Plastique in his hand" (12-13). In fact, the poet sees revolution against the white society as the religious thing to do. In "Towards a Walk in the Sun," he declares

> I yearn
> To slit throats and color
> The wave with the blood of the villain
> To make a sacrifice to the gods. . . . (37-40)

Kgositsile sees violence in South Africa as necessary; he also sees it as part of a global black revolution. In "When Brown is Black," a poem he dedicated to American black militant H. Rap Brown, Kgositsile rallies all blacks:

> For Malcolm,
> for the brothers in Robben Island
> for every drop of Black blood
> from every white whip
> from every white gun and bomb
> for us and again for us
> we shall burn
> and beat the drum
> resounding the bloodsong
> from Sharpeville to Watts
> and all points white of the memory
> when the white game is over
> and we dance to our bloodsong
> without fear nor bales
> of tinted cotton over our eye[.] (41-55)

Kgositsile expresses an awareness of how his South African black people's struggle is tied to that of black people elsewhere; he also expresses an awareness of how that struggle is tied to language. In many poems, he suspects the very words he writes in, for he knows that these words and the syntax that connects them together are a white-created system. He feels oppressed as a black writer by the very medium he must work in.

In "Random Notes to My Son," he criticizes his fellow revolutionaries for not going far enough. These fellow sufferers are so trapped in the white man's language that their calls and even their intentions become enslaved to the white man's agenda. In "To Mother," he indicts the language of Christianity as well as the language of black militants: the words are "old and impotent" (9); more important, the words are not "our language" (7). But he is at a loss to pinpoint that other language. The only clue he has is his mother's "articulate silence" (21). He unfortunately knows that he himself is trapped: he expresses his frustration in "To My Daughter" and "Sift and Shift." The "unrelenting talking drum" (22) is his word-less alternative in the latter poem. The white man's language is "sterile old shit" (1), he tells us in "Of Yesterday's Tomorrows"; the alternatives–largely beyond language *per se* are song, rhythm, dance. In "Vector or Legacy," he senses that the alternative must go entirely beyond language as he turns to "the pangs in fleshless rib" (19) of starving urban black children and says they are "clearer than glib verse or song" (20).

In "Notes from No Sanctuary," the last poem in *My Name is Afrika*, Kgositsile is still asking "Where then is / the authentic song? The determined upagainstthewallmotherfucker act?" (II, 15-16). As his playing with white-defined word boundaries suggests, he is trying to contort the given language to make it "other." He tries to contort "established" syntax in similar ways in many poems. But these experiments do not seem to satisfy him. He feels, as he says in "Like the Tide: Cloudward," trapped in "The sinister rot our minds must vomit" (8) and "academic masturbation and splitting / Or chiselling words" (15-16). He finally declares that

Words, be they elegant
As verse or song
Robust and piercing as sunshine
Or hideous memories of our
Cowardice in bondage are meaningless unless
They be the solid coil around our desire and method
Or the "most competent rememberer." May we
    Turn here
  Or return there
Where a fractured rhythm from
  The distant past moves us. (19-29)

This "fractured rhythm," the drumbeat, the pangs of starving children, his mother's silence: all of these, if put together, offer him as radical an answer to the problem of an oppressive white-created language as his answer to the problem of an oppressive white-created society. He seems in *My Name is Afrika* on the verge of advocating a kind of language-violence as well as a more clearly defined political violence.

Cry Rage!

James Matthews and Gladys Thomas' *Cry Rage!* (1972), the first volume of poetry banned in South Africa, is not as radical a work as Kgositsile's *My Name is Afrika*. The sixty-five numbered poems that comprise *Cry Rage!* are not as revolutionary on either the political or the linguistic fronts. The collection, taken as a whole, does indeed call for blacks in South Africa to offer a violent response to their systematic oppression. Matthews and Thomas, however, counsel such a course in relatively few poems. In most of their poems, they depict—at times quite starkly—the oppression that justifies, in their minds, violence against the establishment. Nonetheless, the call for violence is strong enough for Shava to refer to Matthews as "the dean of the poets who write poetry" which "espouses armed struggle" (114).

Matthews and Thomas touch on many of the topics treated in the previous chapter: the harshness of labor in the gold and diamond mines; the indignities of domestic employment in the posh suburban homes of South African whites; the passbook laws and the initimidating ways they were enforced; the segregation along racial lines of public facilities; and the over-zealousness of the police. Two areas of black South African life are treated very fully—and vividly—by Matthews and Thomas. Given how much attention they pay to life in the homelands and life in the townships, one might infer that it is these two situations that especially cause them to cry rage and call for violent attacks.

The homelands are territories established by the South African government for various tribal groups to live in, much like Indian reservations in the United States. The government determined what the tribal groupings would be; the government determined where each group's land would be. Although the government seems to have selected the lands to be set aside as homelands so that the tribes would live where or close to where their ancestors had lived, the government also seems to have made sure that all the "good" land went not to the tribes but to white landowners. Once these homelands were established, many blacks were removed—sometimes forcibly—from where they currently resided to these designated places. Poem #5 in *Cry Rage!* laments how the black people "like the cattle" "are herded / to starve on barren soil" (11-12). The land is so poor that, as Poem #8 tells us, "crops of crosses" are "the only fruit the land will bear" (3-4), these being the crosses atop the graves of the young children and the elderly. We are furthermore told that the children who survive are "thin as reeds" (13). This poem also refers to the fact that many of the men, in order to fend off their family's starvation, had to leave the homelands and go to the white-dominated urban areas to work, leaving

> women who lay with aching loins
> their beds empty of men
> with the lion of the kraal
> an ox in the city[.] (15-18)

The men who leave also suffer sexual longing as they live in "the bachelor barracks" (9, 9) of the big cities' black townships—so much so that some are driven to homosexuality. And in these townships, there are other horrors to face, for "the people of the township / in cement cages" (22, 2-3) "in the fire of frustration / they turn upon each other" (22, 6-7), ending in the "slaughter" (22, 19) and "the maim and rape / of township people" (22, 21-22). Matthews and Thomas choose to dwell especially on the violence women suffer in the townships, where the young men "are born to violence / and the young maidens their prey" (23, 11-12). These young men, "a ravishing band / [of] mother-fuckers" (44, 2-3) use the "penis [as] a slashing blade" (44, 9), "turning [their victims'] body and mind / into a bloody and bruised mess" (44, 12).

The Afrikaner government created these homelands and townships. The government draped their creation in rhetoric suggesting that they would be better for the blacks. The homelands would permit "separate development" that honored tribal ways; the townships would be nicer than the close-in slums they replaced. Many, however, would argue that both policies served white interests by, first, freeing up needed real estate for white development and, second, establishing protective buffer zones between the whites and the feared black majority. Whether the Afrikaner government was duplicitous or not, the policies ended up creating hardships, not benefits, for the black South African people. The severity of these hardships is what leads Matthews and Thomas to call for revolution.

In Poem #13, they recall the ways the white man has wronged the "black man": in the first stanza, they tell how the white man "stripped us of our land" (2); in the second, they talk about the various actions of the police forces; in the third, they note how the white government has tried, through law and terror, to "make of us mute men" (9). Each stanza ends with the prediction that "the walls of Jericho will fall" (4, 8, 12). The last stanza transforms this prediction into a more explicit threat:

> terrifying like thunder will be
> the trumpet roar of our rage
> that will rent prison cages asunder
> as the walls of Jericho fall[.] (13-16)

Amidst Matthews and Thomas' mixed metaphors, note the allusion to the roaring lion, violently emerging from his cage.

Poem #62 in *Cry Rage!* follows much the same pattern. The first three stanzas address themselves to "white man" and tell him all of the evil things he has done. The last stanza tells "white man" that revenge is in the offing:

> white man my wrath will find you
> thunderbolts of truth to pin you
> naked in your guilt
> the exploitation of our fair land[.] (11-14)

The most violent call for revolution is, however, in the collection's concluding poem. Its first stanza calls for the spilling of white blood:

> rage sharp as a blade to cut and slash
> and spill blood
> for only blood can appease
> the blood spilled
> over three hundred years[.] (65, 1-6)

The poets know that the white government will respond to violence with violence, but the number of attacking blacks will be so overwhelming that "your prisons [will] not [have] cells / enough to hold us" (65, 15-16) and "the land has not graves / enough to contain us" (65, 13-14). Then, in a rhetorical flourish, the poets repeat verbatim the call for revenge of the initial stanza.

In the Fog of the Seasons' End

Alex LaGuma's 1972 novel will surprise many "Western" readers, especially if they have read, in prose or poetry, depictions of life in townships such as those that comprise Soweto. The poetry we have examined thus far in this chapter, for example, presents a hellish vision of black slum life. LaGuma's novel, however, takes us to the non-white residential districts of Cape Town and portrays them in terms that are not altogether unpleasant.

After a disturbing "Prologue" (about which I'll write a little later), LaGuma takes us into a world of parks and cafes, of carnivals, of flirtatious young black men and women. Now perhaps the District 6 in Cape Town, which he is recreating for us, was, in reality, a better place to live than the now destroyed close-in slums of Jo'burg or that city's or Cape Town's "new" outlying townships. But, at least in what he chooses to stress in the early chapters of the novel, LaGuma seems to be making a quite conscious choice to depict a world of simplicity and innocence. We learn day-to-day details about black life in Cape Town, and these details, if considered carefully, do indeed reveal that the economic straits of the residents were just a tad above dire. We do not, however, focus on their hardships; rather, we focus on their at times even joyous mood. The atmosphere is the first third of the novel (if one ignores the "Prologue") is very much that of late spring and summer. The carnival setting of some of the early chapters helps create this atmosphere.

But, of course, summer yields to fall and winter; and the novel's title, *In the Fog of the Seasons' End*, suggests that we will move into and through these darker seasons before the novel is finished. And atmospheric changes do indeed occur–gradually–as the novel progresses, literal atmospheric changes *and* figurative atmospheric changes.

The novel tells the story of two men. One, young Beukes, dominates the earlier chapters. The other, a confirmed revolutionary named Elias Tekwane, becomes increasingly important as the novel progresses. Beukes, at times very much a part of the spring-summer atmosphere of the early chapters, is gradually drawn into the revolutionary underground. As he is drawn in, his life becomes connected with Elias Tekwane's. Thus, from about midway through the novel on, what initially seemed to be two separate stories become merged.

Beukes changes, but the changes are subtle. There is no epiphany for him; rather, he slowly becomes convinced that he cannot ignore what the government is doing to his people and try to live a sometimes carefree life. He takes risks; he takes greater risks. He becomes increasingly a loner: he seems to sense that the fewer his personal connections, the better he will be able to serve the cause he is slowly committing himself to. He also seems, as Shava notes, to be discouraged by the inattention of women to the political education he tries to provide. In Beukes' life, we see both the personal costs and the noble determination of revolution.

We also see revolution up-close. So viewed, it looks different from what we might imagine after reading the poems of Kgositsile and Matthews and Thomas. There are no fires or walls tumbling down; rather, there is the quiet by-dark printing and distribution of "subversive" pamphlets and the quiet by-dark shuttling of endangered persons to safety outside South Africa. Some who help Beukes and Elias Tekwane are ones an observer might look at and identify as potential revolutionaries; others are men (and women) with large families and, therefore, a lot to lose if caught. All, very quietly, go about the business of bringing down the system that oppresses them.

The novel is so quiet that the atmospheric shift from the beginning to the ending may not be immediately noticeable. The beginning, despite periodic references to oppressive laws and anti-apartheid demonstrations, is sunlit, in keeping with the spring-and-summer motif implicit in the novel's title. The ending is black yielding to grey yielding, finally, to sunlit. The blackness and the greyness fit the winter the novel has carried us to. The sunlight suggests that there is rebirth coming.

The images at the novel's very end are deliberately contradictory. We have sunlight: "The sun was brightening the east now, clearing the roofs of the suburb and the new light broke the shadows into scattered shapes" (180). As the van carrying endangered revolutionaries to safety departs, Beukes, "stood there until the van was out of sight and then turned back to where the children had gathered in the sunlit yard" (181). But we also see the yard itself and the poverty-suggesting debris in it: "It was quite light now, and the yard was revealing its shape; the piles of tyres, the spare parts, the washlines" (179-80). And we hear a call to war:

> Beukes stood by the side of the street in the early morning and thought, they have gone to war in the name of a suffering people. What the enemy himself has created, these will become the battlegrounds, and what we see now is only the tip of an iceberg of resentment against an ignoble regime, the tortured victims of hatred and humiliation. And those who persist in hatred and humiliation must prepare. Let them prepare hard and fast–they do not have long to wait. (180-81)

Sunlight and children; poverty and war—these are the contradictory poles the end of the novel is pulled between. And since the South African story was, of course, unfinished in 1972, it is indeed appropriate that LaGuma should end *In the Fog of the Seasons' End* somewhat ambiguously. And if "the children . . . in the sunlit yard," the novel's last words, suggest that there will soon be a gloriously successful revolution and this suggestion causes the reader to feel that the novel is an optimistic, revolutionary one, the reader needs only return in his or her mind to the penultimate chapter and the prologue.

The prologue begins the story of Elias Tekwane's arrest and imprisonment and torture; the penultimate chapter completes that tale with more—and more gruesome—torture and Tekwane's ultimate murder at the hands of the security police because he would not yield even though treated brutally. When he not only refuses to cooperate with the police but delivers a speech denouncing their (and the government's) activities, one officer threatens, "'We'll make you piss blood, you baboon'" (6). A minute later, the other officer adds, "'Tell me what I want to know, or I'll have your balls out" (6). When Elias still refuses, they haul him out of the interrogation room and kick him down the stairs. One officer pauses to urinate on Elias, which causes him to vomit. Then, they hang him on a wall and proceed "to batter him mercilessly with [their] fists" (7) as if he were a gymnasium punching bag.

Elias is in intense pain; his shackled legs have gone numb. He tries, desperately, to think of anything other than the pain he feels. Eventually, the officers take him off the wall, move him to another room, shackle him into a chair, and tell him to talk. When he again refuses, one "hit Elias in the face" and "then beat him up methodically, working on him at close quarters" (171). "[A] vast blue-blackness seemed to be coming towards [Elias] through the pain, an almost welcoming darkness" (171). "He felt himself sliding into the darkness that roared like a waterfall" (171).

Elias fell off the chair, and it broke. The officers were still demanding information, and he was still trying to think of things other than the pain. They stripped off his trousers and underpants, plugged in their "electrical apparatus" (172) and applied "the electrodes against bare legs, genitals" (173). "His flesh burned and scorched and his limbs jerked and twitched and fell away from him, jolting and leaping in some fantastic dance" (173). They then dropped him down the stairs again, and when, he still refused to cooperate, they put a sack over his head, and, in the language of one of the officers, gave "it to him good this time, the ____ing baboon" (175). Elias saw his ancestor; he saw a figure emerging "out of the bright haze" and "[h]is mind called out 'Mother'" (175). Then, he died.

If Beukes' story gives us hope for the revolution, Elias Tekwane's makes us realize how much suffering the revolution will necessarily entail. The two stories, taken together, however, inspire revolution. Beukes' story inspires revolution by offering a sunlit vision, a vision suggesting that the innocent, simple spring-and-summer of the novel's early chapters can be brought back—through revolution. Elias Tekwane's story inspires revolution by offering a nightmare, a nightmare that angers one so much that one feels justified in attacking—revolting against—the oppressors.

Amandla

LaGuma's novel does a good job of focusing one's attention on the people who are oppressed and the people—the everyday people—who are involved in the burgeoning revolutionary cause. Miriam Tlali's novel *Amandla* (1975) begins with a similar human focus, depicting the day-to-day lives and the drift toward revolution of numerous residents of Soweto. However, her novel—for better or for worse—takes a didactic turn. It ends up offering more of a Marxist economics lesson and less a human drama. Because it takes this turn, it is ultimately less appealing reading than LaGuma's novel; nonetheless, *Amandla* offers the reader a useful, albeit somewhat dry and academic perspective on revolution.

Before the novel turns preachy, we see different slices of Soweto life. We see how the government used bureaucracy to both harrass and keep in "their proper place" the black residents of the townships; we see the tension and the violence between the men living (as long as they had work) in the hostels and the "official" residents of Soweto. Meanwhile, we follow the stories of the young people who are—to the surprise of their more complacent elders—rebelling. In one scene, a young girl, spots a teargas-spitting "aeroplane" approaching. She and other "little ones" screamed "'Power! Amandla!" and "hurled their clenched fists into the air." As the aircraft "vanished by degrees into the white mass," they, their fists still held high, "bade it a rowdy, protesting farewell, shouting . . . in deafening unison: 'Amandla!—Power! Ngawethu—Is Ours!" (128).

The police, of course, chose to act against these children. The events of June 16, 1976 are well known; less well known are the smaller assaults. *Amandla* chronicles one (fictitious or not, we don't know) launched against teenage girls:

> They pulled the blankets off the bed and shouted, "komaab uit!," hitting her with the butts of their guns across the face. She screamed for help, calling loudly: "Ma, they're killing me, Help me!: They pulled her out, kicking her all over. "Waar's sy, waar's die ander een? Julle was twee, komaan waar's sy?" She pointed at the kist in a corner of the bedroom and they opened it and pulled out the other girl. They dragged them both out, hitting them, and pushed them into a van full of sobbing kids, and drove them to Protea Police Station. And there it's hell, they say. They locked them—about forty of them—into a small room with black-painted walls. They kept them there, confined in that small space, for hours and hours on end. It would become *so* hot, sweat was just running all over their bodies, terrible! Like being baked in an oven. (186)

This prison room is compared to Hitler's gas chambers and the bottom chambers of slave ships. The girls were, one by one, offered their freedom, if they had sex with the police officers. Some then left pregnant; some left so traumatized that they still suffer years later. Despite crackdowns such as this one, the children become increasingly militant, declaring boycotts—for example—and acting against their elders who refuse to heed the call.

Just as the events of June 16, 1976, are well known, so is *the* focal point of the chidren's protest that day: the insistence, under the government's Bantu education program, that black children learn Afrikaans and be taught some of their lessons in that language. But, as one of the young revolutionaries in the novel notes, "Education is only one small part of the system" (212). This statement serves as the jumping-off point in the novel for the lessons that dominate its last third.

We are told, at length, about "the most vicious system any oppressed people has ever had to deal with" (213). A young revolutionary teaches the young people who have gravitated to him about all the laws that make up "[t]his apartheid monster" (213): the Land Act of 1936, the Colour Bar Act of 1926, the Native Administration Act of 1927, the Conciliatory Act of 1924, as well as more recent, more well-known laws. This revolutionary voice then tries to teach his "students" how all the pieces fit together. "You see," he says, "things remain what they are mainly because of the existing economic system" (238). He then proceeds to talk about "our capitalist economy" and how it stands in the black majority's way. He then proceeds to denounce those who call for either "peaceful change" or "non-violence." These approaches will not work, he says, because those who are defending apartheid are using violence. He defines this "violence" broadly and radically: "it is not only what the police do with their batons and guns"; it is the "starvation, alcoholism, malnutrition, kwashiokor T.B., gastro-enteritis, and many other forms of what Andrew Young calls 'passive violence'" (239) that the system inflicts upon the black people. He debates with his "students" whether foreign nations, such as the United States or the Soviet Union, can be called upon to help. They seem to reach the conclusion that, in one student's words, "'We must do it. We must take the initiative'" (153).

Unfortunately, the clear vision of the long political, economic lesson does not hold sway. Tlali returns to Soweto reality, and, as the novel ends, shows us chaos, not clear-headed revolution, descending on the townships. Still, and despite how didactic the many pages of lessons are, it is the revolutionary vision that dominates *Amandla*. The kids have the right ideas, Tlali seems to be saying; but the right ideas cannot prevent the internal tensions, the alcohol, the human passions of Soweto from taking over the scene. Not yet.

The Soweto I Love

The chaos of Soweto, 1976, inspired much of Sipho Sepamla's collection of poetry entitle *The Soweto I Love*. One might expect the events of that year to have inspired anger. Surprisingly then, the mood of most of Sepamla's poetry is sadly quiet, bitterly quiet. He can no longer write with wit, as in his earlier poems, but, as Barnett notes, violence does not "fit" Sepamla's personality (61). Thus, the call for revolution is muted; nonetheless, it's present. Not surprisingly, the collection was banned.

Sepamla's poems, like other collections we have examined in this and the preceding chapter, catalogue the many abuses South African blacks have suffered. Not surprisingly, given the police crackdown after the 1976 Soweto riots, he devotes a good deal of attention to the abuses suffered by those who were imprisoned under the nation's security laws. Also not surprisingly, given the events of June 16th, he devotes a good deal of attention to children as victims.

"At the Dawn of Another Day" and "Bullets" glance most directly at the schoolchildren's demonstration against being forced to learn in Afrikaans and the police's reaction. In the former poem, Sepamla writes

> it was on the day children
>   excused the past
>   deploring the present
> their fists clenched full of the future
>
> at that moment when students were taking the
>   forward pace
> the police stood shattering the peace[.] (13-19)

In the latter poem, Sepamla tells us how "bullets / pierced the backs of kids killed and / killed and killed" (14-16), the repetition of "killed" suggesting that the murdering of unarmed schoolchildren went on and on.

But there were other children who were victimized. "How a Brother Died" talks about a decent young man who just happened to be in the wrong place at the wrong time and was killed; we are not sure by whom. In "A Child Dies," a curious child runs toward a burning shop

> until he fell smack
> into the hands of a towering giant
> he was grabbed
> he was hurled to the ground
> like grain
> he was pounded and pounded
> with a gun-butt[.] (18-24)

Elsewhere in the poem, the "towering giant" is referred to as "a monster" (9). This word gives us a clue to the murderer's identity, for in "Like a Hippo," the bizarre-looking armored vehicles used by the South African forces to suppress riots, the vehicles known as "hippos," are termed "nature's ugliest monsters" (4) and "prehistoric monster[s]" (19). This association between "monster" and the Afrikaner government's power is also made in "I Saw This Morning," where "little children clasping schoolbags" (3) are depicted, fleeing, screaming, from "an unseen monster" (10).

The abuses that Sepamla records in *The Soweto I Love* are hard to describe, for, as he tells us in "Talk to the Peach Tree," "words have lost meaning" (7). Not only have words lost their power to describe the injustices, but they have lost any power they might have had to deal with the injustices. This is the point the poet makes at some length in "Words, Words, Words." Words have been used to manipulate the black people, to make them think, for example, that the homelands policy is a promise of independence "which deserves warm applause" (14). Words have been used by the government so often in this way that the poet declares "words / . . . stalk our lives like policemen" (23-24).

The failure of words to deal with the injustices leads Sepamla to call for action, for revolution. In "At Sunset," he praises the "youth embraced in unity / shouting a delirious cry / Power! Power! Power!" (19-21). The young people's tragic fate—death—inspired the older onlookers to recall what they had suffered, and these onlookers "swore to pay the debt with defiance" (30). Similarly, in "All That Gold," what black laborers suffered in the mines is recalled. The poem ends by noting that there is a "debt to settle" (13).

The revolutionary impulse seems in Sepamla's poems to be kept pent-up within, ready to explode. "On Judgment Day," a poem whose very title suggests the settling of debts, the poet refers to "the storm raging within us" (11); in "The Exile," the voice of a young man refers to "man's willpower" (20) and "strength" (25) as lessons he has learned from his exiled father that will now be useful since "my life offers no alternatives" (23).

"The Island" is a curious poem in so far as the voice delivering the poem is the white South African nation. The voice speaks of how "Mandela & Sisulu have grown grey" on Robben Island "but their spirits still defy me" (20-21). Still defied, losing its courage, white South Africa says "rumour has it I'll be deserted one day" (25). The white nation then senses the revolutionary impulse that will lead to its defeat. The black boy, who is the speaker in "Shop Assistant," reiterates this prediction when he tells a condescendingly racist shop assistant, "go ahead / your time runs out" (25-26).

"On Fear" starts by talking about the fears the black people have known, but then, after noting that "fear is all-pervasive" (32), the poem suggests that as fear has been "burrowing here today" among the blacks it will burrow "there tomorrow" (33-34) among the whites, as they come face-to-face with a black revolution. As the poet says in "Drum Beats," "for 300 years, life has been shit" (12-13) and the recollection of these centuries of oppression has "charged rage to an unbridled / pitch" (17-18), leading him and others to the point of "ruthlessness" (21). As the poet says matter-of-factly, toward the end of *The Soweto I Love*, "we will have to spill blood" (3).

Sepamla tells us in "A Wish" that he wishes for "peace at all times with all men" (12). Perhaps it is this wish instead of simply his personality or his shock after the Soweto massacre and riots that results in his revolutionary call being somewhat muted. But, even though the call may be quieter or sadder than that found in some of the other works examined in this chapter, it is still there: "we will have to spill blood."

Works Cited

Barnett, Ursula A. *A Vision of Order: A Study of Black South South African Literature in English (1914-1980)*. Amherst: University of Massachusetts Press, 1983.

Kgositsile, Keorapetse. *My Name is Afrika*. Garden City, NY: Doubleday, 1971.

LaGuma, Alex. *In the Fog of the Seasons' End*. London: Heinemann, 1972.

Matthews, James, and Gladys Thomas. *Cry Rage!* Johannesburg: Sprocas Publications, 1972.

Sepamla, Sipho. *The Soweto I Love*. Cape Town: David Philip, 1977.

Shava, Piniel Viriri. *A People's Voice: Black South African Writing in the Twentieth Century*. 1989; rpt. Athens: Ohio UP, 1988.

Tlali, Miriam. *Amandla*. Johannesburg: Ravan Press, 1971.

PART III

Listening to the Lion

7

Ignorance

The bulk of the contemporary literature examined in Part Two of this study was written by black South Africans and focused on the plight of Black South Africans. The white minority is, more often than not, portrayed as the enemy. Another group of works examines the white minority more closely, and the three chapters that comprise the third part of this guide look at this literature and how it portrays the white South African: as ignorant, as guilt-ridden, and as inspired to act.

Ignorance, the focus of this particular chapter, takes many forms. Richard Rive's 1971 radio play *Make Like Slaves* examines the ignorance of those who want to help the oppressed majority. The naivete that characterizes this ignorance is funny at the same time that it is sad. Expatriate Sheila Roberts' *The Weekenders* (1981) deals with the affluence, decadence, and racism of the privileged white minority. The ignorance most of the people portrayed by Roberts exhibit is fueled by an insensitivity that is appalling. Roberts' intention is to satirize—viciously—this attitude. Nadine Gordimer's 1984 novella *Something Out There* returns to the tone of Rive's play. White ignorance is laughable. However, the racism that undergirds the white society often surfaces in all its ugliness. The fact that Gordimer's work is set after the 1976 Soweto riots and the police crackdown that followed these riots does cause the reader to be a bit more disturbed at the ignorance.

Make Like Slaves

Rive's brief radio play features two voices, referred to in the script as "He" and "She." They had met en route to Cape Town from London. Now, months later, she comes to his apartment to ask for help. She has been trying to help the black people of South Africa by organizing a group of them into a theatrical troupe and having them perform a play that depicts, in three acts, the African's story:

> The first act is set in Africa. They sing indigenous African songs. You should hear my Nyanga Players. The throb of the primitive. Dancing and rhythm. Palm-frons and jungle drums. Africa. . . . Act two is literally and dramatically the centre. The middle passage. They are captured and in a boat going across the Atlantic. An overcrowded boat. Chained down, whipped, abused. The longing for home. . . . And then the finale. They make like slaves. . . . They make like slaves. Oh, it's a bit of drama school slang I picked up when I was studying in London. They make like slaves. They sing sorrow-songs. Spirituals. (166-67)

The black players she has assembled, however, are not cooperating with her. They are always late; they seem to resent either her or the script or both.

She turns to He because, as a colored South African, he might be able to serve as an intermediary between white and black. Being "brown," he might–she naively assumes–be able to understand the two other colors:

> You're in the middle so to speak. Being brown you can speak to them and to me. They'll understand. I'll understand. They'll listen to you. (167)

As the play progresses, however, we learn that the colored man she has turned to knows very little about the black South African people:

> I have very seldom been inside an African location and I have certainly never been inside Nyanga. . . . I knew one or two [blacks] at university, but that is all. Do you realize that isolation in this country is by no means a white monopoly? We Browns are isolated from both Whites and Blacks. I've lived within a few miles of Nyanga most of my life, and yet I have never been there. But I have been to London, Rome and Paris. I've lived in the houses of Whites in Europe and never in the houses of Blacks here at home. (176-77)

He tries to blame his isolation on the system, but the audience realizes that it is more a reflection of his personal decision not to get involved. However, one cannot help but interpret Rive's "he" as a commentary on the many South African coloreds who have *not* found common cause with their black brethren. This comment on South Africa's colored population, however, is secondary in the play to its portrayal of white ignorance.

"She" comes across as sincere: she wants to help the oppressed black people. She cannot, however, come to terms with cultural differences. She is obsessed with punctuality. Again and again, she brings up the fact that the blacks do not arrive for practice on time. "Eight o'clock is eight o'clock in anybody's language" (178), she says. She is blindly unaware that different cultures have different attitudes toward time and that her insistence that the blacks be punctual is her imposition of her European culture (a neurotic version of it) on them.

She also cannot understand why the blacks in her theatre company might dislike the play–and her. Rather than allowing the players to develop the script, she imposes it on them. Not only has she denied them freedom, but she has interpreted their history for them, repeating the mistakes of many colonial and post-colonial historians of Africa. Her doing this *for* them reflects condescension on her part. These players, unlike *real* actors and actresses, she tells us, cannot do just anything, but this play is "the type of thing they can do" because it's "the type of thing they can feel." Slavery is, she tells us, "part of their experience, a part out of their past." When "He" suggests that the players might resent the reenactment "being done at the whim of some foreigners," she misses his point entirely and says, "They might or might not enjoy it, but they can certainly do it . . . and with conviction" (175).

"She" seems sincere, but her imposition of her culture's values on the troupe *and* her decision to interpret the African's history for the African reveal that she is entrapped by a continuing colonial mentality. "He," as distanced from the African as he is, is capable of not only revealing that entrapment but getting at the racist resentment that lurks just beneath her seemingly sincere surface. When "He" is not as upset at the blacks' lack of punctuality as "She" is, "She" flies into a rage:

> Well, haven't I made enough allowances already? How much more must I sacrifice because I'm white? Am I responsible for their oppression?

> Did I put them in locations? Must I suffer their unpunctuality in silence? Smile at their sneers? Enjoy their snide remarks in a language they know I can't understand? (179)

When "He" tells her, "Your acute martyrdom is showing" (179), "She" responds:

> Whose side are you on? What more do you people want? Must I change my colour? Move to a location? Throw bombs? (179)

"She" starts talking about "sides"; "She" uses the loaded phrase "You people." The racism that is within her, despite her good intentions in coming to South Africa, surfaces. But "She" learns little from her outburst, for when "She" and "He" arrive at the troupe's practice, she refers to the lack of punctuality of most of its members sarcastically and she tells the players to practice the third act and "to make like slaves" (181). Early in the play she hears the *Missa Luba* in the colored man's apartment. Impressed by the music but ignorant of what it is, she appropriates it as the accompaniment to the third act's portrayal of work on the plantations in the New World. In so doing, she creates an incongruous, ironic picture to conclude the play with. The irony, of course, rebounds on her and reveals the extent to which she doesn't "get it." She doesn't "get" the *Missa Luba* or his brief discussion of Countee Cullen or his explosion of her reliance on racial or national stereotypes: she remains naively oblivious to much of what the play reveals. Most importantly, she doesn't "get" that she is, not very far beneath her superficial liberalism, quite racist.

The Weekenders

Sheila Roberts' 1981 novel, *The Weekenders*, very effectively uses multiple narrators to give the reader a viciously satiric look at the white South African. Sometimes, Roberts uses a third person omniscient voice to talk about the events of a weekend trip to a posh resort in a now indepedent homeland and to show the white South Africans on the trip for the superficial, selfish, racist, and callous people they are; sometimes, Roberts uses the voices of the characters themselves. Among these, the initial voice, that of American academic Joe Johnson, and the concluding voice, that of Joanne Robinson, are the only two who come across positively: both are sensitive human beings who, despite their flaws, see the situation in South Africa clearly. The other voices all succeed, much like the personae used by Robert Browning, in satirizing themselves.

A bit of background is necessary to understand the situation the novel depicts. As I noted in Chapter One, the white South African government "created," as part of its separate development doctrine, homelands for the several African tribes that comprise the black population. To these homelands, blacks were—sometimes forcibly—removed. The plan was to grant these homelands independence once they were ready. Four achieved independence before the government put the homelands policy on hold a few years ago: Transkei, Ciskei, Bophuthatswana, and Venda. No foreign governments recognized these as independent states; however, South Africa did. With South African recognition came the possibility of these now independent states having different laws than in South Africa *per se*. South Africa, governed by the rather Puritanical Afrikaners, did not allow gambling, interracial sex, or "blue movies." All of these illicit pleasures were, however, legal or at least tolerated in the homeland of Boputhatswana. South African businesses, sensing that South Africans would pay for these pleasures and a general atmosphere of decadence, built large resorts in this homeland. And to them white South Africans have indeed flocked. Famous (or infamous) for these resorts is Sun City in Boputhatswana, a short drive from Jo'burg or Pretoria. Although Roberts' novel names its homeland Tshithaba and its resort city Kwa' Metse, it is probably Sun City that she has in mind.

The white South Africans who assemble themselves for a free weekend at the new Champagne Inn are a decadent lot. The American academic Joe is able, because he is a foreigner, to comment on "the antics of a load of brainless, vulgar barbarians." Joe had not been in the country long, but he already "despised most of the white people he had met in South Africa for their worship of the worst aspects of his own country, its cult of glamour, youth and pleasure, and its love of money, of *things*" (47). These white South Africans, Joe observed, were "sooner or later scathingly yet jocularly critical of the government" but then behaved with hedonistic abandon "almost as if [their] bawdy contempt had fulfilled a duty and [they] were free then to enjoy [themselves]" (23).

The Champagne Inn was not really ready to receive guests: many areas looked unfinished, and there were still problems with hot water and electricity. However, the lodging, the food, and the alcohol were all free. Nonetheless, there was grumbling. The affluent white South Africans "expected the best of everything and became ill-mannered and angry when the best was not forthcoming" (55).

Surfaces were all, it seemed, that the white South Africans saw or cared about. Late in the novel, we find out that Joe and his South African host, Tim, have been detained on suspicion of terrorism because of their appearance. As Tim observes, "Our clothes are crumpled! Joe has a beard and an unusual walk, so we are suspect! Insane!" (118). Joe and Tim are, of course, released; however, the appearance of wrongdoing was enough, Tim tells us, to undermine his academic career:

> Things are not going too hot for me in the Department. The Chairman was not happy about seeing Joe's face and my ugly mug in the papers in connection with such a dreadful affair. My old, ongoing criticisms of the Government seem to him to have subtle, subversive significance now, even though both Joe and I were cleared. I shall have to start looking around for another job, I think. (119)

This general portrait of the white South African as decadent and superficial is reinforced by the numerous sketches of individuals that Roberts offers. Champagne Inn executive Charles Vetter is, for example, upset that his wife has chosen to attend the gala weekend because "[h]er presence would certainly inhibit the full expression of his own animal enjoyments" (33). Bisexual orgy-enthusiast Bronwen Mostert tells her husband Fred that she is "sick of this holy-moses business, this big South African guilt trip" (28) over the treatment of blacks: she wishes that people would be people and see other people as people. Despite this desire for color blindness and racial tranquility, she delights at the prospective dramatic "scene" when the black chieftain of the homelands and his family "crash" the first night's banquet: "A black chieftain and his wife or retinue or whatever? People are going to be furious" (59).

Charles Vetter and Bronwen Mostert receive potshots from the pen of satirist Roberts. Another couple, Bob and Stella, are satirized more extensively. Bob is attacked for his sexism:

> He wanted [Stella] at home, her tall leggy ballet-trained grace enhancing the furnishings and objets d'art in his home, and her wifely presence discounting in business circles the gossip that he was not quite normal, not quite one of the boys, in spite of his old Michaelhouse school-tie. (26)

We never find out for certain if Bob is gay, as some of his business colleagues suspect; we do, however, discover what seems like hatred for women in his desire to keep them subordinate when we are told "he enjoyed the subservience his wealth created in [Stella]" (26). This hatred again surfaces when, held captive by a group of black men, "he took to taunting his wife about her imminent consecutive rapes by four black men" (116).

Stella is a racist, mouthing statements so stereotypical that she comes across almost as a parody of a racist. She complains about the independent homelands saying that she doesn't "feel very comfortable being out of the Republic" because "These black African states are all so . . . well, *African*, and dirty, and inefficient, and honestly, hardly civilized, I'd say" (24). She becomes indignant when Venner acts cordially toward the homeland's chieftain. ". . . do we have to watch Venner play barman to a couple of wogs" (60), she asks. If she had her way, she'd have nothing to do with blacks: "I hate talking to these people," she tells Bob; "I hate having to look at them and smell them. They make me sick" (104).

Early in the weekend, Stella attacks Joanne Robinson for having a "liberal" attitude: "And, let's face it, Joanne, you *always* take the part of the blacks. You liberals never think . . ." (57). The reader, however, thinks that she, Stella, is the one who never thinks. This view is reinforced when a reporter interviews her after Joanne is brutally raped by the four black men who had captured Joanne, Tim, Bob, and herself when they were on a Sunday morning horseback ride:

> I must say this first. I am dreadfully, *dreadfully* sorry for Joanne but . . . doesn't it strike you as kind of, well, poetic justice that it should be Arthur Robinson's wife who was . . . er . . . beaten up . . . I mean, really, it was *his* fault we all had to endure this awful weekend. He was in charge of building operations, he told Charles Venner the new Inn would be completed. (106)

Her comment is appalling–to suggest that Joanne, somehow, deserved to be brutally raped because the guests at the Champagne Inn had, in Stella's own words, been denied hot baths and had to eat "Sara Lee cakes for desert three times a day for three days" (106).

Roberts also chooses to give the reader a rather full satirical portrait of a minor character, Annette, who is one of the hostesses at the Champagne Inn. Early in the novel, in a stretch narrated by the third person omniscient voice, we hear Annette complaining about the black trainees that she thinks she will have to work alongside at the new inn. Late in the novel, in a stretch that she narrates, we learn why she has taken the job at the Champagne Inn:

> I used to be a nurse but I didn't finish my training. It's not nice work, you know. Man, you're on your feet the whole day and the pay's not good. And after a while people get you down, always wanting attention for the slightest thing. You don't get used to pain and blood and all the mess, people wetting themselves, old people who can't wait for the bedpan, the enemas, the bedsores, the catheters, and having to wash the dead. A lot of girls think they'll end up marrying doctors, but I can tell you, the students'll screw and drink with you but they mostly end up marrying their senior partners' daughters once they've finished with their internship. Some of the younger doctors are already caught: they married so that their wives could work and help put them through med school. And the older doctors usually have a lot of bloody kids. They're not even worth having affairs with. The Afrikaners are building up the South African nation, the Catholics won't use birth control, and the Jews don't believe in abortion. Another thing, if a doctor can stick up a family photo with a ton of kids in it, his female patients think he's a nice guy and they don't mind stripping.
>
> Nursing's no life, man. They say you get hardened to all the cruelty and misery in life, but I don't know. Maybe I didn't stay long enough to test

> the truth of that. I just gave it up after two years. I think my talent is for getting on with people. I like people, especially men. (110-11)

She seems devoid of human sympathy. Therefore, Annette's expressed desire to work with people is surprising. Not surprising, however, are her comments about "[t]hose bladdy black bastards" (113) who assaulted Joanne and her threat to "cut off their pricks with a blunt scissors" (112). One can perhaps understand her anger, given what the men did to Joanne; however, one finds her statement that she "can't associate with a black on equal terms" (111-12), her desire to "kill" the Tshithaba men who "make passes at me in the street" (112), and her opinion that "Joanne Robinson should have screamed and screamed like hell to begin with and she would have got off with just being raped" (115) difficult to tolerate.

A final lengthy portrait is that of Arthur Robinson. Others evaluate him as unfeeling. Jim says, in the novel's opening section, that "It was fortunate that she [Joanne] had not seen the strange look of revulsion that had overtaken the initial expression of fear on the man's face as he had joined the crowd at the steps" (14) when her battered, almost-dead body was dumped in a sack at the front of the Champagne Inn. Annette also comments on Arthur's reaction to Joanne's rape. She says, ". . . he just stood there, looking down at her as if it all was her own fault" (114). Unfortunately, Joanne *did* see Arthur's face. Later in the novel, she thinks to herself, "Had my hair been there, matted and tangled and filthy perhaps, but still there, would Arthur have looked down at me in that way, horror, pity, anger, but most of all repulsion, moving across his features?" (128).

These observations by others paint Arthur as superficial and selfish. More damning are his own words. In this short section he narrates, he talks about how relieved he is that Joanne asked for a divorce and moved out:

> I feel an immense relief being able to come home at night to smiling faces and not having to anticipate solemn discussion about poverty and misery and the political cock-up when all I want to do is relax with my family. Gretchen is also a fine woman to have in bed. She rouses easily, expresses her enjoyment, and comes without any difficulty. I've never understood why so many women turn sex into a complicated business when it's essentially a very simple human activity.

Arthur is free from serious discussions of South Africa's problems; Arthur has his new play*thing* in the croupier girl he was having an affair with while he and Joanne were still married. He is relieved that she, Joanne, asked for the divorce:

> . . . I am certainly glad she decided to leave. I mean, after *that* experience I could not have asked her to leave and have retained my image with the Company. People, not understanding, would have been disgusted with me. (121)

And, now that Joanne is gone, he feels very free to criticize her. He criticizes her "working-class" manners that made him "uneasy when [he] took her to Company functions" (121); he criticizes her lack of decorating taste, he criticizes her cooking; he criticizes her household management skills; he criticizes her lack of "dress-sense." "She did nothing well" (123), he declares; ". . . she was never quite sexy enough for me; she was obsessed by but badly informed on politics–an annoying combination" (123), he continues. "She had no awareness of how her behaviour could affect my position–she never tried to influence the right people, and Goddammit, she *would* buy me things I didn't like" (123). How appalling, the reader declares, with sarcasm aplenty. Arthur's seven pages should have most readers screaming.

All of these portraits–of Charles and Bronwen, of Bob and Stella, of Annette and Arthur–are disturbing. And they are, as Jim Johnson tells Joanne Robinson, "a microcosm of your country" (65). What we might say of these six characters, Roberts the satirist wants us to say of the white population of South Africa generally.

Joanne objects to Jim's characterization of the hotel guests as a "microcosm," citing herself as the exception. She is unlike the others on the weekend trip, and she is unlike the majority of her nation's white people. She, much to Arthur's annoyance, is upset at the political course the nation is taking; she, much to Stella's annoyance, is supportive of the black people's cause.

Thus, it is sadly ironic that she is the one the four black men brutally victimize. One is left asking why Joanne. It would be "better," one feels, if it had been Stella who had been raped. Then, one could feel a certain justice in the assault. But perhaps

Roberts does not want to set-up a situation in which a rape is, in any way, justified. Or perhaps Roberts wants us to realize that *all* whites are the enemy and *all* whites are privileged and ignorant. Most of the characters in the novel are blatantly so. A close examination of Joanne's life reveals that even she has enjoyed the decadent high life her husband's money had provided her. Furthermore, this close examination reveals that she, as sympathetic as she is to the black cause, is ignorant of particular black people. In thinking about the police proceedings that followed her assailants' arrest, she says, "I knew then the truth of the accusation that all blacks look the same to white South Africans" (134). She could not pinpoint the one of the four who mutilated her; she could not later, when she was a witness for the government against the one who was still alive, definitively say that he—this particular black man—had raped her. "They all look alike. All blacks have always looked alike" (134), she says. Furthermore, she says, revealing how her enlightened view is not as enlightened as one might think, "They are one threat" (134).

Something Out There

Nobel laureate Nadine Gordimer's 1984 novella *Something Out There* deals, in ways serious, comic, and both, with this threat. The story is set in Johannesburg's far-out suburbs. Mr. and Mrs. Naas Klopper moved there many years back because Jo'burg was becoming umpleasant. Fifteen years back, they didn't feel quite safe; "Now," Mr. Klopper says, "it's a madhouse, Friday and Saturday, all the Bantu buses coming into town from the locations, the papers and beer cans thrown everywhere . . ." (122-23). As the novella begins, this couple is playing host to a much younger couple who go by the names of Charles and Anna Roster. They are looking for a place to live and Naas, a real estate broker, has just the place for them.

Charles and Anna are, however, not who they claim to be. They are not a young couple seeking a quiet place to live, one that will perhaps prevent a second miscarriage. Rather, they are terrorists, and their task is to set-up a base of operations near an important power station. From this base, two black men, who will masquerade on the little farm the couple rents as hired black help, will launch an attack on that station. Once the couple and their two black compatriots are in place, the far-out suburbs are no longer the safe haven the Kloppers (and others) assume. There is trouble right in their midst. Of course, they are totally oblivious to it.

The Kloppers' ignorance as to the real use the former Kleynhans place is being put to is suggestive of the general ignorance of the white South African population to the *real* threat: terrorism at the hands of committed revolutionaries with genuine grievances against the South African state.

Gordimer counterpoints, with deliberately abrupt transitions, another story to that of the Kloppers and their new neighbors. This second story is of a baboon. During the same time that the four revolutionaries, Charles, Joy, Vusi, and Eddie, are executing their plan, this baboon is terrorizing white suburban Johannesburg. It appears on roofs, peering in skylights; it attacks pet dogs and pet cats in people's yards. It is seen reflected in the water of a swimming pool, and it is seen crouching down in the rough of a golf course. Whenever the animal is sighted, it makes the white people's newspapers: it's the kind of comic, human interest story that readers like.

The baboon then takes center stage in the novel as the "something out there" that the white population chooses to focus on. A close examination of the language Gordimer uses when talking about the baboon makes it clear that this is not just a beast but a symbolic representation of how the white population has represented to itself the African population of the country and that population's threat. The blacks are seen as being much like baboons; their threat is more comic than serious, more a nuisance than anything else.

Consider what the novel says about the baboon. Gynecologist Arthur Methus "said if it hadn't been for all the newspaper tales they'd been reading, none of them would have got the mad idea it was anything but a man—one of the black out-of-works, the *dronkies* who have their drinking sessions in" (126) the woods surrounding the golf course. A letter to the editor signed "Had Enough" invited the beast to devour her neighbor's dog, whose barking was causing her daughter's *anorexia nervosa*. The next letter, which Gordimer juxtaposes, is from a tourist and tells of an anonymous black man who slapped the letter writer's wife and broke her dental bridgework while snatching her purse; the letter says that the thief "was no better than an uncivilized ape at large" (132). Police Sergeant Chapman thinks the beast is an ape, not a baboon or a black man. Its ability to use its hands suggests it's an ape, not a baboon; its tearing raw venison with its teeth suggests it's an ape, not a black man, for, he says, "Even a black's not going to tear raw meat with his teeth." (159) Ms. Dot Lamb, chairperson of a Residents' Association in an endangered (by the baboon) area notes that the "koppies" that were "such a treasured feature of the suburb" were now being used for hiding by "an escaped ape" as well as alcohol-consuming blacks (171). Mr. Bokkie Scholtz came to his wife's aid when she screamed after being attacked by "a big grey baboon." He reflects on her attack: he says, "You know what Johannesburg is like these days. They are everywhere, loafers, illegals, robbers, murderers, the pass laws are a joke, you can't keep them out of white areas" (194). He never specifies who "they" are; however, they certainly aren't grey baboons. His mind has slipped from baboons to blacks, without even being aware of the slip and the implicit racism.

In all of these instances, note how blacks are always brought in, one way or another, when the ape or monkey or baboon is discussed. What Gordimer is suggesting is that the ignorant whites not only see the blacks as nothing more than baboons, but they see the blacks' situation and the blacks' threat in terms that reveal absolutely no understanding of either. And, just as "All the residents of the suburbs wanted . . . the animal to be confined to its appropriate place" (181), they also want the blacks confined to their townships and homelands, their proper places.

Toward the novella's end, the narrator makes this point about the white residents' ignorance of the blacks' situation: "A left-wing writer . . . wrote a stinging article noting sentimentality over a homeless animal, while–she gave precise figures–hundreds of thousands of black people had no adequate housing and were bulldozed out of the shelters they made for themselves" (189). Also toward the novella's end, Eddie and Vusi's attack on the power plant helps make the point about the white residents' ignorance of the nature of the blacks' threat. The "something out there" is *not* a grey baboon but a seething black nation ready to use violence to correct many injustices.

The story of the baboon, which Gordimer uses as a counterpoint to the story of the terrorists, is comic at times, but what the counterpointing reveals is not funny at all. Gordimer is suggesting that white South Africans view their nation's blacks as little more than baboons; furthermore, she is suggesting that, when it comes to the blacks' plight and the black's threat, the whites just don't "get it."

That Gordimer is using the counterpoint in this fashion is reinforced by the way the blacks in the novella deal with the rampaging baboon. As Gordimer makes clear, the white newspapers find the story of the baboon "good copy," whereas the black newspapers don't even mention the animal's "attacks." The silence of the black media might well be explained by the fact that "the creature never went beyond the bounds of white Johannesburg" (181). However, the black papers' silence *and* the fact that the beast is so localized seem more likely to be Gordimer's way of signalling that the baboon story is part of an ignorant, racist "mythology" that many whites unfortunately have embraced.

Although the black newspapers ignore the baboon, blacks working as servants in Jo'burg do hear about it and talk about. In their conversations about what proves to be a baboon, note how they signal its irrelevance to them:

> Since no one actually saw whoever or whatever was watching them–timid or threatening?–rumour began to go round that it was what (to reduce any power of malediction it might possess) they called–not in their own language with its rich vocabulary recognizing the supernatural, but adopting the childish Afrikaans word–a spook.
>
> An urban haunter, a factory or kitchen ghost. Powerless like themselves, long migrated from the remotest possibility of being a spirit of the ancestors just as they themselves, that kind of inner attention broken by the batter and scream of commuter trains, the jumping of mine drills and the harangue of pop music, were far from the possibility of any oracle making itself heard to them. (148)

In this passage, Gordimer accomplishes three goals. First, she distances the baboon from the blacks by noting that they do not even use a word in their native language for it, even though a rich vocabulary exists. Naming it in Afrikaans, when there is a Xhosa alternative, strongly suggests that the baboon–and what it stands for–belongs to the white consciousness. Second, she distances the baboon from the blacks by noting how the "spook" is so far removed from "the ancestors" that the baboon, if it were in theory a symbol or an oracle, could not make itself understood to them. Meeting these two goals reinforces Gordimer's point that the baboon story–and the racism and ignorance it suggests–are an unfortunate part of the white "mythology."

The third goal is deftly met: Gordimer gives as she taketh away; Gordimer *makes* the link between the baboon and the blacks as she takes away the possibility that this link is meaningful to the blacks. She accomplishes this paradoxical feat by drawing an analogy between the spook's distance from its roots and the black people's distance from their roots. This distance, as already noted, means that the spook can offer no message to the blacks; however, the fact that the distance is shared between the spook and the blacks suggests common suffering. This sharing reinforces the link the novel has already made between whatever it is that's haunting the white suburbs of Jo'burg and the blacks; furthermore, it reinforces the novella's largely implicit message about black oppression by noting what the spook and the blacks have had to endure in the urban areas. Finally, the link adds to the list of what the blacks have suffered by going beyond grueling labor and long (sometimes dangerous) commutes to the distant townships and noting how, as the South African whites brought the black people into the urban areas because their (cheap) labor was needed, the whites destroyed the vital links between the blacks and their ancestors and blacks and their gods, both of which were rooted in the land the blacks had to leave.

Gordimer's point is that most white South Africans do not realize what they have done and, worse, don't care to learn. They want the blacks, like the baboon, "to stay chained in a yard or caged in a zoo, its proper station in life . . ." (189). We laugh at a lot of what Gordimer includes in *Something Out There*; however, when we realize what she is saying about white racism and ignorance, it is very difficult to smile any longer.

Works Cited

Gordimer, Nadine. *Something Out There*. New York: Viking Press, 1984.

Rive, Richard. "Make Like Slaves." In *Selected Writings: Stories, Essays, Plays*. Johannesburg: Ad. Donker, 1977.

Roberts, Sheila. *The Weekenders*. Johannesburg: Bateleur, 1981.

8
Guilt

Richard Rive, Sheila Roberts, and Nadine Gordimer—the authors whose works were discussed in Chapter Seven—all believe that there are many white South Africans who are ignorant of what their government has done and is doing to the black inhabitants of South Africa. Some are ignorant because they have not discovered the truth; others are ignorant because they have *chosen* not to discover the truth. Some white South Africans, however, have found the truth, and finding it has led to a flurry of emotions, the most prominent one being guilt. The two works examined in this chapter reveal the process of discovering the truth and the emotions the discovering prompts. The two works are very different in kind, however. One, J. M. Coetzee's *Waiting for the Barbarians* (1980) is a novel and is decidedly post-modern in its rejection of formal realism; the other, Athol Fugard's *"Master Harold" . . . and the Boys* (1982), is a play and is quite realistic.

Waiting for the Barbarians

Although I will discuss Coetzee's 1980 novel *as if* it were about South Africa, I need to preface my remarks my noting that the novel is not *just* about South Africa. If one pays attention to the details in the novel and then tries to place it in time and space, one will have, as Paul Rich has noted, some difficulty. Some details suggest we've moved back in time to, perhaps, the turn of the century; other details, for example Colonel Joll's ultra-modern sunglasses, suggest we are in the present. Some details —for example the desert-like landscape—could be linked to certain sections of the South African nation; other details—for example the snowbound mountains—suggest a location considerably farther away from the tropics than South Africa is. Although one might argue that the landscape of the novel is strikingly like that of the Asian reaches of the former Soviet Union, the landscape is probably a surreal creation, designed to evoke many places simultaneously. Similarly, the time of the novel is equally "open," so that the novel can examine totalitarianism or colonialism whenever it raises its ugly head.

A useful clue to the novel's indeterminate time and place is found in Coetzee's biography. After graduating from the University of Cape Town with a double major in literature and mathematics, he went off to London, where he worked as a computer programmer for IBM. That work evidently did not satisfy his aesthetic yearnings. They were somewhat satisfied by the films of Ingmar Bergman to which Coetzee became almost addicted. Bergman's films often create a dreamscape in which highly symbolic action occurs. One is not supposed to ask such realistic questions as "Where?" and "When?"; rather, one is supposed to accept the dreamscape as no place and every place and no time and every time and attend to the symbolism and the message that the symbolism conveys or tries to convey. This description of how one should respond to Bergman could be applied profitably to Coetzee's novel. *Waiting for the Barbarians* depicts a dreamscape (perhaps "nightmare-scape" would be the better term) that is no particular place and every place and no particular time and every time. It is loaded with symbolism, and one feels that deciphering the code of this symbolism is the way to get at the novel's message/s. Of course, South Africa and *now* are subsumed within this description of the novel's scene, so, in a sense, the novel is about South Africa. And, as we will see, the symbolism, although it has resonance beyond South Africa, does indeed seem to interpret the South African situation. I will be talking about Coetzee's novel then *as if* it were *about* South Africa; however, do keep in mind that the reading I offer is only one—and perhaps the most limited one—of the readings that are possible. Also keep in mind that, as Lance Olsen has argued in *ARIEL*, *any* interpretation that is based upon reading the symbols may be, in a sense, superficial in so far as it fails to recognize the way the heavily symbolic language seems to deconstruct itself.

Interpreted perhaps superficially then, *Waiting for the Barbarians* is the story of an evil empire. The story takes place in a frontier fort far from the empire's center. In this fort the empire is represented by a magistrate who is so near to retirement age that one would expect him to just drift through his remaining years of service:

> I am a country magistrate, a responsible official in the service of the Empire, serving out my days on this lazy frontier, waiting to retire. I collect the tithes and taxes, administer the communal lands, see that the garrison is provided for, supervise the junior officers who are the only officers we have here, keep an eye on trade, preside over the lawcourt twice a week. For the rest I watch the sun rise and set, eat and sleep and am content. When I pass away I hope to merit three lines of small print in the Imperial gazette. I have not asked for more than a quiet life in quiet times. (8)

Unfortunately for him, he develops a guilty conscience. Fueled by rumors of subversive activities by barbarians beyond the frontier, imperial forces directed from the center, not by the magistrate, have come to the fort to investigate. Their methods of investigation include brutal torture of dark-skinned native people who, in the eyes of the magistrate, are quite innocent of any wrongdoings.

Gradually, the magistrate is drawn into action on behalf of these barbarians and against the empire. Although the empire's brutality in general upsets him, it is the cruel treatment of a young barbarian girl in particular that prompts him to act. He takes her in, tries to heal her wounded feet and legs, and then decides to return her to her people in the distant mountains.

Sexual tension mounts in the novel. He is attracted to her. She has been abused by her captors so much that she expects his sexual advances. She seems to feel obligated to pay him for his kindnesses with sexual pleasure. She even acts jealous when he refuses her advances but seeks out pleasure from the fort's young prostitutes. Consider the following sequence of quotations:

I

> When I have washed her feet I begin to wash her legs, For this she has to stand in the basin and lean on my shoulder. My hands run up and down her legs from ankle to knee, back and forth, squeezing, stroking,

moulding. Her legs are short and sturdy, her calves strong. Sometimes my fingers run behind her knees, tracing the tendons, pressing into the hollows between them. Light as feathers they stray up the backs of her thighs. (29-30)

II

First comes the ritual of the washing, for which she is now naked. I wash her feet, as before, her legs, her buttocks. My soapy hand travels between her thighs, incuriously, I find. She raises her arms while I wash her armpits. I wash her belly, her breasts. I push her hair aside and wash her neck, her throat. (30)

III

I feel no desire to enter this stocky little body glistening by now in the firelight. It is a week since words have passed between us. I feed her, shelter her, use her body, if that is what I am doing, in this foreign way. There used to be moments when she stiffened at certain intimacies; but now her body yields when I nuzzle my face into her belly or clasp her feet between my thighs. She yields to everything. (30)

IV

She lies on her back with her hands placidly over her breasts. I lie beside her, speaking softly. This is where the break always falls. This is where my hand, caressing her belly, seems as awkward as a lobster. The erotic impulse, if that is what is has been, withers; with surprise I see myself clutched to this stolid girl, unable to remember what I ever desired in her, angry with myself for wanting and not wanting her. (33)

V

I have not entered her. From the beginning my desire has not taken on that direction, that directedness. Lodging my dry old man's member in that blood-hot sheath makes me think of acid in milk, ashes in honey, chalk in bread. (34)

VI

She lies naked, her oiled skin glowing a vegetal gold in the firelight. There are moments–I feel the onset of one now–when the desire I feel for her, usually so obscure, flickers into a shape I can recognize. My hand stirs, strokes her, fits itself to the contour of her breast. (40)

VII

There is no link I can define between her womanhood and my desire. I cannot even say for sure that I desire her. All this erotic behaviour of mine is indirect: I prowl about her, touching her face, caressing her body, without entering her or finding the urge to do so. I have just come from the bed of a woman for whom, in the year I have known her, I have not for a moment had to interrogate my desire: to desire her has meant to enfold her and enter her, to pierce her surface and stir the quiet of her interior into an ecstatic storm; then to retreat, to subside, to wait for desire to reconstitute itself. But with this woman it is as if there is no interior, only a surface across which I hunt back and forth seeking entry. (43)

VIII

Whether she guesses where I have been I cannot decide; but the next night, when I am lulled almost to sleep by the rhythm of the oiling and rubbing, I feel my hand stopped, held, guided down between her legs. For a while it rests against her sex; then I shake more of the warm oil on to my fingers and begin to caress her. Quickly the tension gathers in her body; she arches and shudders and pushes my hand away. (44)

IX

There are moments during the day, in my office behind the courtroom, when my attention wanders and I drift into erotic reverie, grow hot and swollen with excitement, linger over her body like a moony lustful youth; then reluctantly I have to recall myself to the tedium of paperwork or walk over to the window and stare into the street. (44-45)

X

"Wouldn't you like to do something else?" she asks.

Her foot rests in my lap. I am abstracted, lost in the rhythm of rubbing and kneading the swollen ankle. Her question takes me by surprise. It is the first time she has spoken so pointedly. I shrug it off, smile, try to slip back into my trance, not far from sleep and reluctant to be diverted.

The foot stirs in my grip, comes alive, pokes gently into my groin. I open my eyes to the naked golden body on the bed. She lies with her head cradled in her arms, watching me in the indirect way I am now used to, showing off her firm breasts and her sleek belly, brimming with young animal health. Her toes continue to probe; but in this slack old gentleman kneeling before her in his plum dressing-gown they find no response.

. . . She slips open my gown and begins to fondle me. After a while I push her hand away.

"You visit other girls," she whispers. "You think I do not know?" (55)

The magistrate is attracted, but, at the same time, unattracted. He seems to know, without explicitly articulating the knowledge, that having sexual intercourse with her would be further victimizing her. He therefore resists his desires and her invitations. Until they are on the long road toward her mountain village. Then, he gives way to his lust; she seems very willing:

> Then, wide awake, I feel her hand groping under my clothes, her tongue licking my ear. A ripple of sensual joy runs through me, I yawn, stretch, and smile in the dark. Her hand finds what it is seeking. "What of it?" I think. . . . Beneath her smock she is bare. With a heave I am upon her; she is warm, swollen, ready for me; in a minute five months of senseless hesitancy are wiped out and I am floating back into easy floating oblivion. (63)

However, the power imbalance is such between the magistrate and the barbarian girl that he, in reality, rapes her—regardless of what the scene looks like. Of her other sexual relationships while in captivity she says, "'Yes, there were other men. I did not have a choice. That was how it had to be'" (54). This same comment could be applied to her sexual relationship with the magistrate.

He succeeds in returning her to her people, but, deep down inside, he knows he has victimized her at the same time. "I wanted to do what was right," he says. "I wanted to make reparation: I will not deny this decent impulse, however mixed with more questionable motives . . ." (81). So, with mixed emotions, he returns to the frontier town where the imperial forces are waiting to apprehend him as a traitor. He is thrown in jail, tortured, and eventually mocked and "crucified" at the command of the Empire's Colonel Joll. Along the way to the mortification (but not death) of the scene the magistrate interprets as the enactment of a scapegoat ritual, the magistrate's defiance of the Empire continues and his understanding of his complicity in the Empire's evil deepens. The magistrate uses Joll's questions about wooden slips he (the magistrate) has collected as an opportunity to indict the Empire's actions. Later, the magistrates abandons all subtlety:

> "*You* are the enemy, Colonel!" I can restrain myself no longer. I pound the desk with my fist. "*You* are the enemy, *you* have made the war, and *you* have given them all the martyrs they need—starting not now but a year ago when you committed your first filthy barbarities here! History will bear me out!" (114)

This passage precedes the "crucifixion" scene in which the magistrate sees himself as scapegoat or martyr. This latter scene strikes a clear parallel between the magistrate and Christ, but before we ask whether this allusion is serious or ironic, we need to discuss what has already transpired in South African terms. The evil empire suggests the Afrikaner-dominated South African government; Joll (whose name is vulgar Afrikaans, meaning "fuck") suggests the stereotypical white South Afrikan government security officer. The magistrate is unnamed, suggesting that he could be any white South African who, after years of blind, loyal support of the government's actions, realizes that the government is oppressive. The barbarians suggest the blacks whom white South Africa portrays as primitive and has moved as far as possible from the white center of the nation—to the homelands or to the outer limits of the major urban areas. The unreasonable, unjustified fear the empire has of the barbarians suggests a similarly unreasonable, unjustified fear the South African government has of its black majority:

> Of this unrest I myself saw nothing. In private I observed that once in every generation, without fail, there is an episode of hysteria about the barbarians. There is no woman living along the frontier who has not dreamed of a dark barbarian hand coming from under the bed to grip her ankle, no man who has not frightened himself with visions of the barbarians carousing in his home, breaking the plates, setting fire to the curtains, raping his daughters. (8)

The empire's methods of dealing with suspected barbarians suggests the South African government's methods of dealing with suspected blacks in the months and years following the Soweto massacre and riots of 1976. The really dangerous barbarians, who are somewhere beyond the empire's controlled area, suggests the many black militants who fled to neighboring countries such as Botswana and Mozambique and were indeed arming themselves so that they could terrorize and destabilize and perhaps one day attack South Africa.

Since this South African allegory is not *the* meaning of Coetzee's *Waiting for the Barbarians* but, rather, one particularized reading of the novel's timeless, placeless depiction of totalitarianism, one does not know how far to push the allegory. Pushed just a bit farther, the closer-in, more civilized "fisher folk" could well represent South Africa's historically more docile colored people, and the language on the wood slips the magistrate finds in the "fisher folk"'s village could well be the language of either the San or the Khoi, which are as obscure to the magistrate as the language of the barbarians (the blacks) will become if the empire is able to do the barbarians (the blacks) what it did long ago to the San and Khoi peoples.

I take the allegory as far as these slips because they and the barbarian girl's battered feet have struck most readers as begging for symbolic interpretation. The slips seem to suggest how the empire (and all empires) destroy the language and thereby the culture of the people it (they) conquer or colonize. The battered feet seem to suggest how the empire destroys the freedom to move and thereby other freedoms, such as the freedom to flee tyranny. The "fisher folk" have been successfully fixed in their place; the barbarians are still on the run, but the empire's goal is to fix them and control them (or kill them).

The barbarian girl's battered feet also sets up the recurring scenes in which the guilt-ridden magistrate bathes and massages them. These scenes, as we have already seen, have an increasingly erotic quality, as his bathing and massaging proceeds from the girl's feet to her entire naked body; however, before the scenes become perverse erotica, they also evoke Christ's washing of the feet of his apostles on the night of the Last Supper. It is almost as if Coetzee is trying, in these scenes, to mix, as they might in a dream, the two forces that are at war in the magistrate's mind. Will he give way to lust and join the victimizers of this poor girl, or will he resist his body's desires and become her redeemer?

As we have already established, he gives way to the lust and, in essence, rapes her as he is returning her to her people. Thus, when he returns to the village and the imperial force that waits to arrest him and "crucify" him, he has lost the potential to redeem her or anyone. His "crucifixion" then is ironic. He suffers–and almost dies–but for nought. Coetzee seem to be suggesting that even if white South Africans discover the truth and try, inspired by guilt, to redress wrongs, they will probably find themselves so tainted, one way or another, by their complicity in the oppression that they will not be able to accomplish anything. Just as the magistrate's complicity in victimization is clear only after one puts his act of sexual intercourse with the barbarian girl within the context of power "politics," the sympathetic South Africans' complicity is clear only when one steps back and realizes that all of the advantages white South Africans have (posh houses, fancy cars, etc.) are an affront to blacks whose exploitation allowed white South Africans to acquire those advantages.

The magistrate's relations with the barbarian girl (and with women in general) can be contextualized in two other ways that shed additional light on what Coetzee's *Waiting for the Barbarians* says about South Africa in particular and colonialism or totalitarianism in general. Both W. J. B. Wood and Joan Gillmer, writing in *Momentum,* see the novel as a commentary on the Cartesian-based "Western" mentality that both South Africa and colonialism and imperialism are based on.

Wood's essay discusses how the Cartesian mind-body split affects the magistrate. Unable to reconcile the two, he demonizes the latter. Thus, a healthy attitude toward the physical becomes perverted into the Empire's negative depiction of the barbarians as grossly physical, into Joll's torture of the body of the prisoners he takes, and into the magistrate's lust toward and abuse of–rape of–the bodies of young girls. Gillmer's essay dovetails nicely with Wood's, for Gillmer argues that the West's abandonment of "those elements of human nature that are traditionally ascribed to the nurturing feminine principle–qualities such as love, mercy, forgiveness, intuition and creativity" (110) is figured in several of Coetzee's works by "those images of violation and injury of women and children which appear so enigmatically and apparently so gratuitously . . ." (110). Gillmer's comment helps us see why the magistrate's wrestling with his complicity in imperial oppression is linked in the novel with his lustful desire for young girls. Furthermore, the comment provides us with a further link between the magistrate's lustful reflections and his recurring dreams of innocent but in some way battered (female) children. One of the magistrate's most revealing reflections cements this link between the barbarian girl and other young girls he has used and young (female) children:

> What have I been doing all this time, pressing myself upon such flower-like soft-petalled chidren–not only on her [the barbarian girl], on the other one too [a young prostitute at the fort]? (97)

The magistrate's dreams of young children are not further evidence of the magistrate's perverted desires but rather a reflection of his inner desire to end the oppression and restore the "feminine" elements of human nature that the Empire has virtually destroyed. To the extent that the magistrate is and has been a beneficiary of the Empire's mentality, he is tragically unable to fulfill this desire—for either himself or for the land. He is compelled to demonstrate his complicity by acting against, not for, the children.

Waiting for the Barbarians then becomes the story of the failure of the guilt-ridden to effect redemption for their victims or themselves. They fail because guilt alone is not enough. They must renounce all of the advantages that the victimization of others has gained them, but that is difficult if not impossible to do. How do you turn back the clock? How do you erase history?

This last question is relevant to the reflections the magistrate offers as the novel closes. He realizes that the barbarians have been the victims of history; he realizes that he is a victim of history. He also suggests that once historical actions initiate the process, events simply occur, much as the wind blows, without humans who come along later having much control. His reflections invite us to ask whither the wind is blowing as the novel ends. The wind *seems* to be on the verge of blowing the existing order apart. The imperial forces have fled in a panic at the rumored invasion of barbarians, leaving the village unprotected. But there are no barbarians yet, and, from what we've discovered about the people the empire so fears, we wonder if they are coming. The novel ends with all uncertain: is the evil empire about to dissolve, or will Joll and the imperial troops return? are the barbarians about to launch a brutal raid, or are the feared barbarians an imperial fiction that became so real in the imperial mythology that the empire finally believes the fiction it created to be real? We are left waiting, waiting for the wind of history to bring about a predetermined fate.

Having created this expectation, Coetzee further complicates matters by undermining it. The wind dies down, and we are left with the picture of children building a snowman, a process the magistrate will not interfere in. This picture, which concludes the novel, counterpoints the disheartening reflection on historical inevitability. Maybe the children are not trapped and can act; maybe they can build a better nation; maybe the elements of human nature that children represent in the text can be restored. Maybe.

"Master Harold" . . . and the Boys

Athol Fugard's 1982 play, *"Master Harold" . . . and the Boys,* also looks to the children. The adults in and out of the play seem trapped. Young Harold's racist father is trapped in his degenerate behavior; the black tea room workers, Sam and Willie (the "boys" of the title) are trapped in apartheid. Only young Harold seems as yet free to determine what will characterize his life.

Like most of Fugard's plays, there are very few parts–three to be exact, Sam, Willie, and Hally (Harold's nickname). Before I discuss these three and the important results of their interaction, I want to discuss a fourth character, one who never appears or speaks, Hally's father.

Hally's father stands in the play for a large segment of the adult white South African population. He's an embarrassment and a nuisance to Hally: on more than one occasion, Hally has had to help his drunk father home from the pubs; before his recent hospitalization, Hally has had to wait on his now-crippled father. When he hears from Sam the possibility that his father is coming home from the hospital, he is distraught; when he hears that his father is actually home, he is angry–so much so that he lashes out at Sam. Hally has long yearned for a real father, a man he could admire, but instead he has a drunken cripple who blurts out horribly racist jokes and fills up vile-smelling pisspots, which Hally has to empty. (Fugard is suggesting that the jokes and the pisspots are much the same.) Without Hally knowing it, Sam has served as a substitute father to the boy for many, many years. After school, he would help Hally learn his lessons. Initially, Sam played the role of the poorly educated black and let the proud schoolboy teach him and thereby learn. Later, Sam changed his role and became more of an equal, still, occassionally, letting Hally turn teacher and feel superior. Sam also played with the boy, something his father couldn't or wouldn't do. Sam also helped the boy cart his drunk father home from the pubs and tried to make the boy feel proud of himself when his father's degenerate behavior made him feel self-ashamed.

Sam is a man of vision. He has a vision for Hally: he will be a white South African *unlike* his father and his father's fellows. He also has a vision for the future of South Africa. This vision is twice expressed in the play.

One version of the vision involves dancing. Sam and Willie's great recreational passion is dancing—oddly enough, ballroom dancing. The play opens with the two of them practicing their steps; the play closes with the two of them dancing. In between, there is a great deal of conversation, back-and-forth, between Sam and Willie concerning the upcoming dancing contests. Sam, about halfway through the play takes ballroom dancing and turns it into a vision of international and racial harmony—everybody moving together on the dance floor so perfectly that there are no collisions: "There's no collisions out there, Hally. Nobody trips or stumbles or bumps into anybody else" (45). Sam continues, talking about the dream's opposite:

> But instead, like you said, Hally, we're bumping into each other all the time. Look at the three of us this afternoon: I've bumped into Willie, the two of us have bumped into you, you've bumped into your mother, she bumping into your Dad. . . . None of us knows the steps and there's no music playing. And it doesn't stop with us. The whole world is doing it all the time. Open a newspaper and what do you read? America has bumped into Russia, England is bumping into India, rich man bumps into poor man. Those are big collisions, Hally. (46)

What Sam doesn't realize, however, is how this vision has all people dancing the ordered ballroom dance defined by the white man. This realization turns what was a vision of peace into a vision of (white) law and (white) order—at least for the audience.

The second version of the vision also turns sour. One day, several years before the time of the play, Sam decided to make a kite for Hally. Sam used scraps from his squalid rooms; to those were added a few odds and ends from Hally's mother's middle class household. Hally recalls "[t]he sheer audacity of it":

> Tomato-box wood and brown paper! Flour and water for glue! Two of my mother's old stockings for a tail, and then all those bits of string you made me tie together so that we could fly it! (29)

Then, the two of them went to the park to fly the kite. Hally was sure it would not fly: he had questions about the quality of the materials used in constructing it; he doubted Sam's expertise; he was "shit-scared" (29) of making of a fool of himself with, maybe, other kids around. But the kite does fly. The kite is made of scraps and odds and ends drawn from white and black worlds; the kite is being flown by a "[l]ittle white boy in short trousers and a black man old enough to be his father" (31): it symbolize white-and-black together, flying freely in the sky, the sky which does not know the racist laws of the land beneath it.

Unfortunately, Hally chooses to sit down on a bench in the park. Dejected, Sam leaves Hally there. And young Hally, at that point in his life, does not know why. Toward the end of the play, Hally learns why Sam left and why the optimistic vision of the kite failed: "It was a 'Whites Only' bench. You were too young, too excited to notice then. But not anymore" (58).

His visions fail, but Sam doesn't give up, although he comes very close to giving up during the course of the play. When Hally learns that his father is indeed coming home, he, angry at his father, takes that anger out on Sam when Sam tries to tell Hally he should treat his father with more respect. He repeats one of his father's worst racist jokes, one that turns on the "fair" appearance of a black man's arse. He further demands that "the boys" stop being so familiar with him and start addressing him as "Master Harold." Indignant, Sam lowers his trousers to show Hally what a black man's arse really looks like. Insulted, Hally spits in Sam's face. Himself insulted (and hurt), Sam gives up on Hally and says he will hereafter always call him "Master Harold." No more after-school games; no more kite flying. Sam probably concludes, at least momentarily, that Hally is a lost cause, is like his father. Sam definitely concludes that racism is far more difficult to overcome than he had thought, years ealier, when he befriended the boy. What can one good, shrewd black man do, he might be asking himself, against the prevailing thoughts and culture of a racist people?

The play climaxes at the moment Hally spits in Sam's face; however, the play does not end with this ugly act. Having learned that teaching Hally to be a man unlike his father will not be as easy a task as he had thought (and having cooled down a bit), he again addresses the teenage boy as "Hally" and suggests that they "try again" (59). Hally responds, "Try what?"; Sam says, "Fly another kite . . ." (59). Hally notes that "It's still raining, Sam. You can't fly kites on rainy days, remember"; Sam responds, "So what do we do? Hope for better weather tomorrow?" (59). Hally responds to that remark with a "Helpless gesture" and a repeated "I don't know" (59). Sam ends the conversation by telling Hally one thing he now does know:

> I reckon there's one thing you know. You don't *have* to sit up there by yourself. You know what that bench means now, and you can leave it any time you choose. All you've got to do is stand up and walk away from it. (59-60)

We are left wondering what Hally will do. The text offers no clue. The director and the actor playing Hally have a great deal of leeway in staging Hally's departure from the stage, and how this exit is played will determine, to some extent, whether the audience feels hopeful or hopeless. Either way, one thing Fugard certainly wants to be clear is that Hally has confronted the truth.

The text and certain facts extraneous to the text do give us some cause for optimism. In the text, Sam and Willie return to dancing–not aware that their steps are white-defined. But at least the dancing offers them enjoyment and the possibility of success, and the music they're dancing to is by American black jazz singer Sarah Vaughan. The scene inspires optimism. Her song addresses a "Little man," suggesting Hally, and tells him he "had a busy day" and to "go to sleep now." Her song implicitly promises him a better tomorrow. This song, so interpretted as relevant to Hally, inspires optimism too.

The most significant cause for optimism in the text is the change that the play's events have caused in Willie. Early in the play, we learn he has been beating his girlfriend and dancing partner Hilda. Sam counsels him not to do so: "You hit her too much"; "*Too* much and *too* hard. You had the same trouble with Eunice"; "Beating her up every time she makes a mistake in the waltz? No Willie!" (7). But the events of the play, not Sam's words, convince him; at the end of the play, Willie pledges to apologize to Hilda and "beat her no more" (60).

To understand what causes this change in Willie, one must note, as Sheila Roberts has in an article in *English in Africa*, that beatings are mentioned in several contexts in the play, all of which have the disempowered, be they students or black prisoners or women, beaten by the empowered. One must add to this observation what Errol Durback refers to in an article in *Modern Drama* as "the psychopathology of apartheid," which causes those who are disempowered and abused by those higher up in the system to vent their anger by disempowering and abusing those lower. This "psychopathology" explains, at least partially, why blacks who obtain some power from the white government have often used it against less privileged black fellows and why black men so often abuse black women. Durback describes it as a chain: white man hits white woman hits white child hits black man hits black woman. Willie learns enough from the dramatic events between Sam and Hally to know he must break the chain. This decision by Willie inspires optimism.

Outside the text, there is still further cause for optimism. "*Master Harold*" . . . *and the Boys* was the play Fugard felt he *had* to write, for in it he confesses his guilt. The play is quite autobiographical, and Harold Lanigan Athol Fugard is staging what *he* did in 1950 to the black man Sam who tried to befriend him when he was growing up in Port Elizabeth. He dedicated the play to the real Sam (and to his [Fugard's] father), and when the play premiered in South Africa at the Market Street Theatre in Johannesburg, Fugard tried to get the real Sam to the theatre.

We then know what Hally does after the curtain closes. We know that Hally grows up to be Athol Fugard, who crusades against apartheid and racialism in his plays and who has helped train black performers to create their own plays. In a 1984 article, Rob Amato refers to a curious anonymous paper entitled "Art and Revolution in South Africa: The Theatre of Athol Fugard" that was distributed in 1982 at an academic conference in Gaborone, Botswana. The anonymous author, seemingly disturbed at Fugard's prominence as an anti-apartheid writer, attacks the playwright for being unable to escape the privileges he has based on race and social class and thereby really understand the plight of South African blacks. Fugard's plays, especially because they advocate black perseverance *not* rebellion, do not promote the cultural, political, or economic interests of the black majority. I mention this anti-Fugard article, not because I agree with it, but because it suggests that not all see Fugard as an anti-apartheid hero. But, whether he be anti-apartheid hero or a flawed, perhaps unsuccessful anti-apartheid voice, he is still the play's extra-textual happy ending. Hally confronted the truth; Hally allowed the profound guilt that the truth inspired to transform him from a teenager on the verge of becoming his father's son to a white playwright who at least tries to make matters right.

Works Cited

Amato, Rob. "Fugard's Confessional Analysis: "*Master Harold" . . . and the Boys*. In M. J. Daymond, et al., eds. *Momentum: On Recent South African Writing*. Pietermaritzburg: University of Natal Press, 1984. 198-214.

Coetzee, J. M. *Waiting for the Barbarians*. 1980; Rpt. New York: Penguin, 1982.

Durbach, Errol. "*Master Harold*: Athol Fugard and the Psychopathology of Apartheid." *Modern Drama* 30 (1987): 505-13.

Fugard, Athol. *"Master Harold" . . . and the Boys*. 1982; Rpt. New York: Penguin, 1984.

Gillmer, Joan. "The Motif of the Damaged Child in the Work of J. M. Coetzee." In M. J. Daymond, et al., eds. *Momentum: On Recent South African Writing*. Pietermaritzburg: University of Natal Press, 1984. 107-20.

Olsen, Lance. "The Presence of Absence: Coetzee's *Waiting for the Barbarians*." *A.R.I.E.L.* 16.2 (1985): 47-56.

Roberts, Sheila. "'No Lessons Learnt': Reading the Texts of Fugard's *A Lesson from Aloes* and *Master Harold . . . and the Boys*. *English in Africa* 9.2 (1982): 27-33.

Rich, Paul. "Apartheid and the Decline of the Civilization Idea: An Essay on Nadine Gordimer's *July's People* and J. M. Coetzee's *Waiting for the Barbarians*." *Research in African Literatures* 15 (1984): 365-93.

Wood, W. J. B. "*Waiting for the Barbarians*: Two Sides of Imperial Rule and Some Related Considerations." In M. J. Daymond, et al., eds. *Momentum: On Recent South African Writing*. Pietermaritzburg: University of Natal Press, 1984. 129-40.

9

Action

At the end of Coetzee's *Waiting for the Barbarians*, we leave the magistrate a guilt-ridden, but broken man. His guilt has led him to a futile act of rebellion and into an equally futile act of redemption. At the end of Fugard's *"Master Harold" . . . and the Boys*, we leave Hally a guilt-ridden and confused seventeen year-old boy/man. In the text, there is some hope that his guilt will lead to action; in the theatre, this hope can be strengthened or weakened, depending upon how the director and the actors choose to interpret the script. Only outside of the text and the theatre does hope truly blossom, for guilt over what he did when he was seventeen to his friend Sam led Athol Fugard to act, the writing and staging of the play being *the* particular act (with Fugard's oeuvre being the act on a larger scale).

In this chapter, we deal with two works, both written in 1979, where the action is *in* the text. Nadine Gordimer's *Burger's Daughter* is the more difficult of the two, for Gordimer takes us very much inside the mind of her central character, Rosa Burger. Rosa has lived in the shadow of her activist parents. Now, on her own, she must figure out, first, who she is, and, second, who she is *in relation to* her South African homeland. Andre Brink's *A Dry White Season* is the easier. Although the novel's mode of narration is sophisticated, once the reader gets to the core of the story–the enlightenment of comfortably middle class Afrikaner school teacher Benjamin Du Toit, one is able to follow the plot as if the novel were a suspenseful thriller. The ferocity of Brink's indictment of *his* people and the philosophical depth of the novel's politics do not strike one until the story reaches its conclusion.

Action then is so much a part of Brink's novel that it dominates our mind *as* we read. The action in Gordimer's masterpiece is quieter; nonetheless, it is to what Rosa Burger ultimately *does* that the entire novel points. In both cases, the action is on behalf of the nation's oppressed people—on behalf of the lion; in both cases, the action is premised upon an awareness on the part of the central character of her or his complicity in the oppression.

Burger's Daughter

The bulk of Nadine Gordimer's *Burger's Daughter* is appropriately titled, for, until the very end of the novel, she has no clearly-defined identity of her own. Her father's life, in many ways (and in ways she resented) defined her own:

> My mother is dead and there is only me, there, for him. Only me. My studies, my work, my love affairs must fit in with the twice-monthly visits to the prison, for life, as long as he lives—if he had lived. My professors, my employers, my men must accept this overruling, I have no passport because I am my father's daughter. People who associate with me must be prepared to be suspect because I am my father's daughter. And there is more to it, more than you know—what I wanted was to take a law degree, but there was no point; too unlikely that, my father's daughter, I should be allowed to practise law, so I had to do something else instead, anything, something that would pass as politically innocuous, why not in the field of medicine, my father's daughter. (62-63)

The novel, in fact, is very much an account, told from five if not more narrative perspectives, of her struggle to find this separate identity. Although Gordimer has denied that she is a "feminist" writer, the novel will take us through three phases in this struggle and ultimately demonstrate—in line with a feminist ideology—that, for Rosa, personal and political *must* be connected. The novel will further demonstrate that body and mind (the sensual and the ideological) must be connected.

The novel has three parts. The long first part reviews, in a meandering manner, Rosa's life before and immediately after her father's death in prison. Her father, perhaps—as Stephen Clingman has suggested in his 1986 *The Novels of Nadine Gordimer*—modeled on South Africa Communist Party leader Bram Fischer, was famous for the intense political debates that took place around his swimming pool. All, regardless of race, were welcomed to Dr. Burger's home and to these discussions, and all were treated as equals. Many of these "liberals" and "revolutionaries" brought their families along. When Rosa was growing up, she often played with the children, some white and some black. One in particular, a black boy she knew as "Baasie" (i.e., "little boss"), will prove significant later in Rosa's story. Back when they were children together, there was no awareness of his "otherness" because of either sex or race. Their relationship was a sensual one but not a sexual one. "He and Rosa had often shared a bed when they were as little as Tony . . ."; they "fought for the anchorage of wet hair on Lionel Burger's warm breast in the cold swimming pool" (55). Rosa's father was a surrogate father to the boy; Rosa's mother was a surrogate mother. When circumstances resulted in Baasie's being sent away, Rosa "forgot Baasie. It was easy" (71). But the person she forgot when she was young returns to her mind frequently when she matures. She recalls "a special, spreading warmth when Baasie had wet the bed in our sleep" and how "in the night [she] didn't know whether this warmth that took us back into the enveloping fluids of a host body came from him or [her]" (139-40). When, still later, she feels she has "lost connection" with the human dimension of politics, she re-recalls this "memory of childhood warmth" (172).

Rosa grew out of this asexual sensuality. Soon, politics was ideological and public, and she found herself expected to embrace her father's (and mother's) ideology and to be as comfortable in the public arena as they were. As a young girl, she never really questioned these expectations, but, after her parents' deaths, she did. Largely as a monologue addressed to her dropout friend Conrad, she does so, as she reviews her life thus far, in the novel's first part.

During this first part, politics has a sterile feel. It swirls around Rosa, occasionally occupying her mind. It does not, however, affect her body. But her body, we discover, is central to how Rosa expresses herself and, thereby, *is* herself:

> Rosa Burger's prim thighs closed at the bony outline of pubis in shrunken jeans, a long sunburned neck with the cup at the collarbones where—she sat so still; no nerves, she did not fidget—a pulse could be seen beating: Noel de Witt's girl; also the mistress of a Swede (at least;

> of those that were known) who had passed through, and some silent bearded blond fellow, not someone who belonged, not he, either. A body with the assurance of embraces, as cultivated intelligence forms a mind. Men would recognize it at a glance as the other can be recognized at a word. (121)

In just a few movements, one could discern how Rosa's being was wrapped in her body just as, in a few words, one can discern who is and who is not intellectually gifted. The most crucial event of that first part is tied to this sensuality. That event was not her father's death (which liberated her) but, rather, her meeting Marisa Kgosana, the activist wife of an imprisoned African leader. Marissa is dynamic and very sensual–so much so that Rina Leeuwenberg refers to her as "Mother Africa," a figure who, Richard I. Smyer argues, embodies the physicality, the wholeness, and the primal energy that Gordimer's heroines increasingly aspire to or exhibit. Rosa is *strongly* attracted to Marisa–more because of this over-powering sensuality than the "black consciousness" ideology she preaches.

Rosa's initial description stresses Marisa's "half-bare back," "the colour of her skin," "two rounded shoulder-blades," "proud backside jutting negligently at the angle of the weight-bearing hip," and "long legs" (134). Marisa's physical appearance has a powerful effect on Rosa:

> To touch in women's token embrace against the live, night cheek of Marisa, seeing huge for a second the lake-flash of her eye, the lilac-pink of her inner lip against transluscent-edged teeth, to enter for a moment the invisible magnetic field of the body of a beautiful creature and receive on oneself its imprint–breath misting and quickly fading on a glass pane–this was to immerse in another mode of perception. (134)

This kiss causes Rosa to speak of "a sensual redemption" into "a new brotherhood of flesh" (135). She connects the sensuality she feels in Marisa's presence with her earlier relationship with Baasie: "I felt it in Marisa's presence; the comfort of Baasie in the same bed when the dark made that house creak with threats" (135).

Unfortunately, as Leeuweberg goes on to note, Rosa cannot be like Marisa in the patriarchal white society of South Africa which insists (albeit at times subtly) on female passivity. There is, Rosa thinks, no *place* for a white woman like Marisa. Since she wishes to become a white woman like Marisa, this means that there is no *place* for her. Furthermore, political South Africa, even though Lionel is dead, is still the place it was while he lived. This political place is not Rosa's *place* either: it's too public. So, Rosa, seeking a private place where she can be assertively sensual, leaves South Africa for France. Her linking of political with public leads her to set aside politics—for the time being.

The second part of *Burger's Daughter* is the French interlude. There, Rosa explores her sensuality fully. Perhaps, Rosa seems to be thinking in this section, which (according to Margot Heinemann) is addressed to her father's first wife Katya, Rosa's lover Bernard, and Rosa herself, that France—Nice, in particular—can be her *place*. It certainly is a sensual place, for there she finds herself "[d]issolving in the wine and pleasure of scents, sights and sounds existing only in themselves, associated with nothing and nobody . . ." (222). The exterior space was "filled with the peppery-snuff scent of celery, weak sweet perfume of flowers and strawberries, cool salty secretions of sea-slippery fish, odours of cheeses, contracting the nasal membranes; the colours, shapes, shine, density, pattern, texture and feel of fruits and vegetables; the encounters and voices of people handling them" (244). A sensual feast! The interior space, the guestroom at Katya's villa, was "clear with different qualities of light," had "a long cane chair to read the poetry and elegant magazines in, a large low bed to bring a lover to," and was the perfect place for "[a] girl, a creature whose sense of existence would be in her nose buried in flowers, peach juice running down her chin, face tended at mirrors, mind dreamily diverted, body seeking pleasure" (229-30).

Bernard is a crucial figure in this second section of the novel: he alerts Rosa to pleasures and appetites that she never knew she had. As a result, it is clear, as Margot Heinemann suggests in *The Uses of Fiction* (1982), that she is very much *physically* in love with Bernard. Their initial lovemaking is described in terms that evoke Eden:

> They emerged for each other all at once: they had never seen each other on a beach. . . . He might never have been presented with a

> woman before, or she a man. Tremendous sweet possibilities of renewal surged between them; to explode in that familiar tender explosion all that has categorized sexuality, from chastity to taboo, illicit license to sexual freedom. In a drop of saliva there was a whole world. He turned the wet tip of his tongue round the whorl of the navel Didier had said was like that of an orange. (277-78)

And after that initial experience, there were many others. They yearned for the few times when they could forget the rest of the world and enjoy "the experience of being alone, a couple in the pure state," pure "because the night-and-day presence of the other, sensation and rhythm of breathing, smell, touch, voice, sight of, interpenetration with was total provision" and "becomes in itself one single unifying demand" (305).

And when he offers to set her up as his mistress in a stylish apartment in Paris, she finds the proposition very appealing. Perhaps this apartment can be her *place*.

I keep emphasizing "place" for a reason. As Lorraine Liscio has stressed in an article in *Modern Fiction Studies*, Gordimer precedes the novel *per se* with the following epigraph from Claude Levi-Strauss: "I am the place in which something has occurred." However, about halfway through the novel, Rosa talks about "A 'place'" as "somewhere to belong," as "something that establishes one's lot and sets aside much to which one doesn't belong" (149). This latter quotation suggests that Rosa is still looking for a literal place—a some*where*; a some*thing*, not realizing yet what Levi-Strauss' words suggest, that she *is* the place—by definition private and (especially now in France) sensual, but not yet political or ideological.

What completes her search is her encounter—in person and then by telephone—with her childhood playmate Baasie. Zwelinzima, as Baasie is now known, forces Rosa to see him (and, by extension, other blacks) as she really had never seen him before. As Clingman notes, Zwelinzima, by viciously attacking her father's legend and her comfortable liberalism, forces Rosa to see him as "other."

Zwelinzima had been offended earlier in the evening by the way people treated Rosa's father as noble (because he had gone to prison) and Rosa herself as noble (because her father had died in prison). Many black men, including his father, he reminds her, had gone to prison; and many blacks, including himself, had fathers who had died—had been murdered—in prison:

> There are dozens of our fathers sick and dying like dogs, kicked out of the locations where they can't work anymore. Getting old and dying in prison. Killed in prison. It's nothing. I know plenty blacks like Burger. It's nothing, it's us. . . . (320)

He had also been offended by Rosa's addressing him as "Baasie," "little boss," the unintentionally offensive nickname he had acquired in the Burger household, not the noble name his father had given him. This nickname encapsulated to Zwelinzima the shallowness of Burger's liberalism. He recalls his childhood in terms very unlike those used earlier by Rosa:

> . . . your parents took the little black kid into their home, not the backyard like other whites, right into the house. Eating at the table and sleeping in the bedroom, the same bed, their little black boss. And then the bastard was pushed off back to his mud huts and tin shanties. . . . One of Lionel Burger's best tame blacks sent scuttling like a bloody cockroach. . . . (320)

Seeing him this way—as someone patronized and then discarded by white liberalism—results in Rosa, for really the first time, seeing herself as white and all that entails. She realizes the truth in Zwelinzima's rhetorical question, "why do you think you should be different from all the other whites who've been shitting on us ever since they came?" (322) Her body literally revolts at the realization (which is reinforced for both of them when she first asks him if he wants money and then can't even pronounce his Xhosa name correctly):

> . . . she ran to the bathroom and fell to her knees at the lavatory bowl, vomiting. The wine, the bits of sausage—she laid her head, gasping between spasms, on the porcelain rim, slime dripping from her mouth with the tears of effort running from her nose. (323)

Shortly thereafter, she commits herself to doing whatever is necessary to obliterate the gap between black and white, between Zwelinzima and herself. The first step, she realizes, is to return to her native South Africa. There she lets her body, as Judie Newman has suggested in her 1988 *Nadine Gordimer*, reject the male genital-sexual definition of sensuality. Rose then replaces it with a more all-body-encompassing definition. Her body then leads her to work as a physiotherapist among black children. Poignantly, she notes that, after the Soweto massacre and riots, there are many black children in need of more than just physical therapy:

> In the second half of 1976 those who were born deformed were joined by those who had been shot. The school riots filled the hospital; the police who answered stones with machine-guns and patrolled Soweto firing revolvers at any street-corner group of people encountered, who raided High Schools and picked off the targets of youngsters escaping in the stampede, also wounded anyone else who happened to be within the random of their fire. (342)

In the hospital, she busied herself "[e]xtracting bullets from the matrix of flesh, picking out slivers of shattered bone, sewing, succouring, dripping back into arteries the vital fluids that flowed away in the streets with the liquor bottles smashed by children who despised their fathers' consolations . . . " (343). As she chooses this course of action, she also is choosing a political ideology. This ideology is not, however, one rooted in the abstract theorizing that occurred around her father's swimming pool but rather in the battered bodies of the black children of Soweto. As several commentators have noted, Rosa seems to be suggesting that, post-Soweto, her father's white liberalism is no longer going to be sufficient.

Once back in South Africa, it little matters where Rosa does her chosen work. The literal *place* is not important, for Rosa has found within herself a place that merges personal and political, private and public, body and mind, sensual and ideological. From this place, Rosa hopes that she can obliterate one more bipolar dualism, that between "white" and "other." Although Gordimer claims not to be a "feminist," she seems to suggest that the way to achieve this final dissolution is through the common bond as "other" shared with blacks by women.

Rosa, as she embraces *her* kind of political action in the novel's third and final section, proves to be her father's daughter, However, the course she has taken in the novel has led her to a kind of political action unlike her father's before her. That activism finally find her in prison. There, although physically separated from women of other colors, she finds ways through "tiny scrolled messages," through shared gifts, and through songs both religious and revolutionary, to unite the different groups:

> . . . the prison was so old that actual physical barriers against internal communication were ramshackle and the vigilance of the female warders . . . could not prevent messages, the small precious gifts of prison economy (cigarettes, a peach, a tube of hand-cream, a minute electric torch) from being exchanged between the races. Or songs. Early on, Marisa's penetrating, wobbly contralto announced her presence not far off, from her solitary confinement to Rosa's, and Clare's. She sang hymns, piously gliding in and out of the key of 'Abide with me' to ANC freedom songs in Xhosa, and occasionally bursting into Miriam Makeba's click song—this last to placate and seduce the wardresses, for whom it was a recognizable pop number. The voices of the other black women took up and harmonized whatever she sang, quickly following the changes in the repertoire. (355)

Marisa would later complain about a spinal ailment, and Rosa would be recruited to provide Marisa with twice weekly therapeutic massages. "Laughter escaped through the thick diamond-mesh and bars of Rosa's cell during these sessions" (355).

This prison *place* may seem to be the one Rosa finally finds, but its similarity to her father's last place should signal us that this literal place is a coincidence. Rosa *is* her own place, and, as Rosa Burger now, not Lionel Burger's daughter, she can address the novel's last section, where she *acts*, to her dead father. She is now acting on her own terms, acting as Rosa Burger, not Lionel Burger's daughter.

A Dry White Season

Rosa had to separate herself from her father's shadow in order to act; Benjamin Du Toit will have to separate himself from his entire family, from his entire Afrikaner people. He initially, however, is unaware of what the price of action will be.

Ben is slowly drawn into action. His black gardener, Gordon Ngubene, comes to Ben for help. Gordon's son had been arrested during the Soweto riots of June 1976. Gordon wants Ben to help him find out where his son is. When Ben discovers and tells Gordon that his son is dead, Gordon wants Ben to help him recover his son's body so that he may properly bury it. Refusing to accept the police's refusal to produce the body and believing that his son was *not* killed in the rioting but rather in police custody, Gordon begins making inquiries (to the extent a black man can). This investigating quickly lands him in prison, where he, under suspicious circumstances, dies.

Ben cannot rest until he finds out what happened to Gordon. Early on, he is fairly committed to this quest. After he sees Gordon's dead body and the marks of what the police did to Gordon while he was in custody, "[a] barely recognizable face, the left side distorted and discoloured, a blackish purple" (91), he becomes firmly–very firmly–committed:

> Now he had to believe it. Now he'd seen it with his own eyes. But it remained ungraspable. He had to force himself, even as he stood there looking down into the coffin, to accept that this was indeed Gordon. . . . (91)

Ben quickly discovers the costs of this commitment. He becomes the subject of police scrutiny. His home becomes the site of, first, security police searches and, later, security police counter-terrorist burglaries and bombings.

Ben is becoming an embarrassment to the Afrikaner community he has long been a complacent, trusting member of. His church turns on him, so he rejects it. His compatriots at the school where he teaches reject him and malign him because of his "politics." His wife and his married daughters turn on him. His wife eventually leaves; one of his daughters, Suzette, cozies up to her father in order to find out where he is hiding the documents he and other friends of Gordon had been gathering to use against the security police in a court of law. She then tells the police. When Ben catches on and uses his awareness of her unconfessed complicity to outwit the police and mail the documents to a college friend who is now a writer, the police get angry and even. They arrange Ben's murder.

The story thus far is dramatic but superficial. What makes Brink's *A Dry White Season* exceptional is its exploration of the pitfalls that a white liberal who commits to the black cause faces.

Ben—any white liberal—faces at least five dangers. First, he faces losses—losses that will be personally wrenching:

> I was forced to draw up a balance sheet in my mind. On the one side, all the bits and pieces we'd assembled so far. Not an unimpressive list by any means—at first glance. But then the debit side. Isn't the price becoming too high? I'm not thinking of what I have to go through, worried and harassed and hounded day by day. But the *others*. Especially the others. Because, at least partly, it is through my involvement that they have to suffer. (236)

Ben then lists the others:

> The cleaner: "disappeared".
>
> Dr. Hassiem: banished to Pietersburg. Julius Nqakula: in jail.
>
> The nurse: detained.
>
> Richard Harrison: sentenced to jail—even though he's going to appeal.
>
> And who else? Who is next? Are the names written on some secret list, ready to be ticked off as our time comes? (236)

Then, he asks himself an especially scary question: was he, Ben, responsible for what happened to Gordon Ngubene?

> I wanted to "clean up" Gordon's name, as Emily had put it. But all I've done so far is to plunge other people into the abyss. Including Gordon? It's like a nightmare, when I wake up at night, wondering in a sweat: Suppose I'd never tried to intercede for him after they'd detained him—would he have survived then? Am I the leper spreading disease to whoever comes close enough? (236)

Second, he faces excessive ego involvement, an involvement that leads to his acting, not for the sake of the oppressed, but rather for the personal glory he feels he will gain—in his eyes and in the eyes of a few others. Although *we* disagree with much that Ben's racist wife Susan says, we grant that there is some truth when she tells Ben that "all that matters to you is Ben Du Toit. For a long time now it's had nothing to do with Gordon or with Jonathan or anybody else" (261).

Third, he faces over-optimism: believing that he can right all wrong, reveal the truth, restore justice. He needs to learn the wisdom in a remark offered him by a friend: "'There are only two kinds of madness one should guard against Ben. . . . One is the belief that we can do everything. The other is the belief that we can do nothing" (244). Fourth, as this quoted advice suggests, he faces despair when he realizes that he cannot accomplish as much as he thought. This despair is exacerbated by the losses he has suffered.

Fifth and finally, he faces the fact that he is white and therefore privileged and, as a result, damned if he acts and damned if he doesn't act:

> Whether I like it or not, whether I feel like cursing my own condition or not–and that would only serve to confirm my impotence–*I am white.* This is the small, final, terrifying truth of my broken world. I am white. And because I'm white I am born into a state of privilege. Even if I fight the system that has reduced us to this I remain white, and favoured by the very circumstances I abhor. Even if I'm hated, and ostracised, and persecuted, and in the end destroyed, nothing can make me black. And so those who are cannot but remain suspicious of me. In their eyes my very efforts to identify myself with Gordon, with all the Gordons, would be obscene. Every gesture I make, every act I commit in my efforts to help them makes it more difficult for them to define their real needs and discover for themselves their integrity and affirm their own dignity. How else could we hope to arrive beyond predator and prey, helper and helped, white and black, and find redemption?
>
> On the other hand: what can I do but what I have done? I cannot choose not to intervene: that would be a denial and a mockery not only of everything I believe in, but of the hope that compassion may survive among men. By not acting as I did I would deny the very possibility of that gulf to be bridged.
>
> If I act, I cannot but lose. But if I do not act, it is a different kind of defeat, equally decisive and maybe worse. Because then I will not even have a conscience left. (304-05)

Ben faces these pitfalls throughout the bulk of the novel–especially in those sections that he narrates directly in the pages of his diary. To a large extent, he faces them alone. His son Johan provides moral support, but the rest of his family as well as his Afrikaner friends are certainly no help to Ben. He does, however, receive some help from a young journalist named Melanie Bruwer whom he meets at the inquest into Gordon Ngubene's death and from her father, a retired philosophy professor.

To overcome the first two pitfalls, Ben must put the personal aside. Melanie helps Ben do this by sharing with him how she has put the personal aside in her own work on behalf of the oppressed people of southern Africa. Melanie's story is a painful one for her to tell. She was once as idealistic and as naive as Ben is now. Then, on assignment in Mozambique, she was gang-raped by a platoon of black Frelimo soldiers: "One night on my way back to the hotel I was stopped by a group of drunken soldiers. . . . They dragged me off to an empty lot and raped me, the whole lot of them" (132).

Such a personal violation could easily have caused her to retreat from her very public life as an activist. It did not. Rather than flying home, she finished her newspaper assignment in Mozambique. Years later, she is able to "chuckle" (132) about it and to even claim the gang rape "even made things easier for [her]" in so far as it enabled her to "get out of myself. To free myself from my hangups" (133). She later explains what she means by getting out of herself when she differentiates between her body and her self. Before she was raped, the two were intertwined; now, she realizes that she is not her body and that, therefore, what happens to her body does not happen to *her*. Personal hardships, losses, and vile indignities are relevant to her body, but not to *her*. She can continue on with her important political work. Ben similarly must realize that the personal hardships, etc., that he suffers are relevant to the material Ben but not the moral-spiritual Ben. That latter Ben, the *real* Ben, can continue on with his important political work. If Melanie Bruwer can put aside what she had suffered, Ben can certainly put aside what he has.

Later, Melanie talks more about her personal losses—in particular her quickly approaching loss, as a thirty year-old woman, of the potential to bear children. She tells Ben, "This country doesn't allow me to indulge myself like that. It isn't possible to lead a private life if you want to live with your conscience" (246). Not only can she and Ben cast aside the personal, they *must*, given the situation in South Africa.

Events take care of over-optimism, the third pitfall. The fourth and the fifth are more troublesome. To overcome them, Ben must keep foremost in his mind the flesh-and-blood realities that abstractions and systems and even words can mute. Melanie and her father, in very different ways, help Ben focus on flesh-and-blood. This focus gets Ben past despair and past the dilemma he faces as a privileged white South African.

Professor Phil Bruwer, when we first meet him, is working in the earth of his garden. Both the scene and the earthy condition of his attire suggest his attachment to the natural:

> At first sight I took him for a Coloured gardener, squatting on his haunches beside a flower bed, pulling out weeds. Soiled corduroy trousers, black beret sporting a guinea-fowl feather, khaki shirt, pipe in his mouth, and the filthiest pair of mud-caked shoes—worn without socks or laces—I'd ever seen. . . .
>
> His wild white mane couldn't have been combed in months. Small goatee stained with tobacco juice. The skin of his face dark and tanned like old leather, like an old discarded shoe; and two twinkling dark brown eyes half-disappearing below the unkempt eyebrows. . . .
>
> He grinned, exposing his uneven, yellow-stained teeth, many of them mere stumps. (185-86)

Ben and Professor Bruwer begin talking history teacher to philosophy professor, but, as soon as the discussion drifts into abstractions away from the natural, the earthy, the physical, Professor Bruwer launches into a lecture indicting abstractions. He prefaces it by talking about how "the more one gets involved in philosophy and stuff, in transcendental things, the more surely you're forced back to the earth" (186). Then, he talks about how the twentieth century is "living in the spell of the Abstract. Hitler, Apartheid, the Great American Dream, the lot" (186). The abstract leads some people to commit inhuman actions and other people to ignore inhuman actions. He saw it in the '30s when he was in Nazi Germany; he is seeing it now in apartheid South Africa.

The way to overcome the evil that abstractions lead to—"[t]his sickness of the Great Abstraction" (187)—is "to come back to the physical, to flesh and bone and earth" (187). "We're running after the *verbum*, forgetting about the flesh" (187), he tells Ben.

Once you've refocused on the flesh and blood, then it becomes impossible to tolerate the oppression of human beings that *is* South Africa under apartheid. The lesson Professor Bruwer offers then is really an extension of what Ben learned when he went to Soweto (for the first time in his life) to see Gordon's battered corpse. When you see the human flesh-and-blood reality of oppression, you know you must act, even if you also know how very little your actions can accomplish.

Ben requires more than just Professor Bruwer's eloquent words. He needs contact with flesh-and-blood as well as a lecture about it. Melanie decides to provide this flesh-and-blood contact by making love with Ben. How Brink presents their love-making is important. He emphasizes Ben's desperate state in the way he has Ben narrate the event; Ben uses and then rejects various *words* in trying to explain things. Words, it seems, are inadequate to explain what is very much a matter of the body. And it is Melanie's body—and her gift of it to Ben—that Ben ends up emphasizing:

> The candour of her body. Her presence was total, and overwhelming. I feel quite ridiculous trying to grasp it now with nothing but words. How paltry it sounds, almost offensive, reduced to description. But what else can I do? Silence would be denial.
>
> Her hair undone, loose and heavy on her shoulders. Her breasts so incredibly small, mere swellings, with dark, elongated, erect nipples. The smooth belly with the exquisite little knot in its hollow. Below, the trim triangular thicket of black hair between her legs.
>
> But it is not that. Nothing I can ennumerate or adequately name. What mattered was that in her nakedness she was making herself available to me. The incomprehensible gift of herself. (272)

Ben continues, delighting in the physical reality of Melanie's body in print as he delighted in it that night. He celebrates "[t]he full frank miracle of her body," "the unbelievable reality of her body," "the marvel and mystery of the flesh" (273). Like a priestess in a ritual of the flesh and blood, she leads him through an experience he describes as "[a] newness, as of birth" (272). In a sense then, Melanie is leading Ben to the rebirth within him of a necessary awareness of (in her father's words) "flesh and bone and earth" (187).

Unfortunately, Melanie and Ben's lovemaking, although it may help Ben maintain the necessary contact with flesh-and-blood and remain a revolutionary actor, leads to the final collapse of his personal Afrikaner world. The security police, spying on Ben and Melanie, take pictures of the couple having intercourse and send these picture to Ben's employer and Ben's wife. Work and family (except Ben's young son) turn on poor Ben DuToit. He does not, however, react as he might have earlier. Helped by Melanie to overcome the pitfalls of pride and despair, he accepts his losses and pursues his revolutionary action with undiminished determination.

Ben Du Toit ultimately fails in so far as he is killed. His failure to succeed does not, however, diminish the fact that he acted *and* he managed to reveal the truth to a wide public. Here, we need to discuss the manner in which the novel is narrated. We begin and end *A Dry White Season* with the voice of Ben's college roommate. We learn a great deal about this man: primarily, we learn that he has very complacently accepted his lot as a white South African. He clearly has literary talent, but, thus far, he has put it to little serious use. He has spent "half a lifetime devoted to writing romantic fiction" (9) and thereby achieved some fame—enough to be bothered by members of the public who want him to write their story and flattered by members of the opposite sex who want their (to borrow from Kenyan writer Ngugi wa Th'iongo) "moments of glory" in his bed. But, at the moment Ben reestablishes contact with him after a hiatus of several years, he is experiencing a creative drought, a "dry white season." As he faces the pile of papers, newspaper clippings, and photographs Ben posted to him days before Ben was killed, this writer finds his energy returning.

This unnamed writer (perhaps Brink's semi-satiric version of himself) manages to assemble and tell, from the third person point of view, Ben Du Toit's story. The pace quickens. Eventually, it seems as if this narrator no longer feels he has the leisure to assemble Ben's story, so he shifts from third person narration to the first person narration of Ben's journal. This shift also suggests that he has found the objective stance impossible to sustain and now must merge his voice with Ben's voice. Ben has, posthumously, converted his friend to the cause.

When the writer's voice returns at the novel's end, he is clearly changed. He is feeling some of the same feelings that

Ben felt—that he is being drawn into the swirling vortex of oppression just as Ben was; that he must do something, but he can't do much:

> Is everything really beginning anew with me? And if so: how far to go? . . . Is it really just a matter of going on, purely and simply? Prodded, possibly, by some dull, guilty feeling of responsibility towards something Ben might have believed in: something man is capable of being but which he isn't very often allowed to be?
>
> I don't know.
>
> Perhaps all one can really hope for, all I am entitled to, is no more than this: to write it down. To report what I know. So that it will not be possible for any man ever to say again: *I knew nothing about it.* (315-16)

The writer does, however, succeed in accomplishing two tasks. First, he gets the story out; second, he draws us, the readers, into that same swirling vortex.

As I've already suggested, the novel's title is relevant to the narrator's situation. But, of course, its relevance goes beyond that. Brink borrows the title from Mongane Wally Serote's poem "For Don M.—Banned," in which Serote links "a dry white season" to the pain of a time in the course of revolutionary action when nothing, either constructive nor destructive, seems to be happening. Brink, however, has Ben explain the novel's title in the agrarian terms of the Afrikaner as "[t]he drought that took everything from [Pa and me], leaving us alone and scorched among the white skeletons." Ben refers to that time when, as a young boy, he saw all the sheep die as a defining point in his life. Now, he says, "it seems to me I'm finding myself on the edge of yet another dry white season, perhaps worse than the one I knew as a child" (163).

Brink is suggesting that South Africa is now facing a dry white season, the word "white" serving as a wicked pun. The season suggests a kind of death. Ben, before facing his literal death, avoids a moral one—by acting. Similarly, the unnamed writer avoids a kind of death by acting. If we are pulled into the novel, we also—Brink hopes—can avoid a moral death by first knowing and then acting. Serote tells us that "seasons come to pass," suggesting that the dry white season *will* yield to another season. It could be bloody; it could be peaceful. Brink himself offers much the same suggestion in his earlier novel *Rumours of Rain*, in which we are never sure whether the rumored change in weather will be violently destructive or nourishing. Brink seems to hope that, through action on the part of the nation's white population, the more peaceful alternative will prove to be the future.

In the next section of this survey, we address the question of that future more explicitly. As we will see, some works of contemporary South African literature in English share Brink's hope; others, however, offer a much bleaker view of the future.

Works Cited

Brink, Andre. *A Dry White Season*. 1979; rpt. New York: Penguin, 1984.

Clingman, Stephen. *The Novels of Nadine Gordimer: History from the Inside*. London: Allen & Unwin, 1986.

Gordimer, Nadine. *Burger's Daughter*. 1979; rpt. New York: Penguin Books, 1980.

Heinemann, Margot. "*Burger's Daughter*: The Synthesis of Revelation." In Douglas Jefferson and Graham Martin, eds. *The Uses of Fiction*. Milton Keynes, England: Open UP, 1982. 181-97.

Leeuwenberg, Rina. "Nadine Gordimer's *Burger's Daughter*: Why Does Rosa Go Back?" *New Literature Review* 14 (1985): 23-31.

Liscio, Lorraine. "*Burger's Daughter*: Lighting a Torch in the Heart of Darkness." *Modern Fiction Studies* 33 (1987): 245-61.

Newman, Judie. *Nadine Gordimer*. London: Routledge, 1988.

Smyer, Richard I. "Africa in the Fiction of Nadine Gordimer." *ARIEL* 16.2 (1985): 15-29.

PART IV

The Freeway

10

The Nightmare

Nadine Gordimer's short story "The Lion on the Freeway" tells us that the lion, symbolic of black South Africans, *is* on the freeway. Note the present tense. Also note both the pun in "freeway"—the way to freedom—and how the lion is depicted as appropriating a symbolic element of the white man's "making" of South Africa, the transportation infrastructure that, among other things, marks South Africa as a land that is developed, modern, "Western." The word "freeway" then suggests two interrelated questions: first, how will the blacks achieve their freedom; second, what will their appropriation of the modern, developed, "Western" nation mean.

The first question is one of peace and war; the second question is a more complex social and economic one. Thus far, South Africa's writers have chosen to focus mainly on the first. In this chapter, we examine two contemporary works that suggest that violence will be necessary as the lion walks the freeway. These two works, J. M. Coetzee's *In the Heart of the Country* (1976) and Nadine Gordimer's *July's People* (1981) present that violent future in nightmarish terms.

In the Heart of the Country

J. M. Coetzee's 1976 novel is more clearly tied to South Africa than his later *Waiting for the Barbarians,* which was discussed in Chapter Eight. We know we are dealing with a rural district of South Africa, the territory that is central in the agrarian Afrikaner mythology that Coetzee's novel, as Sheila Roberts has noted, destroys. In keeping with this pastoral myth, we are dealing with an Afrikaner "Oom" with patriarchal authority over daughter and non-white servants. This patriarchal authority plus the puritanical disposition of the typical Afrikaner community very much creates for us a suppressed and repressed daughter in Magda. She is our narrator: what we're given are her diary entries. By using this mode of narration, Coetzee enriches the novel considerably. First, the journey we take into her mind takes us beyond South Africa *per se* and transforms a localized political novel into a work that treats, more generally, the situation of women within the patriarchy and the situation of an oppressed people within a "colonial" system. Second, the evidence that we have, throughout, that Magda is insane problematizes the story as, in any sense, "real" and causes us to consider the possibility that the events the novel presents are less a prediction of South Africa's political future and more an exploration of the wishes and fears that characterize the warped white South African psyche. Put in other words, the mode of narration may cause us to shift the novel from the category of predictions about the future for apartheid South Africa to the category of pathological studies of apartheid South Africa. Believing that the novel can be both, we will explore the first reading and then, later in the chapter, the second reading. But before we examine either of these localized readings, we need to discuss briefly the readings that transcend South Africa so as not to sell the novel short.

Magda defines herself for us as a writer. She is, however, a struggling writer. We see her struggling with words; we also see her struggling with larger units of composition. For example, early in the novel, she offers us several versions of her murder of her father. *If* the event does really occur, then she is struggling with all the language choices she must make in transforming it from act to verbal artifact. For another example, much later in the novel, she offers us three versions of her rape by her father's non-black servant Hendrik. Again, *if* the event does really occur (is not just a projection of her insanity), she is again struggling with language as she tries to transform act to artifact. Besides giving us multiple versions of events that we are led to believe have happened, Magda gives us multiple versions of events she envisions. For example, after Hendrik and his young wife Anna leave the farm, Magda envisions four versions of what will happen next. In the first, Hendrik, the suspected murderer of Magda's father, is shot. Magda narrates this version but then adds, "[b]ut perhaps they did not shoot them out of hand. Perhaps, having tracked them down, they took them in, tied like beasts, to some far-off place of justice and condemned them to break stones for the rest of their lives to pay for their crimes and the crazed vindictive stories they told" (122). After telling this version, Magda adds, "[o]r perhaps, they did indeed bring Hendrik back to the farm, to confront me, and I have forgotten. Perhaps they all came, the magistrate, the clerks, the bailiffs, the curious from miles around, and marched Hendrik up to me chained at wrist and ankle, and said 'Is this the man?' and waited for my answer" (122). And then, after telling this third version, she adds, "[o]r perhaps I have been mistaken all the time, perhaps my father is not dead after all, but tonight at dusk will come riding out of the hills on the lost horse, and stamp into the house, growling because his bath is not ready, bursting open the locked doors, sniffing at the strange smells" (122). This last version's possibility, of course, undermines much of Magda's narrative.

Magda seems aware of her struggle with words; however, she may not be aware of the extent to which she is trapped within a language not her own. As Josephine Dodd has brilliantly noted, Magda often falls into passages which suggest the classics of English literature and thereby presents relations as those relations are defined by the patriarchy. In so far as the novel reveals this imprisonment within patriarchal definitions, it becomes an account of an everywoman forced to work in forms and in a language defined for her by men, forms and language that privilege these men and disempower her and other women. Read this way, the novel becomes a provocative look at a woman trying to write against the patriarchy and failing, with madness being the result of this failure. The novel joins Jean Rhys' *Wide Sargasso Sea* (1964) in deconstructing a character the patriarchy would label insane and reinscribing her in such a way that we understand how the patriarchy itself is responsible for that insanity.

Coetzee's novel also reflects the alliance that is often found in African literature between the entrapment of women within the patriarchy and that of blacks within colonialism (and neocolonialism). As Magda is trapped, so are the black servants Hendrik and Anna. We do not see them struggling with language; we do, however, see them struggling with symbolic actions. For example, we have Hendrik's sexual exploitation of Magda, but we do not know what this action means for him—revenge against his former white masters; revenge against his adulterous wife; payment for farm work rendered. He fails to communicate the meaning clearly to Magda. In fact, throughout their sexual relationship, he is very silent, refusing to answer Magda's desperate questions, "'Am I doing it right, Hendrik?'" (110) and "'Are you happy, Hendrik? Do I make you feel happy?'" (111). When these actions either fail to communicate or start to imprison Hendrik, he flees. But of course, all that we see of him (and his wife Anna) is through the language Magda tries to use. Perhaps, the patriarchal language is so much a *white* patriarchal language that Magda must figure these two characters, their relationship with each other, and their relationship to her in a language that is so tied to hierarchies and bipolarities that she cannot represent anything connected with Hendrik and Anna without the language betraying her into racism. Magda is perhaps vaguely aware of the language gap separating her and the non-white characters:

> Hendrik, I cannot speak to you, but I wish you well, you and Anna both, I wish you the cunning of the jackal, I wish you better luck than your hunters. And if one night you come tapping at the window I will not be surprised. You can sleep here all day, at night you can walk about in the moonlight saying to yourself whatever it is that men say to themselves on a piece of earth that is their own. I will cook your meals, I will even, if you like, try again to be your second woman, it is surely not beyond me if I put my mind to it, all things must be possible on the island out of space, out of time. You can bring your cubs with you; I will guard them by day and take them out to play at night. Their large eyes will glow, they will see things invisible to other folk; and in the daytime when the eye of heaven glowers and pierces every shadow we can lie together in the cool dark of the earth, you and I and Anna and they. (123)

Her initial remark about not being able to speak to Hendrik is literally true: he has left. However, it may reveal more. Certainly, her comment about "whatever it is that men say to themselves on a piece of earth that is their own" suggests her awareness of words that are not hers to understand. Similarly, her suggestion that she "try again" to be his "second wife" suggests her awareness of a culture that is not her own. Once the land is *his*, then, with a new language will come a new culture, one that she will desperately try to fit into. *But*, to the extent that she figures this new culture as an "island out of space, out of time," she defines herself as Ariel and Hendrik as Caliban. Prospero may be gone, but the new culture she creates for Hendrik and herself (and Anna) to inhabit is *still* defined in the terms of the Western literature she falls unwittingly into so often in garnering the language and the forms she uses.

Reading *In the Heart of the Country* in these feminist or postcolonial ways takes us away from South Africa, except in so far as South Africa participates in or represents an extreme case of patriarchal, colonial oppression. These readings are important and give Coetzee's novel much of its compelling power. However, the novel is equally compelling if we put aside the poststructuralist concern with language and forms and consider *In the Heart of the Country* as either an allegorical prediction of what awaits the South African nation or a symbolic picture of what infects the Afrikaner soul.

The plot of the novel, stated simply, begins with Magda's patricide. Infuriated by her father's hypocritical, disolute behavior as well as by his exploitation of the black servants on the disintegrating farm, she kills him. It is his rape of his servant Hendrik's new bride, Anna, whom he views as *his* property just as Hendrik is *his* property, that seems to push her from hatred to homicide. The father then represents the white South Africans who institutionalized racism in apartheid; Magda the new generation of white South Africans who reject that system; Hendrik and Anna the non-white (they are colored) victims of that system.

Like Rosa Burger in Gordimer's *Burger's Daughter* and Ben Du Toit in Brink's *A Dry White Season*, Magda realizes that simply rejecting apartheid is not enough. She believes, as they do, that she must do more because, to the extent she was privileged by the system, she was herself a victimizer of the non-whites. Rosa Burger chooses service and solidarity; Ben Du Toit chooses to continue acting, even if so doing is in so many senses futile. Magda chooses a different course: she decides to expiate the sins of her father (of the white South African fathers) by changing places with the servants. She will become the victim.

Committed to her own victimization, she allows Hendrik to rape her. Then, she allows him to use her sexually repeatedly over a period of months. She feels no pleasure; what she feels is humiliation:

> He turns me on my face and does it to me from behind like an animal. Everything dies in me when I have to raise my ugly rear to him. I am humiliated; sometimes I think it is my humiliation he wants. (112)

As this passage reveals, she is ashamed of her body, finding it old, foul, unresponsive, and ugly. She notes early in the novel that,

> Even decades of mutton and pumpkin and potatoes have failed to coax from me the jowls, the bust, the hips of a true country foodwife, have achieved no more than to send my meagre buttocks sagging down the backs of my legs. (21)

Later, while involved with Hendrik, she says,

> I am eating badly, growing even scrawnier, if that is possible. I suffer from rashes about the neck. I have no beauty to lure him on with. Perhaps that is why he will not allow a candle, perhaps he thinks he would be put off by the sight of me. . . . He stays with me more and more briefly, sometimes only for the minute it takes him to release himself inside me. He does not take off his shirt. I am too dry for this kind of activity. I have begun with it too late in life, streams that should be running dried up long ago. I try to moisten myself when I hear him at the door, but it does not always work. I cannot honestly see why he leaves his wife's bed for mine. Sometimes the fishy smell of her comes to my nostrils when he undresses. I am sure they make love every night. (111-12)

Her hatred for her body, as well as her lack of comfort with it, is apparent in this passage. Exposing this body to Hendrik is part of the humiliation she seems to seek. Being second to Anna in every sense is another. What he does to her sexually—the intercourse that gives her no pleasure, the cunnilingus that she finds disgusting, and the animal-like position he sometimes puts her in that (she feels) degrades her are still other parts.

She not only feels no pleasure (only humiliation and disgust), but feels none of her guilt departing from within her. Her act, as a ritual of expiation for the sins of her father, is not succeeding. And that's the ultimate humiliation—to allow one's self to be so humiliated *for nought*.

Expiation is not—it seems—Magda's only goal in allowing herself to be the victim. She felt that, if she reversed roles with the black servants, some genuine communication and connection with them would eventually develop. She tries to develop a relationship with them, but they shun her. They see her as either victimizer or victim, not as a fellow human being. As victimizer, Magda was to be tolerated; as victim, she is to be used—until useless.

Magda becomes useless to Hendrik and Anna when three events coincide. First, Hendrik, who turns to Magda sexually for reasons we're never sure of (revenge against whites, revenge against his wife [for sleeping with Magda's father], payment for his farm work), begins to feel she is so pitiful as to no longer be an object that can inspire hatred or, even in the dark, desire. As hatred and desire turn to disgust, Hendrik is no longer interested in playing a role in her ritualistic humiliation. Second, the food and other supplies (and the money to pay for them) they had access to by staying on at the farm begin to run out. And it looks to Hendrik and Anna (accurately) as if Magda has no access to any additional food or money. Third, Magda begins acting like the madwoman she has already been for a while. Her bizarre behavior frightens them. What will the madwoman do next, they wonder. Not wanting to find out, they leave.

They leave her alone. Alone, she begins engaging in activities that clearly show she's on the edge. She starts hearing voices from above. She begins trying to communicate—in a kind of Spanish—to airplanes passing far overhead (the imagined source of the voices) by arranging stones shaped like pumpkins into words.

This is a scary story of an individual's descent into madness. Interpreted in South African political terms, it is also a scary story. Magda tries, like many "new generation" whites, to right past wrongs. Disgust and guilt lead them to bring down the order their fathers had established–to kill it. Given how much blacks have suffered in the past, these whites are willing–perhaps, inspired by guilt, more than willing–to suffer now. "Redistribution of wealth," the phrase around which so much of the South African future today hinges, could mean not only new government spending patterns that favor the non-white majority, but almost-punitive taxes on white wealth and the confiscation of some white assets. All of this and more will be assented to by these guilty "new generation" whites to expiate their collective guilt. And if the future non-white majority government feels it must in some ways humiliate the former white masters, then so be it.

Unfortunately, reversing the victim-victimizer relationship will work no better in this case than in the case of Madga and Hendrik and Anna. Non-white hatred will fade into disgust, and, as the wealth that can be seized diminishes and whites become increasingly distraught, the non-whites will simply cast their former white victimizers aside and, since the spoils are exhausted, move on themselves, leaving South Africa a wasteland. There will be no new relationship between the races featuring communication or connection; there will be no multicultural nation.

White South Africa will then be left in a state much like Magda's at the end of Coetzee's novel. White South Africa may, insanely, try to resurrect the ways of the fathers, or white South Africa may try to reach other "Europeans"–asking for help or understanding. The "Europeans" will be as far away as the passengers on the airplanes Magda tries to signal, and white South Africa's cries will prove as futile and as silly as Magda's pumpkin stone-writing.

The vision of the future that Coetzee offers in *In the Heart of the Country* is nightmarish. If one chooses to assume that the events of the novel did not happen but are rather Magda's necessary fictions, the picture is equally nightmarish. Magda, representing the sons and daughters of the white South Africans who say they built the country and did build apartheid, is trapped in a bizarre love-hate relationship with her father, who of course represents that older generation. Her sexual jealousy when he brings home a new bride suggests a love that is warped because the puritanical codes of the nation have prevented her from developing a mature, healthful sexuality. Joan Gillmer in an article in *Momentum* discusses the incestuous undercurrent in the novel fully. Put very simply, Magda is, upon her mother's death, assigned the wife's role. She, largely unconsciously, desires the sexual part of this role. When her father remarries or beds his servant's bride, Magda feels that, in so far as these women have been intimate with her father, they have and he has demoted her from surrogate wife to housemaid. She thus dislikes them and hates him. Her desire to murder him and the repeated act of murder suggest the hatred.

The way Magda envisions the new relationship with Hendrik and Anna suggests additional ways in which she is disturbed. She feels guilty; she seeks victimization, humiliation. She detests the physical–her body, any body. She desperately desires to communicate–thus her journal–but she does not know how to. She uses sex to attempt to communicate with Hendrik, but to no avail. She uses stones shaped like pumpkins to spell out words in Spanish to airplanes far overhead, but to no avail.

What then has white South Africa wrought? At the same time it has oppressed and angered its non-white population and alienated itself from most of the rest of the world, it has given birth to sons and daughters of privilege who perversely love and violently hate their parents' ways, who are guilt-ridden and desire (deep down inside) to be victimized, humiliated, used, who detest the physical, and who cannot successfully communicate. To the extent that this psychopathology of the new generation of white South Africans rings true, there would seem to be little hope for a happy future for the nation.

These two readings, the novel as political prediction and the novel as psychological portrait, work together. If you believe Magda invents the events of the novel but still see her as a representative figure, then her psychopathology, shared by those she is representative of, would lead to a scenario much like those in the novel. So if the events are the product of Magda's mind, the fact that she has a mind that needs to create those events suggests that the events–or ones much like them–are likely to occur. Both of these "allegorical" readings are also compatible with the broader interpretation of the novel as an indictment of patriarchy and colonialism, for patriarchy and colonialism figured greatly in the creation of the psychological portrait and the political prediction. Coetzee thus offers us a novel that can be read compatibly by post-structuralist and more traditional critics. In fact, part of the beauty of *In the Heart of the Country* is that it addresses the questions of language and forms–and the connected power–that matter in much post-structuralist discourse without abandoning what many readers feel is the artist's obligation to say something important about the here-and-now. Perhaps Coetzee's failure to abandon what used to be called "reality" is an indication of how morally compelling, in South Africa, that reality is.

July's People

Nadine Gordimer often talks about how morally compelling the South African situation is–about how this situation made her a political writer almost against her will. And, in *July's People*, she achieves the same balance between the new and the old in literary art as Coetzee. Her novel raises questions about language and power, but it also presents *a* future for South Africa that is doubly frightening. It is frightening because, first, it involves a descent into chaos and, second, just when a new, better order seems possible, that new order is dashed.

July's People is the story of a wealthy, liberal white couple, Bam and Maureen Smales. They are living in their comfortable suburb of Johannesburg when civil war breaks out in South Africa. Although details are sketchy, it seems as if rampaging blacks are attacking white businesses, white homes, and whites throughout the Witwatersrand. Fearing for their lives, whites were fleeing–to wherever safety might be found. The Smales' loyal black servant, a man known to them as July, took the Smales and their children under his protection. With him, they returned to his homeland, probably Venda in the northern Transvaal.

There, Bam and Maureen and their children try to adjust to very new circumstances. They handle the task in different ways, with different degrees of success.

The least successful is Bam. He initially strikes us as very attached to his property. We gradually discover that this attachment is because his identity and, in particular, his identity as a male is tied to this property. Thus, he finds himself engaged in a power struggle with July over control of "his" car and, late in the novel, with another black named Daniel over "his" gun. July is not trying to disempower Bam; rather, July is trying to achieve some status in the homeland by flaunting the jeep-like baakie, which he now, in a sense, "has." Daniel is also not trying to disempower Bam; rather, he wants to join the Azanian forces trying to free oppressed blacks in South Africa and thinks he should join the army already armed. The result of July and Daniel's seizure of Bam's "things" does, however, disempower Bam, turning him into a "man who had nothing, now" (145). Bam's disempowerment is figured in his becoming sexually impotent. Connected to both Bam's self-definition through his "things" and his impotence is what seems at times to be emerging as competition between Bam and July for Maureen, another of Bam's "things." Although this competition stays beneath the surface, one might suggest that, in his mind, Bam has already lost. His inability to have sexual relations with Maureen (to put his "thing" to its proper use) suggests that he has already lost it. It is furthermore significant that, when the gun is stolen, it is Maureen, not Bam, who confronts July about its disappearance; Bam, a broken man, just crawls into bed, face down, and perhaps cries.

Some of what I have just said, referring to Maureen as a "thing," may well have offended some. What I was doing in the preceding paragraph is representing Maureen as Bam sees her: the sexism and the materialism then is part of Bam's being. And in so portraying Bam, Gordimer is offering a negative judgment on many white South African males. Gordimer fairly consistently treats her female characters as being open through their physicality and sexuality to "Africa." Since, as Richard I. Smyer notes in *ARIEL,* women's openness is a threat to the patriarchy, Bam and other South African males respond to it by treating women, increasingly, as possessions. If Bam had been less possessive of all of his "things," he might have handled the transition to life in Venda more successfully. As it is, he's a failure, and, curiously, the novel, as it moves toward its conclusion, pays less and less attention to Bam. In fact, the novel pays progressively more attention to Maureen. This shift in focus occurs, I would suggest, because Maureen comes *close* to adjusting successfully.

What makes the difference is only partially her being not so attached to material possessions as Bam. She seems much more aware, as both John Cooke in *The Novels of Nadine Gordimer* (1985) and Stephen Clingman in *The Novels of Nadine Gordimer* (1986) suggest, of the language problems she is having: she becomes aware that she doesn't know the language because she doesn't know the culture it grows out; she becomes aware that her language (and some of the loaded terms in it such as "boy" and "master"), no matter how she intends to use it, is a language of oppression to the villagers. What also plays a major role in her near-success is her ability to redefine her being in new terms, terms that recognize–are tied to–the body. One might suggest that as a woman, she had never renounced her body as completely as Bam had. The bodily experiences of sexual intercourse, childbirth, and menstruation kept her in touch with her physical being. This measure of bodily awareness led Maureen forward: she stopped being as embarrassed, as other white people, by their bodily smells and functions; she began relying more and more on body language to communicate. Some of her use of body language–for example, her flirtatious, seductive use of her body to sway July–is unsuccessful because it is not use of the body *per se*, but use of the body in the enculturated manner of the village that she must learn. By examining her attempts at non-verbal communication with July, one can see her failing as often as succeeding. Some of the failures give the text an inter-racial sexual dimension that has not escaped notice. Several commentators (Christopher Heywood; Rowland Smith; Dorothy Driver) have noted the sexual suggestions in the Maureen-Bam relationship; one–Susan M. Greenstein writing in *Novel*, has closely examined the sexual dimension within the larger context of communication between the two and the verbal and non-verbal miscues that characterize and problematize it. Her examination quite properly deflects attention from the issue of inter-racial sex (which is peripheral, at best, in the novel) and toward the problems of using the body to communicate in an alien culture.

Maureen's heightened awareness of and comfort with her body could well have led Maureen to the point where she was not only able to communicate but able to fit in with the villagers. This potential is suggested in the scene in which she joins the women at work immersed to their knees in the village's muddy fields:

> The women hitched up their skirts in vleis and their feet spread, ooze coming up between the toes, like the claws of marsh-birds; walking on firm ground, the coating of mud dried matt in the sun and shod them to mid-calf. She [Maureen] rolled her jeans high, yellow bruises and fine, purple-red ruptured blood-vessels of her thighs, blue varicose ropes behind her knees, coarse hair of her calves against the white skin showed as if she had somehow forgotten her thirty-nine years and scars of child-bearing and got into the brief shorts worn by the adolescent dancer on mine property. . . . Why should the white woman be ashamed to be seen in her weaknesses, blemishes, as she saw the other women's? (92)

Her so doing not only signaled her willingness to abandon the aloof sanitized, deodorized white culture and plunge her body into the earthy water but her willingness to join in the community of village women on equal terms.

July's People ends up focused on Maureen. Her success or her failure becomes very much *the* story—until it is rudely interrupted. Before I turn to that interruption, I should note that Maureen is not the most successful adapter in the Smales family. The most successful adapters, as Jennifer Gordon notes in *African Literature Today*, are the children. After an initial, short-lived period of disorientation, they jump right into village life, which for them meant village play. How Gordimer describes their new life-style is instructive. They quickly abandoned most of their clothes; they learned how to wipe their bottoms using stones. What is clear is that the white children do not yet have either the materialism or the lack of comfort with the bodily and the earthy that characterize their parents. They learn the appropriate body language quickly; they learn the appropriate African words quickly. They are very much what Maureen was on the verge on becoming—natural, communicative. Maureen

Smale's transformation is interrupted by a passage that reader after reader has found puzzling. Suddenly, there appears in the sky a helicopter. According to most readers, it is a mystery to whom the helicopter belongs:

> The sound is not the fairly familiar one of a troop carrier or reconnaissance plane passing. . . . The chuddering grows behind it [a cloud], her eyes try to follow her ears. A racket of blows that shakes the sky circles and comes down at her head. . . . A high ringing is produced in her ears, her body in its rib-cage is thudded with deafening vibration, invaded by a force pumping, jigging in its monstrous orgasm—the helicopter has sprung through the hot brilliant cloud just above them all, its landing gear like spread legs, battling the air with whirling scythes. (158)

The helicopter might be an indication that white South Africa is on the offensive, reestablishing control over black areas; it might be an indication that nearby black African nations, such as Mozambique, have entered the war on behalf of the blacks and have sent their aircraft in. It might be a Cuban helicopter or an American helicopter. It could be from the U.K. or the U.N. The villagers run around in confusion while Maureen runs toward it, and, in confusion, the novel ends.

Amazingly, only a few readers—for example, Judie Newman in *Nadine Gordimer* (1988)—have paid close attention to the language Gordimer uses to describe the helicopter. It is described in male sexual terms. And, in the novel's terms, this male orientation is very much associated with the white South African world represented best in the novel by Bam. A female orientation is more of the body and of the earth and is associated with the black villagers. Read symbolically then, the helicopter is not only reasserting the male white South African power but it is raping the villagers and Maureen. This reading is reinforced in the very next paragraph when Maureen is said to be "[u]nder its belly, under the beating wings of its noise" (158) This allusion to Yeats' "Leda and the Swan" is to another violent rape.

This reassertion of white, male power and this violent assault occur at the very moment when Maureen seems to be on the brink of a breakthrough, a breakthrough that is not just for her but is, symbolically, for all white women *if* they will recognize they are flesh and blood—bodies that eat and defecate, procreate and give birth, and eventually join the earth that feeds them. There is a great deal of potential in the common ground that Maureen and the village women find. And, maybe, men can reach this common ground as well. But the helicopter's sudden appearance shatters the potential. The image that replaces Maureen and the village women in the earthy water working together as equals is the image of the technological thing—technology being, as Paul Rich suggests, engendered in Western civilization as masculine—thudding, bamming, raping from the sky.

Maureen runs after the helicopter—the words "running" and "run" are repeated several times in the novel's long last paragraph. She runs *through* water that is "tepid and brown and smells strongly of earth" (159-60), suggestive of the rebirth into the natural that was almost hers. She runs *past* the fig tree that is rooted in this water—perhaps, in so far as a fig tree symbolizes Christ, another suggestion of the redemption she's rejecting. She runs through what now seems like an imaginative landscape—farmland yielding to houses with kitchens yielding to "the artful nature of a public park" (160). And as she moves *toward* the "unnatural," "[s]he runs . . . like a solitary animal at the season when animals neither seek a mate nor take care of young, existing only for their lone survival" (160). Her rejection of the natural then is also a rejection of community, of all but herself. Unfortunately, we who can read the language Gordimer uses in the novel's last paragraph see Maureen's running as a defeat—for her and, to the extent she suggested the potential for other women and even men, for others as well. The potential has been lost; an incipient dream has become a terrifying nightmare.

Why does Maureen fail, after coming so far? This question, not the symbolic significance of the helicopter, it seems to me, is the true puzzle at the end of *July's People*. We are left with clues, but no clear answer. What does Gordimer stress in the novel's last pages? Gordimer stresses how Maureen, after trying to exhibit such sensitivity in dealing with July, poses seductively on the hood of the baakie, sending a message to July that is probably unclear to her and is certainly unclear to him since the pose "meant nothing to him, who had never been to a motor show complete with provoctive girls" (153). Gordimer stresses the *gumba-gumba* machine playing "the old music of Soweto, Daveyton, Tembisa, Marabastad" (154). Gordimer stresses how Daniel took the gun "*for himself*" (155) and left presumably for the Witwatersrand to join the revolutionary forces. Gordimer stresses the helicopter and Maureen's running toward it.

At first, it is difficult to discern any pattern at all in these concluding events. And perhaps there is no pattern: the end of the novel dissolves in chaos: that is Gordimer's point. However, there is a common thread. All of the events represent an intrusion of the urban world on the rural landscape—the auto shows, the *gumba-gumba* music, the battle raging in the cities, and the helicopter flying out from the cities and inspiring in Maureen's mind a vision of urban landscapes. This pattern suggests that the urban world is invading and destroying what is there *for all* in a rural, agrarian outlook on life. Oddly, this message of defeat takes us back to some of the early works we considered, works such as Peter Abrahams' *Mine Boy* and Alan Paton's *Cry, the Beloved Country*. Gordimer is suggesting that if we do not grab at the natural and human connectedness that is at the core of rural, agrarian life, we will be plunged into the nightmare of violence that has captured the urban areas and is spreading outward, like a blight.

Works Cited

Clingman, Stephen. *The Novels of Nadine Gordimer: History from the Inside*. London: Allen & Unwin, 1986.

Coetzee, J. M. *In the Heart of the Country*. 1977; rpt. New York: Penguin Books, 1982.

Cooke, John. *The Novels of Nadine Gordimer: Private Lives/Public Landscape*. Baton Rouge: Louisiana State UP, 1985.

Dodd, Josephine. "Naming and Framing: Naturalization and Colonization in J. M. Coetzee's *In the Heart of the Country*." *World Literature Written in English* 27 (1987): 153-61.

Driver, Dorothy. "Nadine Gordimer: The Politicisation of Women." *English in Africa* 10.2 (1983): 29-54.

Gillmer, Joan. "The Motif of the Damaged Child in the Work of J.M. Coetzee." In M. J. Daymond, et al. eds. *Momentum: On Recent South African Writing*. Pietermaritizburg: University of Natal Press, 1984. 107-120.

Gordimer, Nadine. *July's People*. New York: Viking Press, 1981.

Gordon, Jennifer. "Dreams of a Common Language: Nadine Gordimer's *July's People*." *African Literature Today* 16 (1987): 102-08.

Greenstein, Susan M. "Miranda's Story: Nadine Gordimer and the Literature of the Empire." *Novel* 18 (1985): 227-42.

Heywood, Christopher. *Nadine Gordimer*. Windsor, England: Profile Books, 1983.

Newman, Judie. *Nadine Gordimer*. London: Routledge, 1988.

Rich, Paul. "Apartheid and the Decline of the Civilization Idea: An Essay on Nadine Gordimer's *July's People* and J. M. Coetzee's *Waiting for the Barbarians*." *Research in African Literatures* 15 (1984): 365-93.

Roberts, Sheila. "Character and Meaning in Four Contemporary South African Novels." *World Literature Written in English* 19 (1980): 19-36.

Smith, Rowland. "Masters and Servants: Nadine Gordimer's *July's People* and the Themes of Her Fiction." *Salmagundi* 62 (1984): 93-107.

Smyer, Richard I. "Africa in the Fiction of Nadine Gordimer." *ARIEL* 16.2 (1985): 15-29.

11

The Dream

The nightmarish prospects presented in J. M. Coetzee's *In the Heart of the Country* and Nadine Gordimer's *July's People* are both frightening and tragic. Although both works focus much more on white South Africans, these novels suggest that neither whites nor non-whites possess what it will take to provide a peaceful future for South Africa or Azanaia. In *In the Heart of the Country*, racism has so scarred both victim and victimizer that the only future seems to be a frightening, tragic role reversal that, ultimately, satisfies neither party. In *July's People*, there is hope in the natural, earthy, *human* life of the homeland villagers–a life Maureen Smales almost joins, but, in the end, she runs from this life back to the technological, the urban, the oppressive world she knew in suburban Johannesburg. Meanwhile, in the village, the chief is ready to join with white South Africa in combat against his revolutionary black brethren because they are communists and he has been indoctrinated to believe that communists are, by definition, evil.

The scary predictions of these two novels from 1976 and 1981 do not present the only possibilities, however. Expatriate Mazisi Kunene's *The Ancestors & the Sacred Mountain*, a collection of over one hundred poems, presents an optimistic forecast for black South Africans. He does not say much about the nation's whites; however, what he does say suggests that they will be the victims of violence as a new black nation emerges. Nadine Gordimer's *A Sport of Nature* (1987) goes farther. Although it does suggest that revolution will spill blood, the novel evades the details of the emergence of the black nation of Azania and focuses on one white character, a young woman named Hillela, who is able to join with the revolutionaries and the nation's new leaders because, in some significant ways, she is different from most of South Africa's white population.

The Ancestors & the Sacred Mountain

Mazisi Kunene's poetry is ultimately hopeful, but he admits in "Journey into the Morning" that "the vision of a new era is born of the nightmare" (18). That nightmare will, he tells us—albeit briefly—in other poems, entail violence. "First Day after the War," "To a Friend Whose Family Was Killed," and "Brave People" all allude to the fighting that will be necessary; "The Rise of the Angry Generation" refers to the blood "red feathers" (7) of the "great eagle" (1) that is embelmatic throughout Kunene's poetry of the new black nation. "The Master and the Victim" is more explicit, speaking about "[t]he child [who] has chosen to avenge his parent" (18); both that poem and "252 or At the End of a Volume" refer to the violent explosions that will accompany the emergence of the new black nation. Still more explicit is "The Torturer," in which Kunene declares:

> You will die early at dawn
> When the sun is red and the children are walking
> And people are shouting to the morning.
> You will die at dawn
> When the crowds are running to the festival. (1-5)

Late in the collection, Kunene seems to take inspiration from the children of Soweto. "From them," the poet says in "Vision of Peace," "we must learn to create the unending movement" (20). To do so, his fellow black South Africans must listen to the "curse" that the dying children uttered:

> "Those who have killed without mercy,
> Those who are without fear of the victim's eyes,
> Those who laugh at the tumbling skulls,
> Shall walk the chameleon's path into the holocaust" ("Mercy," 10-13)

Kunene, however, devotes relatively little time to discussing these violent prospects; similarly, he devotes relatively little to indicting either the white oppressor or blacks who have "sold out" to Western ways. Most of *The Ancestors & the Sacred Moun-*

tain is devoted to presenting a rich, elaborate vision of the emergence of a glorious African nation in what is presently South Africa.

To fully appreciate Kunene's poetry, one must have some knowledge of Zulu lore and Zulu beliefs, for the poems refer to many legendary figures and play off of the Zulu attitude toward the earth, the mountains and waterways of their native land, and the songs and tales passed on from past generations. I am not going to attempt to deal with these enrichening dimensions of Kunene's poems. Rather, I'm going to summarize what seems to be the poet's vision for the future of southern Africa, a future he presents through an accumulating flood of imagery as he moves from poem to poem in *The Ancestors & the Sacred Mountain*.

Kunene suggests that, for a time, the African spirit has been asleep. Now, however, that spirit is awakening. The spirit seems to find its origin in the earth and, more particularly, in the grand mountains that thrust the earth upward into the skies and toward the sun. The spirit is that of the ancestors, and they, although dead, reside in these mountains. The mountains are, thus, sacred, and, from them, descend the waters that are also sacred. Kunene's poetry speaks often of "morning" and "birth," and he associates the new generation of black South Africans with these beginnings. The present generation–*his* generation–has lost the African spirit of the ancestors; the new generation, however, has rediscovered this spirit. That rediscovery is the occasion for celebrating, feasting. Kunene figures this rebirth, early in the collection, by talking about the eagle's triumphant flight. Later in the collection, Kunene re-figures the rebirth in cosmic terms: the rebirth of the African spirit is akin to the birth of a new planet.

Rather than examine each of the images that constitute Kunene's vision, I want to glance at seventeen individual poems–in the order they appear in the collection. These seventeen most fully present this vision.

"A Heritage of Liberation" leads off the collection. The poem is addressed to Kunene's contemporaries, telling them that they must "[t]ake these weapons for our children's children" (3). The "weapons" are not, however, guns but, rather, the legends from the ancestors. As Kunene and his brethren retell these stories of freedom fighting from the past, they will "let our children live with our voices" (6). Kunene goes further. So that "generations hereafter / May inherit our dream of the festival" (14-15), Kunene's generation "must follow the trail of the killer-bird" (12) into revolutionary action. If not, both they and their children will "sleep the sleep of terror" (13). Kunene and his fellows may well die in the fighting; if they do, he tells the new generation to "bury us in the mountain" (8), which is sacred. Through their fighting and perhaps their death, they will "bequeath to you [the new generation] the rays of the morning" (19).

"A Heritage of Liberation" refers to the eagle; "The Rise of the Angry Generation" uses that fierce but beautiful bird as its central image. The eagle, symbolic of the black African people, will build "its nest with old leaves" (5) (suggesting the lore of the African past), inspired by "the dream" (1) and focused on the glorious "morning" (3) that is to come. From this nest will emerge "the mysterious young bird" (10). At this birth, "[t]he once proud planet shrieks in terror" (9), for the planet knows that "the merciless talons of the new generation" (11) will "not [be] deterred by false tears" (12) and will *act* exhibiting "the wrath of the volcanic mountains" (16) and "the abiding anger of the Ancestral Forefathers" (17).

Both of these early poems in Kunene's collection present his vision with a violent edge. More pacific is "Journey to the Sacred Mountains." In this poem, the persona narrates an imagined journey into the mountains where the ancestors "walk eternally on earth" (7). Among them are "The Holy Ones" (10), and they speak. Notice how the images of mountains and water are used:

> Their voices broke through the waterfalls
> Anthems echoed from the mountains
> They eddied to the horizon like a great wave. (12-14)

"The whole earth was [then] enveloped in their dream" (15), the persona tells us. Within this dream,

> . . . we listened to the great epics

> We heard the voices of the ancient poets
> We were basking in the legends of our Forefathers[.] (18-20)

The dream affected the persona; more important, it affected "the child on our back" (21). Having heard the legends, he "shall grow without fear / And all things great and beautiful shall follow him" (21-22).

Another poem, "Phakeni's Farewell," a "[t]ribute to Robert Rasha, one of South Africa's greatest political leaders," is neither as violent as the first two poems we considered nor as peaceful as "Journey to the Sacred Mountains." Reading "Phakeni's Farewell," we find ourselves in the chaos before "a gathering storm" (5). In this chaos, the poet notes, "the ancestral song is heard" (7), the eagle can be seen soaring above. However, *this* generation seems trapped in chaos; hope is to be found in "the new generations" Phakeni "stare[s] at . . . with joy and tears" (48). At this moment in time, the key is "To preserve the centric point of our dreams" (73), which will be, for those in the future, "The magic awakening of our lives" (85).

"Changes" is one of the few Kunene poems in which he talks about white South Africa. He spends three stanzas describing the white presence. "The feet of strangers," he tells us, "pass our home / Trampling on our grounds with fierce footsteps" (1-2). "Layers and rings of sand," perhaps that extracted from the gold mines, "strangle the river" (6). Wounded in many ways, the earth swells; as it swells, it "crushes the leaves" (10) and it "breaks the mountain" (11).

After these stanzas, the poem changes dramatically. When "the tale" of old "is told," the message that is meant for us / Opens like the scents of a mountain-flower" (15-17) and "the rivers echo with bird-song" (18) and "New life travels through the veins of the earth" (19). This message is presented as a promise of good times to come; and the sensuous delights that pre-figure these times are termed "the pure gifts of the Ancestral guardians" (27).

A fuller vision of these good times is presented in "Return of the Golden Age." The poet and others of his age begin the poem waiting "for the soft things of dawn" (1). With song and with "the laughter of children" (5), "Dawn came" (10). The sun is depicted as penetrating and enlivening all. Then, in the poem's last stanza, we are told that, during this dawn, "Someone from the past shall touch your shoulder" (22). This "someone" will say, "We are the fathers of the poet we shall rise with the sun / And at her zenith sing her songs of the festival" (25-26). These songs come from the past, and this past "Shall nourish the thin leaves of the young plant" (29). The past, once recalled, will feed the future of revolution and freedom and a new nation.

The philosopher-poet will, as Kunene sees matters, play a crucial role in the development of this future. He speaks of this role in "The Maturation of a Philosopher-Poet." His "day of greatness has come" (1). Like a bird, he will sing. "The children of the earth have assembled" (6), Kunene tells us, to hear the song:

> They have heard your words of wisdom
> They have seen your signs of the morning[.] (7-8)

The dawn will lead these children to embrace the earth; then, as "the great lovers of the earth" (12), they will "by the richness of their gifts, / Enrich our world with new life" (13-14).

The poet serves, Kunene tells us in "To My Elder Kinsman," as a channel between the ancestors and the children. A particular elder kinsman caused "my vision" to rise "like a mountain" (4), Kunene tells us; the heritage he passed on "is like an unending rain" (11). In the poem, Kunene talks about this passing-on:

> As I embraced you I knew then
> An era had ended, an era had begun,
> And those who sat in a semi-circle
> Watched with the eyes of our Forefathers[.] (14-17)

As the heritage is passed from elder kinsman to poet, the poetic vision of the ancestors is also passed on. The poet now shares this gift with the assembled elders.

Kunene envisions himself as being in a line of visionary poets. In "Tribute to Mshongweni," he praises someone much farther back in the line, "A Great Nineteenth-Century African

Poet" named Mshongweni. Kunene tells the dead poet that his voice endures: "Your voice and your voice only / Shall rise from the ruins" (7-8). "Your dreams" (9), Kunene continues, will lead those of Kunene's day to "stampede" (14) to the highly symbolic "mountain springs," which will "burst open their freshness" (16). The springs will inspire "ecstatic minds" (18), and from these minds, "The future song shall be born" (19). This song, he tells us, "is the sun of the earth" (20).

Kunene suggests that there will be, in his day, many voices, many songs. In "Expectations of Freedom," he tells us how to distinguish among them. He says he will

> . . . praise their words
> When their minds have touched the sun
> And its fire has enveloped their dream[.] (1-3)

What distinguishes a dream that is enveloped in fire from an "ordinary" dream? Kunene tells us in the poem. A fire-enveloped dream has survived a long stretch of darkness while the speaker/singer has waited for the symbolic morning; a fire-enveloped dream is dreamt by one who vows "with his children" (12) never to "abandon those who are weak" (13); a fire-enveloped dream is dreamt by one who consorts with just, not "cruel men" (14); finally, a fire-enveloped dream is the dream of the "voices of those who are old / Who have chosen to die / Than to bend to the tyrant's will" (17-19).

"Expectations of Freedom" is ambiguous in one sense: it is not clear whether Kunene is talking about the crafters of poetic words or the crafters of political words. Perhaps the ambiguity is deliberate; perhaps Kunene is trying to suggest that, in the South African political environment of the late '70s, the boundary between poetry and politics that once might have existed is gone because the political realities facing the country's people are *so* compelling that all endeavors, especially art, are necessarily political. The same ambiguity is apparent in "After the Death of Mdabuli, Son of Mhawu." The persona uses the occasion of a death to address his compatriots in strong terms:

> It is us, the descendants of the lions
> Who must rule, without us the earth itself would end. (12-13)

He and his compatriots have "walk[ed] to the mountains" (15) of the ancestors; they have "created . . . flashes of lightning / To raise the proud manes of our children" (16-17). These flashes will enflame this new generation. Also enflaming them will be the song the persona and his compatriots created. A bluebird "had lost its ability to fly" (25); inspired by this song, "It shall open its eyes and raise its wings. / It shall fly into the infinity of the sky" (26-27). The song "shall give it power to live again" (28). Having described his people as a bluebird, the persona shifts metaphor and describes them as a flower:

> The flower that is spreading
> Once was buried under the earth.
> So shall our race rise from the nightmare
> And their shadow shall cover the earth
> From this wound we shall live again. (36-40)

The new generation will restore what *once* was; Kunene's generation will serve as midwives or prophets or heralds or the martyred initial wave of troops.

"My Swazi Boy or Song of the Frogs" seems to look at the role Kunene's generation will play from the perspective of the new generation. The persona seems to be that of a young boy, who has been affected by the "eyes" (2) and the "lightning" (3) of a stranger. This stranger offers "fingers [that] heal the pain" (8) and a "face" that refreshes "like a spring" (9). This stranger's "body glistened at the first sign of the morning" (10). This stranger's mission seems to be to carry the young boy across "the river of dreams" (13) and then to give him "an eternity of light burning from the mountain" (16) of the ancestors. In other words, the stranger is the philosopher-poet of Kunene's generation who connects the ancestors and their noble dreams with the new generation of Africans who will renew those dreams.

The time when ancestors and the new generation connect is referred to as "Communion" in Kunene's poem by that title. The poem features three voices. The first, that of the intermediate generation, narrates. The second, that of the ancestors, prophesies an "Ancestral festival" (17) when the symbolic rains will come, the voice of "the mountain-singer" (21) will be recalled, and "You shall regain the power of the dream" (20). The third voice, a child's, delivers the poem's closing lines, although her words and the those of the Ancestors are ambiguously merged at the very end:

> . . . Now I have learnt to speak to the gods
> I am carried away by the warmth of their fingers
> And the Ancestors came to the river and said:
> The alien prophets of fire shall perish,
> They shall be devoured by the violence in their eyes;
> And the survivor shall come to the cleansing place,
> To the creation of a new earth! (25-31)

The ancestors and the new generations have found communion here, even in the way their words join in announcing the destruction of white South Africa and the emergence of something momentously new afterwards.

Kunene's vision of "a new earth," expressed in this poem and others, suggests that his vision extends beyond South Africa. And it does. Not surprisingly, given that he settled in the United States after departing South Africa, some of his poems deal with the oppressive actions of the United States government. He talks about U.S. involvement in Vietnam in neo-imperialistic terms; in "To a Navaho Boy Playing a Flute," he uses the same terms that he uses in poem after poem about South Africa to deal with the relations between the American government and its native people. A young boy leads the persona to the mountain and "the feast of the Forefathers" (10), who reside there. If the persona can "learn the poems of the Dead" (23), then there is rain, there is dreaming, there is singing, there is a new morning, and there is even a sense of the planet —maybe even the universe—renewing itself. Kunene's vision then is quite transferable, quite global.

Kunene, however, usually keeps his attention focused on the South Africa situation. In "The Sons of the Sun," a voice—identity difficult to pin down—urges someone like Kunene to "Run . . . , run" (12) and "Bring back a cluster of beautiful words, / Bring the song that is born of our dreaming" (2-3). Such a song will "overcome the silences of the earth" (4) and "[c]reate new . . . movements in the wombs . . . (5). The songs will be "of ancient tales" (6) and come "from the high point of the mountain" (7); its music is said to be "like a waterfall" (8).

The real effect of the song, however, is not on the one who requests it but on "the children of the earth" (15). The song's effect is like a "hug" (15), and the singer announces the song's purpose as "To link the past with the present" (22). The singer/poet/priest then mixes the language of religious ceremony with that of a last will and testament to make it clear that the new generation has been bequeathed the ancestral spirit and that the ancestral spirit is sacred.

The poem concludes, again, with the voice of a child. The child notes that he or she

> shall possess these gifts,
> When they have killed my song
> When I am impoverished,
> I shall fill my belly with laughter. (29-32)

The new generation, these lines suggest, *will* face adversity as it acts infused with the ancestral spirit. Nonetheless, the gifts that came from the ancestors to the new generation will endure and will produce joy.

"Patience and Wisdom" shifts the focus once more from the new generation to the intermediate one Kunene belongs to. The poem speaks, quietly, in long lines, of how Kunene and other philosopher-poets of his generation patiently endured their slow search for the ancestral vision.

The last two poems we will discuss, "The Return of Inspiration" and "In Praise of the Ancestors," present that search as ultimately successful. In the first poem, "a great singer" (1) from the past leads the persona to the sacred mountain. There, "my powers broke open" from "the wombs of the earth" (3). These powers are depicted as "travelling up and down my body, / . . . like a clan of ants lost in a forest" (4-5). So empowered, the persona "hurried to the ancestral place / Where all fears are banished through courage" (10-11). There, he seizes his "grandfather's great ugubhu" (13), a stringed instrument, and is "seized by the ecstasy of the song" (16). Through this song, he is led to "the ancestral shrines" (20), where his "heart was opened" (21) and he saw the ancestral spirit incarnate and its "glowing dream" (22).

So inspired, the persona is able to sing in such a way that this dream and the ancestral spirit are again alive. In "In Praise of the Ancestors," the persona tells us that he and others "sing the anthems that celebrate their [the ancestors'] great eras" (23) and that "The Ancestors . . . come to listen" (7) and "have opened their sacred book to sing with us" (14). The bulk of the poem consists of similes and metaphors used to suggest the nature of the celebrated ancestral spirit:

> They are the mystery that envelops our dream.
> They are the strange truth of the earth.
> They came from the womb of the universe.
> Restless they are, like a path of dreams,
> Like a forest sheltering the neighbouring race of animals. (15-20)

The ancestral spirit informs the inspiring dream of a new African nation. This spirit emanates from the earth, if not from the primal dust out of which the universe was formed. This spirit, once it informs a nation, will provide shelter. Led by visionaries of Kunene's generation, the new generation will recover the greatness of the ancestors in this new land.

A Sport of Nature

Kunene's vision is grand, although it implies a period of violent transition prior to the ultimate peace. Nadine Gordimer's *A Sport of Nature* is quite similar. In its closing chapters, we see the glory of the new African nation of Azania. Before we reach this chapter, however, we get glimpses of the violent transition. Gordimer's novel, however, is focused on neither the political story nor the non-white peoples of South Africa. Rather, it tells the story of one white woman who is able to play a contributing role in the transition and in the new land.

Both Coetzee's *In the Heart of the Country* and Gordimer's own *July's People* suggested that it may be impossible for the white man or woman to have a place in a new black South Africa. Foregrounded by these novels, Gordimer's *A Sport of Nature* seems to suggest that it may be possible if. . . . Before I fill in the blank with the necessary conditions, I need to discuss the very different reactions readers have had to Gordimer's 1987 novel. Before I discuss those reactions, I need to offer a brief summary of the novel's plot.

When we meet Hillela, she is a schoolgirl named Kim in a whites-only boarding school in Rhodesia. Because she innocently "hangs out" with a colored boy in town, she is asked to leave the school. She not only leaves the school but leaves her second name of Kim for her true but less fashionable and more ethnic name of Hillela. Her mother, years earlier, had left South Africa and her husband for Mozambique and a passionate non-white lover. So, Hillela returns to just her father and accompanies him on his travels as a salesman. When his new wife Billie and Hillela don't get along, he decides to turn Hillela over to his sisters. She lives for a while with the correct Olga, then for a while with the "politically correct" Pauline. When she is discovered in bed with her cousin Sasha, she is told to leave her Aunt Pauline's house. Then, she drifts—from place to place, from bed to bed. She drifts into politics without thinking very much about politics. Eventually, she ends up married to a black revolutionary named Whaila.

Their marriage ends abruptly: Whaila is assassinated, dying in a pool of blood on their kitchen floor. Having seen the bloody, bodily results of the oppressive politics of white South Africa, Hillela thinks and embraces the liberating politics of the black revolutionaries. She becomes a spokesperson and a fund-raiser for them, travelling, with her daughter by Whaila, throughout Europe and the United States. During this period, she seems to turn her body off. Although she is not celibate, she seems to lack the passion she felt before; she seems to be going through the motions of sex.

Two events force a change in Hillela. First, her American lover, Bradley, suggests they marry and pick out furniture, etc. The safe domesticity of it all just does not strike Hillela as being a life-style that fits her. Second, she makes love with another black revolutionary, Reuel. In short order, she marries him and joins him in the fight to liberate colonized Africa. When the revolution succeeds in his country, he ascends to its presidency. Later, he ascends to the leadership of the Organization for

African Unity (OAU). Hillela takes her place beside him as one of black Africa's leading ladies, despite the fact she is white.

Readers have reacted to this story in two very different ways. A review by Jennifer Krauss in *The New Republic* links Hillela's story to those of Rosa Burger and Maureen Smales. According to Krauss, "In preceding novels, Gordimer has charted the evolution of the white liberal consciousness in South Africa. . . . Her heroines have either made peace with their limited ability to effect change (Rosa Burger in *Burger's Daughter*) . . . or they've run away (Maureen Smales in *July's People*)" (33). According to Krauss, Gordimer's third heroine, Hillela, is "a person whose political purpose is dependent on whom she happens to be sleeping with at the time, a person who becomes very famous by doing very little" (33); "a purely sexual being" (34); "a highly impressionable sexual object" (34). Hillela then is *not* to be taken seriously; she is a parody of a heroine. Thus, the novel becomes "a mock history of South Africa's liberation from apartheid" (33) and, therefore, "Gordimer's most deeply cynical novel" (33).

Another reviewer, Maureen Howard in *The New York Times*, grants the obvious: that "the sexual dimension [of the novel] is thematically central" (20), but argues that "Gordimer unites sexual energy and political energy" (20) in Hillela. So uniting the sexual and the political enables Gordimer to create "a powerful novel of awakening, emergence, and . . . a call for a new order" (19). The ending is not, according to Howard, a cynical mock history but rather "happy," "dreamlike but in no way . . . escapist" (20).

Critic Judie Newman in her 1988 *Nadine Gordimer* takes a position similar to Howard's. She presents the ending of *A Sport of Nature* as a "counter-example to the apocalyptic vision of *July's People*" (93) and the entire story as a celebration of sexual radicalism.

Who is correct? To the extent that an author's intention is relevant to a debate over interpretation, Howard and Newman are. In an interview reported in the *Observer* on 29 March 1987, Gordimer discusses the link the novel makes between political and sexual radicalism; in an interview reported in *The New York Times* on 3 May 1987, Gordimer, although admitting that Hillela's ways are shocking, says that Hillela is "a challenge–and potential antidote–to the stalemated political attitudes of her [white] South African countrymen" (22).

What is it then that makes Hillela different–different from other white South Africans who seem left out as the land tries to effect a transition from white-minority to black-majority rule? Gordimer suggests that Hillela is different in two connected ways. She is rootless, and, as a result, able to escape the attitudes toward race and sex that infect those more connected to the white South African nation.

The plot summary above suggests her rootlessness. Her mother has abandoned her; her father will abandon her. Her aunts tolerate her presence until she does things that prove too embarrassing. Then, she moves from place to place to place. She achieves some rootedness with her first spouse, Whaila, but, when that is disrupted by an assassin, she drifts again. Finally, she finds a place to root in. We'll talk about this place in a minute.

First, I need to note the consequences of her rootlessness. Because she lacked strong connections to family, she also lacked strong connections to the attitudes and values that a family presumably would have enculturated her in. Thus, she simply does not see that the boy she begins to associate with in Rhodesia is colored, and, later in life, she makes few or no distinctions between the races. Bodies are bodies; human beings are human begins–that's the attitude she has and lives by. Similarly, she does not feel that a sexual relationship with her cousin Sasha is wrong. They loved each other; they needed the warmth and the intimacy of sexual intercourse. The thought that what they did was incestuous quickly fades from Hillela's mind:

> The knowledge that they were cousins came up into their eyes, between them; she, his cousin, kissed him first, and slowly the knowledge disappeared in rills of feeling. It washed away as the light empty shells at the Bay were turned over and over by films of water and drawn away under the surf. He touched her breasts. . . . She slid the delicious shock of her strange sisterly hand down under his belt; her fingertips nibbled softly at him and, busy at her real mouth, he longed to be swallowed by her–it–the pure sensation she had become to him: for them to be not cousin, brother, sister, but the mysterious state incarnate in her. (32)

Her rootlessness has resulted in her not having internalized a moralistic code that would condemn her love for and intimacy with Sasha.

Boundaries of race and kinship simply do not exist for rootless Hillela. She did not fully acquire the attitudes and values of her nation's dominant people that would establish these lines of demarcation. She also did not acquire another attitude prevalent among white South Africans. That attitude is a negative one toward the body, toward sexuality. Rather than repress or censor, Hillela celebrates the body and sexuality. She manages to communicate this physicality to others:

> Ah no—sexual knowingness proclaimed itself in her laugh, from the very day she approached him with the bun and the book, in the unselfconscious ease with which she was at home with her body in a way that none of his patients, poor things, were, squeezing her soft breasts past the hard metal filing cabinets, swivelling her little behind as she bent to pick up the pen that wouldn't stay efficiently clipped to the pocket of her white coat. (108)

This physicality gives Hillela power. She exhibits it as she walks along the streets:

> She wandered; her body moved with the suppleness limbered by lovemaking, the pretty loll of breasts and the rhythm of her thighs were a confidence that made another kind of path through people in the streets. Men turned, as if at a reminder, to look at her; it was not her fault. (175)

To others, her physicality or sexuality was powerfully apparent; to herself, it was her "cache of trust" (294): she relied on it to help her judge others. It was "the bread of her being" (295): she kept herself "alive" through the multi-faceted pleasures of sexuality.

If Hillela was just a libertine, she would not be a hero (and Jennifer Krauss might be correct in her view of Hillela as sluttish). However, Hillela merges her attitude toward the body and sexuality with politics. When she sees Whaila's dead body on the floor of their kitchen, she *sees* the bodily consequences of politics; when she makes love with him, she realizes that all bodies are equal, and equally beautiful. Those who draft laws denying this basic equality are obsessed, she says, with insignificant differences:

> Lying beside him, . . . she examines his body minutely and without shame. . . . The laws that have determined the course of life for them are made of skin and hair, the relative thickness and thinness of lips and the relative height of the bridge of the nose. That is all; that is everything. The Lilliesleaf houseparty is in prison for life because of it. Those with whom she ate pap and cabbage are in Algeria and the Soviet Union learning how to man guns and make bombs because of it. He is outlawed and plotting because of it. . . . The laws made of skin and hair fill the statute books in Pretoria. (184)

Hillela comes to believe that laws and politics that deny the equality of *all people* by citing insigificant differences must be challenged, for, if some bodies are treated as less, their beauty will be destroyed through both the resulting impoverishment and the inevitable police suppression through violent means. And Hillela finds bodies beautiful.

The structure of the novel, it should be noted, reinforces this story of Hillela's "education." The novel divides into unequal thirds, with Whaila's dead body and Reuel's beautiful body as the two transition points. In the long first part, rootless Hillela is very much a physical, sexual being. Her mind, however, seems disengaged. In the second part, her mind is engaged, as she works long hours in Europe and the United States for the revolutionary cause. The shock of Whaila's dead body, which her mind keeps returning to, causes Hillela during this part to turn her body off:

> Of course Hillela had the body. . . . The body quickly knows–is the first to know–it has not been shot. It is still alive, alive in the Eastern European snow as in the tropical sand-bed. But it also knows when it is being ignored. Neglect of the body doesn't mean not washing or cutting toe-nails. It's a turning away from its powers. It's using it like a briefcase, to carry oneself around, instead of living through it. (253)

Marrying Bradley would represent a permanent "turning away from its powers." In the third part, she becomes a physical, sexual being once again. In this part, however, her mind is also engaged. And, in her marriage to Reuel, she unites the physical and the political and, in the process, obliterates the bipolarity.

"Place" is an important concept in Gordimer's fiction. In *Burger's Daughter*, Rosa Burger looks for a place that is *hers*. She ultimately realizes that "place" is not a location but rather something within that she can manifest in a South African women's prison in solidarity with other women of all races. In *July's People*, Maureen Smales loses her place in posh suburban Jo'burg and then tries desperately to find a new place in a black homeland where she and her family have taken refuge. She comes close to finding that place when she embraces the communal work of the village women as *her* work, but she fails, as the novel ends, to gain sufficient comfort in this new place to resist being raped by the technological, urban, male order she had fled. Hillela will prove to be more like Rosa than like Maureen. Hillela will move from place to place to place, looking for one that fits her. Like Rosa, she will eventually realize that "place" is not a matter of geography. She will realize that her place is the place where physical and political merge: ". . . inside each other, making love, that's the only place we can make, here, that's not just a place to stay" (147). Hillela is indeed different. The title clues us into that, and to help us interpret that clue, Gordimer uses as an epigraph to the novel the *Oxford English Dictionary*'s definition of a "sport of nature." The entry reads, "A plant, animal, etc., which exhibits abnormal variation or a departure from the parent stock or type . . . a spontaneous mutation; a new variety produced in this way." Hillela is this "departure." Whether she is "a new variety"—i.e., whether there will be others like her—is an open question as the novel ends. The challenge that Gordimer claims she is offering her fellow white South Africans is to follow in Hillela's footsteps. Gordimer is not suggesting libertinism for all; rather, she is suggesting that Hillela's attitude toward the beauty of the body (regardless of color) and her ease with the physical may well be valuable if not necessary prerequisites to white involvement in the new nation that the black majority will create.

The novel ends with the celebration of that new nation. Gordimer offers her white readers hope by noting that, although the celebration is an African one, "there are thousands of whites among the blacks" (353). Then, Gordimer shifts the focus to the podium and, on that podium, the white wife of the Chairman of the OAU. Then, Gordimer describes what it is that Hillela and the others are watching:

> Cannons ejaculate from the Castle.
>
> It is noon.
>
> Hillela is watching a flag slowly climb, still in its pupa folds, a crumpled wing emerging, and–now!–it writhes one last time and flares wide in the wind, is smoothed taut by the fist of the wind, the flag of Whaila's country. (354)

The language Gordimer uses is interesting. She suggests what the blacks–what the lion–has suffered in "crumpled" and "writhes"; she suggests the violence that will accompany the lion's movement down the freeway in "flares" and "fist"; she suggests birth after a period of imprisonment in the image of the butterfly emerging from "its pupa"; *and* she suggests the sexual radicalism that the novel associates with political radicalism in "ejaculates." Just as an ejaculation spreads the spermatazoa that can fertilize an awaiting ovum, the independence celebration spreads the joy that will fertilize the nation and help it prosper, grow. Just as orgasm is the profound moment of being for Hillela, this celebration is the profound moment of being for a new South Africa. It is then appropriate that the "Cannons ejaculate" from the Castle of Good Hope," for the novel's ending does indeed offer "Good Hope." That this castle should figure in the novel's end is, furthermore, suggestive of not only the end of the colonial domination of South Africa but of the continent as a whole, for this castle, built in 1679 by Jan van Riebeeck, represents the first colonial intrusion on *both*.

The lion of black Africa will walk the freeway, and, in the end, create a new kingdom. This nation will prosper, grow. This nation that Gordimer dreams of will admit whites who can learn some of what Hillela has come by naturally, because of her rootlessness.

Works Cited

Gordimer, Nadine. *A Sport of Nature*. 1987; rpt. New York: Viking Penguin, 1988.

Howard, Maureen. "The Rise of Hillela, the Fall of South Africa." *The New York Times Book Review*. 3 May 1987. 19-22.

Krauss, Jennifer. "Activism 101." *The New Republic*. 18 May 1987. 33-36.

Kunene, Mazisi. *The Ancestors & the Sacred Mountain: Poems*. London: Heinemann, 1982.

Newman, Judie. *Nadine Gordimer*. London: Routledge, 1988.

Uhlig, Mark A. "Shocked by Her Own Heroine." *The New York Times Book Review*. 3 May 1987. 22.

Bibliography

Primary Works

Abrahams, Peter. *Mine Boy*. 1946; rpt. Oxford: Heinemann, 1963.

Brink, Andre. *A Dry White Season*. 1979; rpt. New York: Penguin, 1984.

Brutus, Dennis. *Letters to Martha*. London: Heinemann, 1968.

Coetzee, J. M. *In the Heart of the Country*. 1977; rpt. New York: Penguin, 1982.

——. *Waiting for the Barbarians*. 1980; rpt. New York: Penguin, 1982.

Dikobe, Modikwe. *The Marabi Dance*. Oxford: Heinemann, 1980.

Essop, Ahmed. *Stories*. 1978; rpt. London: Readers International, 1988.

Fugard, Athol. *A Lesson from Aloes*. New York: Random House, 1981.

——. "*Master Harold" . . . and the Boys*. 1982; rpt. New York: Penguin, 1984.

Gordimer, Nadine. *Burger's Daughter*. 1979; rpt. New York: Penguin, 1980.

——. *July's People*. New York: Viking Press, 1981.

——. *Something Out There*. New York: Viking Press, 1984.

——. *A Sport of Nature*. 1987; rpt. New York: Penguin, 1988.

Gwala, Mafika. *No More Lullabies*. 1982.

Head, Bessie. *When Rain Clouds Gather*. 1968; rpt. Oxford: Heinemann, 1987.

Hutchinson, Alfred. *The Rain Killers*. London: Headley Brothers, 1964.

Kgositsile, Keorapetse. *My Name is Afrika*. Garden City, NY: Doubleday, 1971.

Kunene, Mazisi. *The Ancestors & the Sacred Mountain Poems*. London: Heinemann, 1982. LaGuma, Alex. *In the Fog of the Seasons' End*. London: Heinemann, 1972.

Manaka, Matsemala. *Egoli: City of Gold*. Johannesburg: Soyikwa-Ravan, 1980.

Matthews, James. *Pass Me a Meatball, Jones: A Gathering of Feelings*. Athlone: Blac Publishing House, 1977.

Matthews, James, and Gladys Thomas. *Cry Rage!* Johannesburg: Sprocas Publications, 1972.

Mhlophe, Gcina, Maralin Vanrenen, and Thembi Mtshali. *Have You Seen Zandile*? 1988; rpt. London: Methuen, 1990.

Millin, Sarah Gertrude. *God's Step-Children*. New York: Boni and Liveright, 1924.

Mphahlele, Ezekiel. *Down Second Avenue*. Berlin: Seven Seals Publishers, 1959.

Mtshali, Oswald. *Sounds of a Cowhide Drum*. London: Oxford UP, 1971.

Nkosi, Lewis. *Mating Birds*. New York: St. Martin's, 1986.

Paton, Alan. *Cry, The Beloved Country*. New York: Scribner's, 1948.

Rive, Richard. "Make Like Slaves." In *Selected Writings: Stories Essays, Plays*. Johannesburg: Ad. Donker, 1977.

Roberts, Sheila. *The Weekenders*. Johannesburg: Bateleur, 1981.

Schreiner, Olive. *The Story of an African Farm*. 1883; rpt. Harmondsworth: Penguin, 1979.

Sepamla, Sipho. *The Soweto I Love*. Cape Town: David Philip, 1977.

Serote, Mongane Wally. *No Baby Must Weep*. Johannesburg: Ad. Donker, 1975.

Tlali, Miriam. *Amandla*. Johannesburg: Ravan Press, 19xx.

Workshop '71. *Survival*. In R. M. Kavanagh, ed. *South African People's Plays*. London: Heinemann, 1981. 125-71.

Zwelonke, D. M. *Robben Island*. London: Heinemann, 1977.

Secondary Studies

Amato, Rob. "Fugard's Confessional Analysis: "*Master Harold" . . . and the Boys*." In M. J. Daymond, et al., eds. *Momentum: On Recent South African Writing*. Pietermaritzburg: University of Natal Press, 1984. 198-214.

Barnett, Ursula A. *A Vision of Order: A Study of Black South African Literature in English (1914-1980)*. Amherst: University of Massachusetts Press, 1983.

Clingman, Stephen. *The Novels of Nadine Gordimer: History from the Inside*. London: Allen & Unwin, 1986.

Coetzee, J. M. *White Writing: On the Culture of Letters in South Africa*. New Haven, CT: Yale UP, 1988.

Cooke, John. *The Novels of Nadine Gordimer: Private Lives/Public Landscape*. Baton Rouge: Louisiana State UP, 1985.

Davenport, T. R. H. *South Africa: A Modern History*. 4th ed. Toronto: University of Toronto Press, 1991.

Dodd, Josephine. "Naming and Framing: Naturalization and Colonization in J. M. Coetzee's *In the Heart of the Country*." *World Literature Written in English* 27 (1987: 153-61.

Driver, Dorothy. "Nadine Gordimer: The Politicisation of Women." *English in Africa* 10.2 (1983): 29-54.

Durbach, Errol. "*Master Harold*: Athol Fugard and the Psychopathology of Apartheid." *Modern Drama* 30 (1987): 505-13.

Gillmer, Joan. "The Motif of the Damaged Child in the Work of J. M. Coetzee." In M. J. Daymond, et al., eds. *Momentum: On Recent South African Writing*. Pietermaritzburg: University of Natal Press, 1984. 107-20.

Gordon, Jennifer. "Dreams of a Common Language: Nadine Gordimer's *July's People*." *African Literature Today* 16 (1987): 102-08.

Greenstein, Susan M. "Miranda's Story: Nadine Gordimer and the Literature of Empire." *Novel* 18 (1985): 227-42.

Heinemann, Margot. "*Burger's Daughter*: The Synthesis of Revelation." In Douglas Jefferson and Graham Martin, eds. *The Uses of Fiction*. Milton Keynes, England: Open UP, 1982. 181-97.

Heywood, Christopher. *Nadine Gordimer*. Windsor, England: Profile Books, 1983.

Howard, Maureen. "The Rise of Hillela, the Fall of South Africa." *The New York Times Book Review*. 3 May 1987. 19-22.

Krauss, Jennifer. "Activism 101." *The New Republic*. 18 May 1987. 33-36.

Leeuwenberg, Rina. "Nadine Gordimer's *Burger's Daughter*: Why Does Rosa Go Back?" *New Literature Review* 14 (1985): 23-31.

Liscio, Lorraine. "*Burger's Daughter*: Lighting a Torch in the Heart of Darkness." *Modern Fiction Studies* 33 (1987): 245-61.

Nelson, Harold, ed. *South Africa: A Country Study*. 2nd ed. Washington, DC: Government Printing Office, 1981.

Newman, Judie. *Nadine Gordimer*. London: Routledge, 1988.

Nkosi, Lewis. "Sex and the Law in South Africa." In *Home and Exile*. London: Longman, 1963. 37-43.

Olsen, Lance. "The Presence of Absence: Coetzee's *Waiting for the Barbarians*." *ARIEL* 16.2 (1985): 47-56.

Omer-Cooper, J. D. *History of Southern Africa*. London: James Currey, 1987.

Rich, Paul. "Apartheid and the Decline of the Civilization Idea: An Essay on Nadine Gordimer's *July's People* and J. M. Coetzee's *Waiting for the Barbarians*." *Research in African Literatures* 15 (1984): 365-93.

Roberts, Sheila. "Character and Meaning in Four Contemporary South African Novels." *World Literature Written in English* 9 (1980): 19-35.

——. "'No Lessons Learnt': Reading the Texts of Fugard's *A Lesson from Aloes* and *Master Harold . . . and the Boys*." *English in Africa* 9.2 (1982): 27-33.

Shava, Piniel Viriri. *A People's Voice: Black South African Writing in the Twentieth Century*. 1989; rpt. Athens: Ohio UP, 1989.

Smith, Rowland, "Allan Quartermain to Rosa Burger: Violence in South African Fiction." *World Literature Written in English* 22 (1983): 171-82.

——. "Masters and Servants: Nadine Gordimer's *July's People* and the Themes of Her Fiction." *Salmagundi* 62 (1984): 93-107.

Smyer, Richard I. "Africa in the Fiction of Nadine Gordimer." *ARIEL* 16.2 (1985): 15-29.

Steadman, Ian. "Alternative Politics, Alternative Performance: 1976 and Black South African Theatre." In M. J. Daymond, et al., eds. *Momentum: On Recent South African Writing*. Pietermaritzburg: University of Natal Press, 1984. 215-32.

Uhlig, Mark A. "Shocked by Her Own Heroine." *The New York Times Book Review*. 3 May 1987. 22.

Wood, W. J. B. "*Waiting for the Barbarians*: Two Sides of Imperial Rule and Some Related Considerations." In M. J. Daymond, et al., eds. *Momentum: On Recent South African Writing*. Pietermaritzburg: University of Natal Press, 1984. 129-40.

Index